DETROIT PUBLIC LIBRA
3 5674 01213
P9-ARO-514

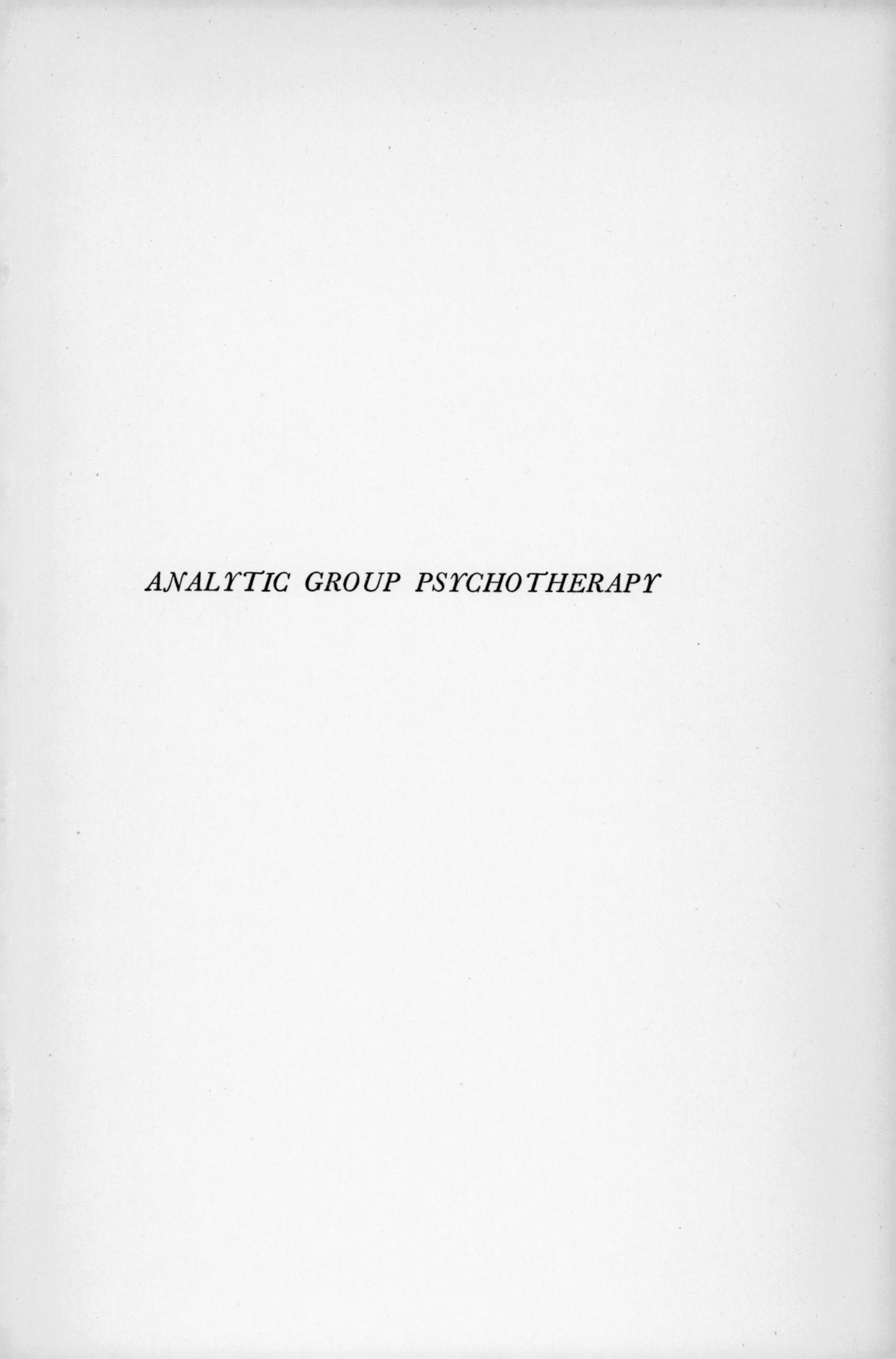

ANALYTIC GROUP PSYCHOTHERAPY

ANALYTIC GROUP PSYCHOTHERAPY

WITH CHILDREN ADOLESCENTS AND ADULTS

S. R. SLAVSON

COLUMBIA UNIVERSITY PRESS
NEW YORK

First printing 1950
Second printing 1951

PUBLISHED IN GREAT BRITAIN, CANADA, AND INDIA BY GEOFFREY CUMBERLEGE
OXFORD UNIVERSITY PRESS, LONDON, TORONTO, AND BOMBAY
MANUFACTURED IN THE UNITED STATES OF AMERICA

PREFACE

THE present volume is a companion to *An Introduction to Group Therapy,* published in 1943. With the exception of the last chapter, the latter was devoted almost entirely to Activity Group Therapy. Contemporaneously with my efforts since 1934 to develop that technique and to report on findings, we at the Jewish Board of Guardians have been experimenting since 1937 with several other types of group treatment as patients indicated special needs. As a result, we have evolved groups for children of pre-school age which we described as *group play psychotherapy.* Another type of group for children in the latency period, who are too disturbed to be placed in activity groups, we designated *activity-interview group psychotherapy.* The term used for a third type is *interview group psychotherapy* used with adolescents and adults. While all these groups are based on precisely similar foundations in psychodynamics and psychotherapy, the techniques are at variance in important respects. The reader will find detailed descriptions of these in the body of the text.

A good part of the present volume has been given over to records of actual sessions. Short extracts from records were selected to illustrate or heighten the meaning of theoretic statements. Full records of six sessions were included with condensed interpretations and brief discussions of dynamics as related to the therapeutic process. Two of these deal with groups of small children of different ages, one with pre-adolescent girls, another with adolescent girls, one with a group of adults, and still another with a group in an institutional setting.

The full records were taken at random and are only a very small part of the many thousands of pages accumulated in our files. They were selected because of age and sex distribution and not because they are of greater clinical value than others. Briefer abstracts have been drawn largely from one group of adolescent girls, and to a lesser extent from another group of younger girls. It was felt that this plan would give a better and more continuous picture of the process and the reactions of individuals than could otherwise be achieved. A listing of references to each of the patients is supplied in the Index so that something approaching a treatment history can be gleaned from reading the indicated passages as a unit.

Perhaps a few words ought to be said about the title of the book. We were faced with the problem of finding a generic term that would include all three types of group psychotherapy—play, activity-interview, and interview—since they are fundamentally similar insofar as they are all based on transference, catharsis, interpretation and insight, and have their foundations in psychoanalysis. After casting about for such a title we arrived at the one used here. We have not considered appropriate the term "Group Analysis," used by some authors, since it connotes a study of the dynamics and processes of social interaction, rather than treatment of patients. Nor did we consider the term we have used in the past, "Interview Group Therapy," adequate as a designation of the content of this book.

We propose that Group Psychotherapy be divided into two main divisions: *activity* and *analytic*. The former refers to groups for school-age children in which manual occupations, free play and unrestricted acting out without restraint or interpretation is the sole treatment process. The latter, Analytic Group Psychotherapy, is to be employed for all types of therapy groups—whether activity

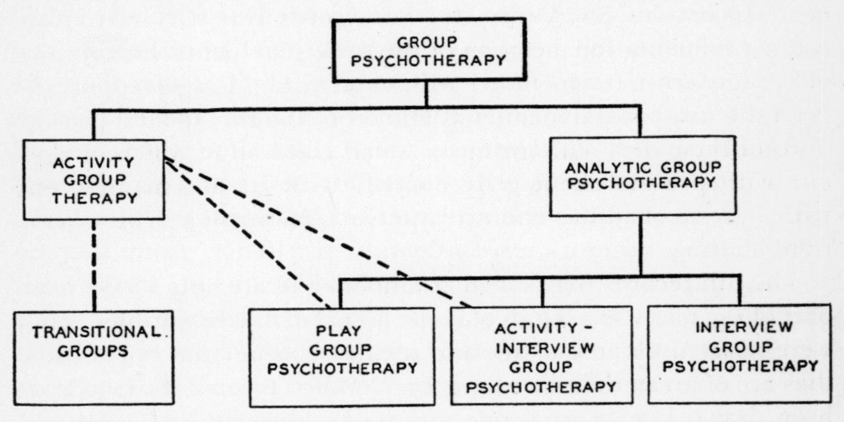

Types of group psychotherapy employed by the author for various age levels and clinical problems. The broken lines indicate use of activity as catharsis in the various types of groups.

or verbalization, for children or adults—in which transference is present and interpretation with a view of evoking insight is the aim.

Some criticism has been leveled at the proponents of group therapy because it has evolved a terminology of its own, emphasized lesser known processes in man's mental and social life, and has developed new techniques. This is unavoidable. No system of thought or practice can escape it. As new phenomena and forces are identified, they are described and, therefore must also be named both for communication purposes and for the sake of clarity. All sciences and technologies have had similar histories. It is inevitable that the interaction of a number of people in a dynamic emotional relation, such as occurs in a therapy group, would give rise to phenomena that do not appear in any other situation, and names had to be given them. A glossary is, therefore, supplied at the end of this volume, as we found it necessary also to do in *An Introduction to Group Therapy*. Despite this terminological accretion, Analytic Group Psychotherapy is in every *basic* respect identical with individual psychotherapy and dynamic psychiatry. The reader will find ample support for this view in the body of this book. Only to the extent to which this similarity exists can group psychotherapy lay claim to being a valid therapeutic procedure.

The present book is based, with one or two exceptions, on the work of the author at the Jewish Board of Guardians, a Child Guidance Agency in New York City. The agency is particularly suited for experimentation because of its traditional unorthodoxy and experimentalism,[1] and its wide resources. The fact that there are between 1,500 and 1,600 individuals—children and adolescents and their parents—in treatment at any given time makes possible the wide choice of clientele necessary for research and experimentation. The Agency also offers a variety of treatment resources, such as psychiatric casework, psychotherapy, psychiatry, group therapy, Big Brothers and Big Sisters, residential treatment, institutions, and camps. It has a large staff of psychiatric caseworkers, group therapists, psychiatrists, psychologists, and other types of personnel necessary in a multi-service agency. Detailed records are kept of all

[1] Gordon Hamilton, *Psychotherapy in Child Guidance* (New York, Columbia University Press, 1947), traces the development of the therapeutic technique at the Jewish Board of Guardians in the last thirty years.

individual interviews, group sessions, psychiatric conferences, referral summaries, intake interviews, progress summaries, integration conferences, and other treatment contacts and activities too numerous to list here. Because of these resources and the general attitudes of the staff and administration, it was possible to test a number of departures that seemed reasonable, and from which this and other volumes have resulted.

I wish to express my deepest appreciation to the Jewish Board of Guardians and its Directors and to my many associates and colleagues, especially to Betty Gabriel, Fanny Millstein, Rena Schulman, Dr. Hyman Spotnitz, and Dr. John H. W. Van Ophuijsen. The first three for their painstaking work with groups; to the latter for the many stimulating and enlightened discussions and suggestions. Thanks are due to the Community Service Society of New York for permission to use several abstracts from their group therapy records.

I am especially grateful to Dr. Nolan D. C. Lewis of the New York State Psychiatric Institute, who despite a very busy professional life took the time to read the full manuscript and make a number of helpful suggestions.

I am indebted to the many professional journals and other publications in which some of the ideas and theories contained in this volume first made their appearance. Chief among these are the *American Journal of Orthopsychiatry, Mental Hygiene, The Nervous Child,* and the *Psychoanalytic Review,* as well as publications by Grune and Stratton, Inc., International Universities Press, and Child Care Publications.

I am indebted to Herschel Alt for his encouragement and other help in facilitating the publication of this book, and to Mrs. Arthur D. Schulte, a member of the Executive Board of the Jewish Board of Guardians, for continued and steadfast faith in our work. As in my *Introduction to Group Therapy,* I again wish to express my appreciation to Dr. John Slawson, whose pioneering spirit made my first experiments in group therapy possible fifteen years ago.

My thanks go to Marcia Kinstler for devoted and intelligent secretarial help.

New York
July, 1949

S. R. SLAVSON

CONTENTS

CHAPTER ONE

HISTORIC BACKGROUNDS AND CURRENT PRACTICES

UNLIKE activity group therapy for children, which was first introduced in 1934, the use of "conversational" groups in the treatment of various types of medical and mental disorders has a comparatively long history. Scientifically oriented practitioners cannot consider, however, as therapy the many magical, semi-religious, revivalist and religious-evangelical activities of "inspired" persons in ancient, medieval and modern times. Shamans, medicine men, and miracle workers have undoubtedly affected "cures"—probably in cases of hysterical conversions; but the elements of planfulness, understanding, and control of the dynamic factors involved in a scientific practice were absent from their activities. Although the precursor of all science is magic, and modern psychotherapy was preceded by incantation and suggestion, it is necessary that we draw a sharp line between the two. This is especially important in the light of some "savage survivals" in present-day mental and social sciences, and in the administration of corrective efforts.

While the treatment of psychotics by the group method has a somewhat longer history,[1] this work with non-psychotic mental patients is in its very beginnings. Unlike most other techniques in psychiatry, which had their beginnings in various European countries, group psychotherapy has had its origin in the United States. This is quite understandable in the light of American culture, which is essentially a free group culture. Here have also evolved other important organized group movements such as labor unions, social group work, and group recreation. Democracy is not, as is

[1] See Chapter XV, p. 246.

frequently emphasized, the triumph of the individual, but rather that of the free group.

In 1905, J. H. Pratt introduced the "class method" with a group of patients suffering from pulmonary tuberculosis in what came to be known as "thought control" clinics. Dr. Pratt was impressed, as were many others before him, with the effect of mental attitudes of patients on the rate and thoroughness of recovery from somatic illnesses. While this relation had been noted before, his use of a group for stimulating recovery from a physical illness was as new as it was unique.[2] Later the "class method" was adopted for other types of physical maladies by a number of physicians in general practice.

These groups are rather large, in some cases consisting of as many as a hundred or more patients. The procedure consists of an explanation as to the nature of the disease from which the patients suffer and the meaning and intent of the medication and other therapeutic measures. Such intellectual understanding is designed to induce better cooperation on the part of the patients in treatment. Patients who understand the effect, and therefore the importance of a special diet, rest, and care recommended, may be expected to abide by them more scrupulously than those who follow a routine blindly and who have no appreciation of the effects of breach of instructions.

Of greater importance in recovery is a patient's unwillingness to improve from an incapacitating malady that yields to him secondary gains. Physical illness is not infrequently the only means an individual has of punishing persons in his environment by inconveniencing them and causing them worry and anguish: it is a tool in retaliatory hostility. Illness sometimes becomes chronic because through it patients with infantile, dependent characters gain the attention which they always craved; they have discovered, acci-

[2] J. H. Pratt, "The Home Sanitorium Treatment of Consumption," *Johns Hopkins Hospital Bulletin,* May, 1906; "The Class Method of Treating Consumption in the Homes of the Poor," *Journal of the American Medical Assoc.,* August 31, 1907; "Results Obtained in the Treatment of Pulmonary Tuberculosis by the Class Method," *British Medical Journal,* October 10, 1908; "The Class Method in the Home Treatment of Tuberculosis and What It Has Accomplished," *American Climatological Assoc.,* Vol. XXVII, 1911; "The Tuberculosis Class, an Experiment in Home Treatment," *Proceedings of the New York Conference Hospital Social Service,* Vol. IV, 1917; "The Principles of Class Treatment and Their Application to Various Chronic Diseases," *Hospital Social Service,* December, 1922; "The Influence of Emotions in the Causation and Cure of Psychoneuroses," *International Clinic,* December, 1934.

dentally perhaps, an unfailing means of getting what they want. Other patients use physical symptoms to control people around them and thus wield power as well as a means for exploiting members of one's family and the community. The sense of power gained through such means is highly gratifying and one, unconsciously, perhaps, resists or discards measures to eliminate the conditions that yield these welcome results.

Depth psychology has taught us also that emotional conflicts can be converted into physical symptoms and hostility can be displaced on the organism itself. Very often there is present in many chronic patients, especially in the functional group, a masochistic, self-pitying, and at the same time self-punishing quality that renders them either inaccessible to medical treatment, or at least retards it when applied. It is necessary to find some means of altering this attitude toward the self and free the psychic energies (libido) from their anchorage in the patient himself and activate them to flow outward. Finally, there are patients who become inured to an illness which serves to protect them from a life of effort and responsibility. Through it they escape the need to exert themselves and face the strain and danger of an active life.

A further analysis of the basic motivations of such chronic patients discloses elements which properly belong to the period of childhood. The patients are helpless, dependent, unable to face the actualities of life; they seek infantile gratifications of power-drives and hostile feelings. These associated psychologic concomitants have to be dealt with by psychologic means at the same time that medical treatment is carried on.

Dr. Pratt's "classes" attempted to correct attitudes that impeded recovery from physical illness. To do this he gave inspirational talks that would lift the patients out of their inertia, introspection, and self-pity. He called upon them to describe their own efforts, very much on the style of testimonies at revivalist meetings. Patients who had made acceptable progress were moved up to the front benches and finally were advanced to sit on the platform with the doctors. These were the "star patients." All this had the effect of encouraging other patients to improve, both because of the examples set and the striving for similar recognition in the group by the doctor. Before and after the regular sessions patients were encouraged to mingle freely, talk to one another, exchange experiences, and reactions, share views, encourage and help each other. In his evaluation of Pratt's work Harris gives the following account of the dynamics: [3]

1. Loss of self-consciousness by
   a. Group association, demanding change from an introvertive to an extravertive attitude.
   b. Desire for approval of leader, promoting a spirit of rivalry for maximum improvement.
   c. Identification of patient with leader.
   d. Realization that others have like problems.
   e. Increase in sense of importance from promotion for faithful attendance and successful readjustment to, finally, the honor bench.
   f. Appeal to immature emotional side of the patient's nature.
   g. Early establishment of goal in life, that is, good emotional habits.
2. Sthenic (inspirational) suggestion to whole group by
   a. Reading progress slips.
   b. Testimony of members who adjusted themselves to their problems.
   c. Informal talk following relaxation when receptivity is at a maximum.
3. Establishment of rapport with leader by
   a. Roll call.
   b. Enthusiasm of readjusted members for leader.
   c. Occasional personal chats with leader following meeting.
4. Reinforcement of all factors operative by
   a. Heightened suggestibility of group.
   b. Removal of extraneous stimuli through relaxation.
   c. Constant repetition of chief thought chosen for the particular class session.
5. Friendly relations established among members—of special value for those with limited social opportunities.

Buck used a similar plan of "class instruction" with patients suffering from hypertension.[4] Chappel, Stefano, Rogerson, and Pike [5]

[3] H. I. Harris, "Efficient Psychotherapy for the Large Outpatient Clinic," *New England Journal of Medicine,* July, 1939.

[4] R. W. Buck, "Class Method in Treatment of Essential Hypertension," *Annals of Internal Medicine,* September, 1937.

[5] M. N. Chappell, J. J. Stefano, J. S. Rogerson, and F. H. Pike, "Value of Group Psychological Procedures in Treatment of Peptic Ulcer," *American Journal of Digestive Diseases and Nutrition,* January, 1937.

found these classes effective with patients who had peptic ulcers, and more recently Hadden reported on his work in "group instruction" for tubercular, diabetic, neurosyphilic patients as well as with patients without organic diseases.[6] As early as 1920, Greene found free group activities in addition to group discussions effective in the treatment of stutterers. In this connection Greene [7] states:

> our group approach is of paramount importance. This group approach was developed because it was found that individual therapy proved ineffective in the stutterer's case. The stutterer suffers from a social neurosis, and the narcissistic barrier that he has built between himself and others makes it impossible in most cases for him to cooperate with the therapist under orthodox psychiatric procedures. However, when the stutterer is part of a group, all of whom have the same problem, this barrier is soon broken down. Having thus established a more or less "neutral" atmosphere, we can force him to overcome his symptom and his anxiety. In this way the stutterer in time acquires an emotional stability that enables him psychologically to bridge the gap between our special environment and the regulation environment of the outside world.

As we examine the fairly widespread use of "the class method," we see clearly that the basic dynamics operating in these groups are suggestion, temporary ego-strengthening, rivalry, and the desire to please the father (which is a modified form of transference). Each feels that if someone else can accomplish something—in this case, improvement—so can he. He is further placed in rivalry with those of the patients who "make the grade." Those who are moved up to the front benches and finally accepted in the inner (family) circle on the platform next to the therapist (father) are the envy of the others, who are thus motivated to attain a similar status (sibling rivalry). Here also submission to the father for the bounty (affection) he bestows is ever present. If one improves (pleases the father), he is accepted and loved by the father (doctor).

It is clear that the "class method" exploits the patients' regressive trends, such as infantile cravings for love, need to submit, and immature rivalry tendencies. The patients are not helped to mature

[6] S. B. Hadden, "Treatment of the Neuroses by Class Technic," *Annals of Internal Medicine,* January, 1942.

[7] James S. Greene, "Speech and Voice Disorders," *The Medical World,* November, 1939.

emotionally so that they are no longer dominated by these infantile cravings and trends, which is the real aim of psychotherapy. However, in view of the fact that here the group psychological instruction was employed only as adjuncts to *medical* treatment, it cannot have identical aims and objectives as does psychotherapy. Perhaps in this connection it is interesting to note the contrast between this work and that of Greene. Because Greene views stuttering as a symptom of a total personality (not medical) disorder, and the stutterer as one who "suffers from a social neurosis," his groups are more autonomous and self-directing, namely, they reinforce the maturity trends in the individual patients.

The class, or group, method of instruction has been accepted in the treatment of psychotics and to a lesser extent also of psychoneurotic patients. However, because of the nature of neuroses, education and instruction cannot be effective in treatment; rather, the intrapsychic structure of the patient must be the focus of the therapeutic effort, even though social and interpersonal factors must always be considered. There is no record in the literature of any change in the class instruction plan until the publication by Wender of a paper in 1936 [8] and by Schilder [9] in the same year of a technique more suited to the therapeutic needs of psychoneurotics. Wender, who worked with mental patients in a private hospital, saw the use of groups as valid for the total setting of the hospital.[10] He, too, employed the class method for larger groups of patients at first, but later he added the small intimate groups on an interview basis. Wender's general leaning is toward a combination of education and the psychotherapeutic interview.[11] He bases his work quite explicitly on Freudian concepts and draws upon Freudian psychology for the content of the group instruction. He believes that "the human individual is a 'group animal,' seeking a satisfying niche in the social setting; that he is a social product, whose inhibitions and

[8] Louis Wender, "Dynamics of Group Psychotherapy and Its Application," *Journal of Nervous and Mental Diseases,* July, 1936.

[9] Paul Schilder, "The Analysis of Ideologies as a Psychotherapeutic Method, Especially in Group Treatment," *American Journal of Psychiatry,* November, 1936.

[10] See pp. 254–55.

[11] Louis Wender, "Group Psychotherapy, a Study of Its Application," *Psychiatric Quarterly,* October, 1940; "Group Psychotherapy within the Psychiatric Hospital," in *Current Therapies of Personality Disorders,* ed. Bernard Glueck (New York, Grune and Stratton, Inc., 1946).

repressions are motivated by the mores of the group; that difficulties in adjustment and failure to express his emotional troubles are the result of his inability to face the group and to find his place in it." In Wender's practice, the therapist occupies the center of the stage more than is the case in later practices of group psychotherapy, but to a considerably lesser degree than in Pratt's method. Wender leans more on psychological subject matter than on physiological, as did Pratt. Topics like repressions, the unconscious, conversions, sublimations, ambivalence, hostility, the Oedipus complex, and sibling rivalry are presented by the physician and discussed by him and the patients. The therapist presents for analysis and discussion case histories (always anonymous or disguised) of patients present in the group. He directs and guides the ensuing discussions. Wender has a fourfold treatment plan which also constitutes the dynamics of group psychotherapy as he sees it. These are: (1) intellectualization, (2) patient-to-patient transference, (3) catharsis, and (4) group interaction.

We see, therefore, considerable advance toward psychotherapeutic orientation as compared with the physiological and inspirational school inaugurated by Pratt. But this reorientation was quite inevitable in terms of function and aim. Pratt did not use the group for a psychotherapeutic aim specifically. The group was ancillary to medical treatment and not a psychiatric end in itself. Pratt was not seeking to change the psychic structure of his patients but to enlist the psyche as an aid to physical recovery. Since Wender was preoccupied with psychoneurotic and psychotic patients in a sanitarium, it is understandable that his emphasis would be on psychological, rather, than medical topics.

A more strictly psychoanalytical procedure was introduced by Schilder with ward and clinic adult patients in a hospital. His pattern and *modus operandi* followed in every regard the individual psychoanalytical interview. Schilder limited his work to groups of four or five patients in which free association reigned supreme. There was no set plan for these interviews, the therapist introduced no special subject nor were the patients encouraged to do so. The group interviews centered around the patients' personal problems, in the discussion of which all present, including the therapist, freely participated. Schilder believed in the value of ideological clarity as well as emotional change, and centered at times on these.[12]

The following basic attitudes must be uncovered and discussed, according to Schilder, in order to help the emotionally disoriented person to recover from his difficulties: "(a) The need to love and be loved. (b) The tendency to maintain one's own support. (c) The tendency to maintain the integrity of the body (reaction to sudden noises, impressions). (d) The tendency to eat, drink, acquire property, retain. (e) The tendency to expel what cannot be used or what is threatening. (f) The tendency to handle and destroy objects and human beings and to get insight into their structure."

Unlike many of the others who use the group method in psychotherapy, Schilder studied the effectiveness of his group practice and found it to be effective with psychoneurotic patients. He was also the first to evaluate and relate group psychotherapy in terms of clinical and diagnostic categories.[13]

In the early 1940s Benjamin I. Weininger of Washington, D.C., conducted therapy groups in his private practice, but no report of this work has been published. Weininger's method differed from the other practices in the fact that he did not conduct group discussions, but rather confined the entire treatment session to one patient with the others acting as spectators. Alexander Wolf is also reported to have employed group treatment with his private patients much on the lines of Weininger.

The current literature reveals multitudinous devices and artifices employed by therapists. The gamut runs from the authoritarian approach of Low, the confessional-inspirational method of Pratt and his followers, the didactic technique of Klapman, the aesthetic activation of Altschuler, the drama forms of Moreno, the social-educational method of Bierer, and the quasi-analytical approach of Wender and Foulkes,[14] to the psychoanalytic method of Schilder. Other devices are the "call system," "the rotation method," the question-box, reading as therapy, and numerous visual devices.

12 Paul Schilder, "The Analysis of Ideologies as a Psychotherapeutic Method, Especially in Group Treatment," *American Journal of Psychiatry,* November, 1936.

13 Paul Schilder, "Results and Problems of Group Psychotherapy in Severe Neuroses," *Mental Hygiene,* January, 1939. See p. 236.

14 S. H. Foulkes, "Principles and Practice of Group Therapy," *Bulletin of the Menninger Clinic,* May, 1946. S. H. Foulkes and Eve Lewis, "Group Analysis," *The British Journal of Medical Psychology,* Vol. XX, Part 2, 1944.

Many of these were evolved during World War II and have served very effectively with patients who, for the most part, suffered from acute and temporary disturbances. But these artifices are not applicable when transplanted to group psychotherapy in civilian life. When the aim is to overcome acute reactions to fear and excessive strain, any cathartic device is helpful. Such devices are of little or no value, however, when more or less permanent changes in the personality are desired. Even when we succeed in causing symptoms to disappear, as in the so-called "social recovery," there is no assurance that these symptoms or others to take their place will not reappear after treatment is terminated. While education, suggestion, guidance and advice may be helpful in dealing with some types of adjustment problems, they should not be confounded with real psychotherapy, the aim of which is to affect within varying degrees changes within the personality structure.

The serious lack revealed in the literature is the absence of criteria for selecting patients and grouping them. This we consider a very serious defect which perhaps is due to an unjustifiable zeal. The demands on psychiatric resources are much greater than can be met, and it becomes necessary to seek out more economical devices for treatment. This, however, should not cause practitioners to lose perspective. Various types of authoritative therapy may help the dependent, infantilized patient to keep himself in control or alter his behavior, but as soon as the restraints are removed, he is likely to regress. Inspirational therapy may be effective with hysterical symptoms, but the hysterical character is not cured by it.

In the introductory chapter to *The Practice of Group Therapy* I have noted that concepts such as "group emotion," "group symptom," "group formation" have found their way into the literature and I have expressed the view that these do not really apply to therapeutic groups.[15] More recently, esoteric and transcendental attributes have been ascribed to therapy groups, thereby obscuring the specificity of the process and greatly diminishing the instrumental value of groups in therapy. Therapy groups cannot be viewed as groups in the ordinary sense of the word and with the same meaning as applied to social or educational groups. In these

[15] S. R. Slavson, ed., *The Practice of Group Therapy* (New York, International Universities Press, 1947).

the individual is merged with, or better still submerged in, the group. The role each plays, the position he occupies in relation to the others, the group stratifications and the common aims, are all more or less fixed. This I have described as "group fixity." In therapy groups, these rigidities and fixed relations and roles must be prevented or the therapeutic process is completely blocked. The group must always remain *mobile*.

The dynamics in ordinary groups can be described as interstimulation, interaction, induction, neutralization, identification, assimilation, polarization, rivalry, projection, and integration.[16] In analytic groups only a few of these make their appearance, and they do not lead toward unified or cohesive group action. Each patient must remain a detached entity in whom intrapsychic changes must occur. He cannot give up his autonomous identity, as is the case in ordinary groups, but must remain at all times detached and work on his own problems. This changes the concept of the group as commonly understood. In fact a more correct characterization would be "compresence of patients" rather than a group of patients. These principles are amply demonstrated in the records in this volume. Patients talk about their problems and those of the others, as individuals. There never is a group problem or a group project or a group aim.

The therapist as well must keep in mind and seek to understand the latent content of what is being said by *each* patient rather than focus attention or try to understand the "group process." This does not exclude his awareness of the effect members of a group have on one another. Individuals have different effects upon different members of a group. Some overdominate and block the catharsis of the others; some are quarrelsome and antagonistic, and keep the others in a state of emotional turmoil and fear. There are those who compete with the therapist as a sibling or parent figure, and still others who naturally have insight into psychologic processes and exert a beneficial effect on the group interviews.

The present volume is an attempt to set forth group psychotherapy in a *strictly clinical setting* and to base its practice on specific and accepted clinical concepts. An effort has been made to relate

[16] S. R. Slavson, *Character Education in a Democracy* (New York, Association Press, 1939), Chapter IV.

diagnostic categories to treatment procedures. We assume the correctness of the basic concepts of genetic psychology, psychodynamics, and pathology developed by Freud and his associates and the established phenomena of infant sexuality, Oedipal conflict and the structure and function of the unconscious. We also accept the hypothesis of the structure and the dynamic relation of the id, ego, and superego, and the existence and dynamism of the libido, and employ the dynamic elements of process suggested by Freud. These are transference, free association and insight which, of course, are greatly modified through the multiple relations in a group setting and which will be described in detail in the pages of this book.

Basic assumptions are indispensable to any orderly presentation of an idea, for without such essential elements one cannot build a structure of theory and practice any more than a building can be built without bricks, steel, and concrete. The therapist, as well, functions in accordance with his acceptance or rejection and his understanding of these foundational assumptions as his frame of reference. One who rejects the Oedipal conflict as a major source of personality difficulties, for example, would evade exploring that area. If he believes in educational procedures only, he would not encourage patients to uncover their unconscious conflicts; and the therapist who looks askance at the theories of instinct and libido, or denies the existence of infantile sexuality and primary aggression must of necessity employ different techniques and have different treatment aims than one who is in agreement with these facts, theories, and assumptions. In analytic group psychotherapy, as in individual psychotherapy, the orientation of the therapist is of utmost importance, for what he understands to be the foundational dynamics in development of human personality and its malformations will affect his practice.

In 1937, three years after activity group therapy[17] was first initiated, experiments with different forms of group treatment were conducted under the direction of the present writer. These experiments were prompted by the recognition that activity groups were not suited for all the children and pre-adolescents that came for treatment. Because of age differences and the diversity in the clin-

[17] S. R. Slavson, *An Introduction to Group Therapy*, New York, Commonwealth Fund, 1943.

ical picture presented, other therapy methods were found necessary to meet the needs of different patients.[18]

The first departure from activity group therapy was made when a mixed group was organized for seriously disturbed and intensely psychoneurotic boys and girls from eight to ten years of age. The chief difference between this group and the activity therapy groups, then in operation, lay in the fact that the therapist interpreted behavior and attitudes to individual children and to the group as a whole. She encouraged the children to understand each other and their own behavior.[19] Later this work was extended to include both pre-school and older children,[20] adolescents,[21] and mothers.[22]

In this connection it should be noted that group experience holds limitless growth possibilities for children, and to a large extent also for adolescents. In fact, the child develops largely through experience and association, and to a lesser extent through knowledge and ideas. The child is a function-mechanism, and his psychological expansion results from action and not thought. Action, realistic impediments, external control, and affectionate guidance affect intrapsychic changes more than do concepts and ideas. This is especially true of the latency period, when interpretation is displaced by living in a therapeutic atmosphere and by corrective experiences and reactions. We designate this *situational therapy.*[23]

Situational therapy in a group is particularly suitable for chil-

[18] S. R. Slavson, "Current Practices in Group Therapy," *Mental Hygiene,* July, 1944; "Differential Dynamics of Activity and Interview Group Therapy," *American Journal of Orthopsychiatry,* April, 1947; *An Introduction to Group Therapy,* Chapter IX.

[19] See Chapter IX, pp. 138 ff.

[20] Betty Gabriel, "An Experiment in Group Treatment," *American Journal of Orthopsychiatry,* January, 1939. Leon Lucas, "Treatment of Young Children in a Group," *The News Letter of the American Association of Psychiatric Social Workers,* Winter Issue, 1943–44. S. R. Slavson, "Differential Methods of Group Therapy in Relation to Age Levels," *The Nervous Child,* April, 1945; and "Play Group Therapy for Young Children," *ibid.,* July, 1948.

[21] Betty Gabriel, "Group Treatment of Six Adolescent Girls," *The News Letter of the American Association of Psychiatric Social Workers,* Winter Issue, 1943–44; and "Interview Group Therapy for Adolescent Girls," *American Journal of Orthopsychiatry,* October, 1944.

[22] Fannie Amster, "Collective Psychotherapy of Mothers of Emotionally Disturbed Children," *American Journal of Orthopsychiatry,* January, 1944. Etta Kolodney, "Treatment of Mothers in Groups as a Supplement to Child Psychotherapy," *Mental Hygiene,* July, 1944. A brief description of these various methods can also be found in S. R. Slavson, *An Introduction to Group Therapy,* Chapter IX.

[23] S. R. Slavson, *An Introduction to Group Therapy,* p. 16.

dren in the latency period because of their immaturity, undeveloped ideational capacities, and limited language facilities. Acting out and the consequent reactions of others are more natural for these children than is talking out. The period of latency is also the period of the maximum centrifugal emotional growth which follows the Oedipal period. It is at this stage that persons other than members of one's family assume added importance; group therapy utilizes this natural homonomous trend in the therapeutic process. This should not be taken to mean that language has no place whatever in the treatment of young children. (See Chapter VIII.) Direct dealing with them by the therapist is frequently indicated, but it must be subordinated to acting out, and the consequent reactions and responses, through which the young child achieves release from anxiety, cathexis displacement, sublimation channels, substitute gratifications, ego-strengthening, and derivative insight, and establishes ego boundaries.

Group interviews with adolescents and adults were found to be most effective. The conversations are of the same nature as in individual interviews, but the presence of others with similar problems provides mutual support and enables the group members to bring forward latent and repressed feelings. The interviews yield clarification of, and release from, emotional tensions. The therapist helps each member to allay anxieties, gain insight into and understanding of his problems, and develop more wholesome attitudes toward parents, mates, siblings, and the world in general. Occasional questioning, direct and indirect discussion, and interpretation help each member of the group to find release from traumatic disturbances.

In this connection it is well to keep firmly in mind that group psychotherapy is not based on a system of psychodynamics or psychopathology different from any other form of treatment; the bases are the same. It is, rather, a method, and as such must be founded on definite assumptions with regard to man's psyche, the nature and causes of its malformations, and must function within an acceptable framework of general psychotherapy.

A striking observation that forces itself on one is that despite the variation in methods employed in the so-called different "schools" of psychotherapy, favorable results are obtained by them all. Three possibilities come to mind that may explain this incongruity or paradox. One is the suitability of a given method to the skill and temperament of the therapist; a second is that the nature and dynamics of the problems in different patients are such that one method evokes a better response than another; the third is that there are common and basic elements in all of the "schools" of psychotherapy, which are overlooked because of the preoccupation with the differences rather than with the similarities. It is of utmost importance for the further development of psychotherapy generally, and for its increased usefulness in the future, that an effort be made to identify the common elements among these various "schools" and to establish, on a research basis, the suitability of any given type of treatment to a specific type of patient.

The common elements in all sound psychotherapies—and this may explain the reason for their effectiveness, even though the therapies differ in some of their assumptions—are five in number. Present also in analytic group psychotherapy, these are: (1) relation (transference), (2) catharsis, (3) insight, and/or ego-strengthening, (4) reality testing, and (5) sublimation. The presence of all, or a majority of these dynamics in the different "schools" of psychotherapy accounts, in our opinion, for successes in treatment by what are seemingly diverse and even antagonistic approaches. In all of the more acceptable techniques, at least the first three of these elements are present. Individual psychotherapy does not supply reality testing and sublimation as a part of the treatment situation. The patient constantly tests himself, however, against the realities of his own life, and these tests he employs in his recovery. In the world in which he lives he finds for himself either fulfillment or sublimations of his impulses and cravings. Groups, on the other hand, are a tangible reality and supply possibilities for sublimations as well. In order to lay a systematic foundation for analytic group psychotherapy, specifically, each of these separate dynamics will be discussed topically in succeeding chapters.

CHAPTER TWO

TRANSFERENCE AND SUBSTITUTION IN GROUP PSYCHOTHERAPY

THE TERM transference is employed to designate the similarity in the feelings and attitudes a patient has toward the therapist and toward his own parents. The patient *transfers* his feelings from parent to doctor, accepting the latter *in loco parentis* and reacting to him with associated emotions. Most of these feelings and attitudes have been repressed and form the content of the unconscious. Thus repressed and censored, they cannot be brought out to the light of day without a special therapeutic setting. The defenses built up by the ego are too strong to permit their appearance in the conscious; instead, rationalizations, symptoms, and projections are employed to resolve inner conflict. In treatment the patient displaces upon the therapist the prohibited, guilt and anxiety-evoking wishes he has had toward his parents. The basic nature of these attitudes are libidinal (sexual), and dealing with them is a major skill the therapist must possess. They form the pivot of psychoanalytic treatment.

The importance of transference in therapy was vaguely recognized even among the ancients. When Socrates acknowledged the existence of mental as separate from physical illness, he prescibed the remedy of "sweet words." We know that patients respond best to a doctor with a "bedside manner" and that some have what is described as a "therapeutic personality." The fact is commonly recognized that some persons are better able than others to evoke responses and promote improvement in physical and mental illnesses, and that both physicians and psychotherapists possess such qualities in varying degrees. Some easily evoke the confidence of patients and enter into a state of empathy with them; others require a longer time to attain this response. In practice, one finds patients with whom a particular therapist cannot establish a working relation at all, although he receives positive reactions almost instantaneously from others.

The initial empathy the patient feels with the therapist is as good a guarantee as one can have that the treatment will be successful. The fact that during treatment negative feelings will arise toward the therapist, and that hostility toward him will periodically appear, does not detract from the basic solidity of the therapeutic relation. The original sympathetic attitudes of the patient will be of help when these transitory negative phases arise.

Transference is the major dynamic in all forms of mental therapy. This holds true of group psychotherapy, although, here, it is vastly modified both quantitatively and qualitatively. The spontaneous interaction of a number of people inevitably produces a multiplicity of relationships such as domination-submission, parasitic, anaclitic, supportive, equipodal, unilateral, bilateral, and multilateral, and various combinations of these. In analytic group psychotherapy we are largely, though not exclusively, concerned with the unilateral, bilateral, and multilateral relationships.[1]

The phenomenon of transference is not confined to psychotherapy alone. It occurs in social casework and in everyday relations among people. This wider use and understanding of the concept in its varying meanings, both in quality and intensity, has led to the recognition that there can be "levels of transference."

The patient transfers his early libidinal cravings, affections, and aggressions toward his parent of the opposite sex and his resentments toward the parent of the same sex, with the many complex constellations that accompany these emotions. The cravings for various types of gratifications, including the sexual, deeply repressed by the child because of fear of the parent of the same sex and because of the direct denial by the parent of the opposite sex, form the nucleus of psychoneuroses and play an important role in other personality malformations and social maladjustments.

In the treatment of patients, especially children, we are not always faced with definitely crystallized psychoneuroses. Many pa-

[1] S. R. Slavson, "Types of Relationships and Their Application to Psychotherapy," *American Journal of Orthopsychiatry,* April, 1945. See also his "Transference Phenomena in Group Psychotherapy," and "Catharsis in Group Psychotherapy," both to be published in *The Psychoanalytic Review.*

tients have neurotic trends or traits. They react to inadequate parents and siblings, have either deflated or inflated self-esteem (self-image), are hungry for love, crave support and security, or suffer from some form of character malformation. More serious psychoneurotic patients may require thoroughgoing psychoanalytic treatment, but many can be helped by other types of derivative and less intensive therapies, that have been found to be effective in varying degrees, especially when properly suited to a specific patient. In all of them, however, transference is the basis of treatment.

Since the bases of the feelings toward parents which patients live through in the psychotherapeutic relation is essentially charged with libido, we shall designate the transference toward the therapist as *libidinal transference.* Obviously this cannot be as intense in groups as it is in individual treatment. The presence of other members with whom the therapist has to be shared and the relations that inevitably arise among the members themselves dilute it. Another reason is that, in groups, interpretation seldom reaches areas in the patient's personality as deep as in individual treatment. The therapist has to consider here both the dilution of the transference and the differential readiness of the patients. Interpretation that may be appropriate for one may prove disturbing to another. Much of the interpretation, as we shall see from the record material, is given by the patients to each other. By and large, interpretation in groups is directed to the *lowest common psychological denominator.* Additional interpretation, when required, has to be given to patients in supplementary individual sessions, which should always be available to them when necessary.

Another type of transference in therapy groups originates in intermember relations. Some of these relations are of the sibling type, while in some instances a patient may accept another as a parent figure and transfer upon him the feelings he has had toward his parents. Patients reveal in groups the sibling rivalries they had experienced in their childhood; they seek to monopolize the therapist and hold the center of the stage in an unmistaken desire to be the only child. This and similar behavior is accepted by some in the group and resented by others, who challenge and punish the overassertive fellow member by either prying questions, by arguments and disagreement, or by direct attack. Through identification, patients who had themselves suffered through sibling rivalry are likely to support the "victim," others join in the torment, still others remain inactive. Though primary attitudes are vastly modified by later experiences, the behavior of each member is determined by his early experiences with siblings and parents.

The network of feelings among members of a therapy group (in which they transfer their early attitudes toward parents and real siblings) we designate as *sibling transference*. The following situation illustrates this.

> At one point during the twenty-second session, the (adolescent) girls talked in a superficial vein, but what came out of the discussion was that Paula was jealous because the group frequently complimented Reva on her improvement. She wished the girls would help her select a new way of doing her hair. Even her boy friend Jim criticized it, telling her that she would look more attractive if she wore her hair differently. She made a slip of the tongue when she said: "Jim will divorce me if I don't comb my hair more stylishly." The girls burst out laughing at this. Paula appeared embarrassed and was not very coherent when she tried to explain her mistake. . . . Several styles of hair-do were suggested to Paula. Sandra volunteered to help her create one for herself and began to talk about her married sister, who was having marital difficulties. This was not followed up by the girls, as Paula continued with her complaining that unless the group helped her better herself and look more attractive, they were not doing their duty. The girls who sensed Paula's need for attention, gave her a great deal of recognition. They spoke quite spontaneously of the great improvement Paula had made since she came to the group. She now speaks in a well-modulated, pleasant voice; in fact, not once during the entire session did she raise her voice, they said. (Her harsh, brazen speech annoyed the girls when she first came to the group.) She glowed on being complimented and remarked that they were not permitted to raise their voices even on the stairs, where she had worked. (She had worked in a hospital during the summer vacation.) Paula then proceeded to describe a number of different types of surgical operations. The girls were very much interested and listened attentively as she described some of the things she had seen in the hospital.

Identification transference is also very much in evidence in all types of group psychotherapy. The possibility of identifying (and, therefore, also of universalizing) is a major advantage in group treatment. While its base is a narcissistic one, the awareness of similarity of experiences, needs, and feelings helps each to see himself more objectively and encourages him to face and cope with his own psychologic difficulties. Identification serves also to extend the capacity for object relations that is always defective in patients who need psychotherapy. Identification transference is also the foundation for group unity during the negative phases of the transference toward the therapist.

Some illustrations of this type of transference follow:

Anne tells again about the girl around whom she would like to write a play. She refers to her as a "problem girl." In the play this girl would have a friend whom she admires and in whom she confides. As they talk, the first girl finds that her friend, too, has problems. The climax of the play is that both girls become more tolerant of their parents, and in turn the parents more understanding of their daughters. Anne says that if the group could write a play together and bring out these ideas, "the girls would have the satisfaction of knowing that they were helpful."

Anne then goes on to say that she has arguments with her mother, who tries to choose her friends for her, "and we get into an uproar." Betty says she always quarrels with her mother, to which Ella comments: "Girls, can you tell me what girls don't quarrel with their mothers?"

At another session, when Betty was ill, she sent through her sister the book she promised to give Yolanda. The sister explained that Betty had a cold, but would come the following week. When she left, the girls were unanimous about their affection for Betty. They said that though she is very sickly, Betty needs the group and they would visit her if she became really ill.

After the sixteenth session, all the girls, without exception, dressed much better and all looked much nicer. In the past, Anne had been careless about her appearance but was now making an effort to look more presentable. Ella, who proudly wore men's shirts and ties (see p. 105), was now dressing in more feminine fashion, wearing a soft white blouse and an attractive grey suit.

There are also negative manifestations of sibling transference as in jealousy and rivalry.

Reva and Rose seemed very joyful when they first saw each other at the group after a separation of three years. It seemed as though they wanted to catch up in a few minutes with all that had happened to them. They both talked at once and told one another about their recent "stand-ups." Georgia and Phyllis seemed disturbed at being left out of the conversation. Georgia said she had been "rushed" by a boy she met recently and when she finally found time to give him an appointment, he did not show up. Paula, too, had a similar experience, but she didn't care because there's always Jim in the background.

Anne and Ella talked about camp. (Betty, who was present, could not take part in this since, having been an invalid, she never went to camp.) She seemed to be annoyed at being left out, and suddenly interrupted their conversation by boasting about her uncle, a seaman, who had recently been home on a visit. Then she told about another very rich uncle of hers who had graduated from high school at twelve years of age. He had not been very good to them, but the seaman uncle outfitted Betty with very nice clothes.

In groups, the various types of relations may lead to mutual support, to discharge of aggression, or to assuaging guilt feelings. The characteristic clusters and subgroups that develop within the larger group are of definite value to each of the participants. Depending upon the situation, transference in groups occurs in cycles. Both positive and negative feelings tend to be intensified through identification and rivalry. Rivalry manifests itself when patients attempt to please the therapist and vie for his attention and love. But because latent hostile and aggressive feelings toward the parental figure are always near the surface and are easily activated, feelings of guilt and the need for group protection against punishment tend to bring the patients together. It is in the negative phases of the transference that group unity is most evident. The therapist may, therefore, find himself at times the target of hostility and aggression which may be expressed directly or disguised as humor or sarcasm. It may also manifest itself in more passive forms such as indifference, silence, lateness, and absences.

Dilution of the transference toward the therapist is one of the inevitable results of group treatment. The therapist is not the sole focus of cathexis; the transference is divided among fellow patients. This is particularly helpful to those who feel disloyal toward parents or mates when they develop strong attachments such as in individual treatment. Group psychotherapy for such patients is, therefore, less threatening and less guilt-evoking. Dilution of the libidinal component of the transference is essential also for patients who, because of homosexual trends, are afraid to become involved with a therapist of the same sex. It is also advantageous for individuals who have been hurt in their earliest relations and are therefore afraid of emotional attachments. Though transference dilution has definite advantages to many patients, it at the same time reduces the depth of treatment. This is its chief disadvantage.

Expression of hostility toward the therapist in the transference relation is a primary requirement in psychotherapy. Where there is no hostility there is no therapy, for withholding aggression is a form of resistance. In individual treatment the therapist must help patients to articulate negative feelings toward him. In groups the expression of hostile feelings is greatly facilitated because of the *support* patients give each other. This may be the reason why the timid and withdrawn improve so rapidly in all types of group treatment. It is easier for the inhibited to cast off protective taciturnity than it is for the aggressive to curb reactive assertiveness.

Sandra said that she had learned from sad experience that one cannot do everything one wants. The outcomes of her runaway from home were not very pleasant. She paid dearly for her escapades by having to go through distressing encounters at the Childrens' Society, and later in court. The therapist said: "And now you are criticized here." Sandra said she does not look upon this (therapy) as a bad experience: she has always enjoyed coming to the clinic (which she attends by court order). The therapist said that there must have been times when she did not enjoy it, especially when she was angry with the therapist for some reason or other. Sandra insisted that she never hated the therapist, but there were times when she was angry. Lydia cannot recall a time when she was angry at the therapist. The therapist interjected that sometimes it is necessary to admit you are angry, though anger can be expressed in other ways, too. It can be show by the silence, for example. Rose said she was never aware of anger toward the therapist, and as the discussion proceeded Rose seemed to become impatient with the conversation. Paula now spoke of her "unwillingness to talk" and "not keeping appointments" as a way of expressing anger. The therapist said that this was a good point and that, while some of the girls had been unable to express it in so many words, their feelings were often manifested through coming late and staying away.[2]

Despite periodic hostility toward the therapist each patient desires to be loved and accepted by him as a parent surrogate. In fact, this is among the motives for improvement. The patient perceives what the therapist (good parent) would like him to be and strives to please him.

While the attitudes of the patients to each other and toward the

[2] Although the therapist's intention here is to bring forth negative feelings, she presses the point too strongly and too directly. The incident, however, reveals repression and ambivalence in some of the girls, and that they are becoming vaguely aware of this.

therapist may alternate between love and hate, submission and aggression, activity group therapy has demonstrated that a group can have a therapeutic effect only when its fundamental relations are positive or can become so in the course of treatment. Alternation of emotion is inevitable but the conditions for therapy require that the basic attitudes toward the therapist are positive, though at times these feelings may be hostile. To describe these two manifestations, the terms *basic transference* and *transitory transference* are suggested.[3]

The therapist, whether in individual or group treatment, has to be certain that the basic transference toward him is positive before he can use it as a treatment tool. Patients frequently withdraw from treatment because the therapist begins the interpretation before a positive basic transference had been established. The initial period of the treatment relation must be devoted to establishing a transference of this kind. Once this is achieved the therapist can, when necessary, employ authority, criticism, and in rare instances even deprivations.

A very neurotic woman with serious complications in her family life usually talked about the problems of the other members of the group and those of her neighbors, but did not refer to her own difficulties. Once the therapist turned to her and said: "You always talk about other people. You have troubles of your own. Why don't you talk about them?" The patient's face flushed. She appeared deeply hurt and depressed and remained silent throughout the remainder of the session. She spoke but sparsely at subsequent sessions as well.

The therapist had evidently overestimated the transference relation and misjudged the effect the statement might have. The patient sought to hide her own problems behind those of other people and thus reduce her guilt and anxiety. She sought the anonymity that groups provide, and this should be permitted, for varying periods, as a step in the treatment of particularly resistive and stubborn cases. One must give such patients a great deal of time. In the present case, with one brief statement, the therapist swept aside the strong defenses the woman had built up. If necessary at all, it would

[3] I am indebted to Dr. John H. W. Van Ophuijsen for first suggesting these terms to me.

have been more appropriate to make a general statement such as "It seems that all people have the same kind of problems that we do: Mrs. K. (the patient) probably has them too." This would not have been so threatening and anxiety-provoking as was the direct attack.[4]

The positive nature of the basic transference is revealed in the following abstract from a group interview, the twenty-fifth:

Sandra said that she would never lie to the therapist and that is why she told of the possibility of being expelled from school. In back of her mind there was the thought that she ought to graduate from high school. "See," she said to the therapist: "I feel that I have to tell you things. You are like a mother to us." Florence (a visitor) agreed, completely, with Sandra. She said that in all the years she had been coming for individual treatment (she visited the group just once) she had never withheld anything and had never told a lie. Paula said that she had been coming for individual treatment with Mrs. Golden (her individual therapist) about four-and-a-half years, but "I can speak more frankly here [in the group] than I can to Mrs. Golden, because Mrs. Golden is too businesslike." She stamped her feet on the floor in anger and said: "I can't stand it." She said that Mrs. Golden had only herself on her mind. Sandra said that maybe things were happening to Mrs. Golden, too. Paula went on to say: "When I am with the girls, I feel that I am completely devoted to them and that I have nothing else on my mind." Paula was afraid to discuss the group with Mrs. Golden, lest she would take her out of it. "I like the group too much," she added. She would leave the group, if Mrs. Golden wanted her to, but then the truth would have to come out. The therapist asked Paula what she thought she got from the group. It was difficult for Paula to formulate her ideas, but she believed she had learned self-control and how to behave with people. She added that she could learn more by listening to the discussion among the girls than by reading any book.

Interpretation: The conflict in the transference is quite evident. Paula prefers the diluted relation in the group to intensive psychotherapy. Mrs. Golden represents the superego and its restraints, while the group appeals to Paula's pleasure drives (as mother substitute). This conflict was even better displayed at the seventeenth session of a group of girls.

After a lengthy talk about how evil their mothers were, during which Yolanda said she was tired all day at school because of her parents' quarrels at night, a discussion about teachers followed. Most of the girls said they disliked their teachers for one reason or another. Ella suddenly

[4] It is necessary to differentiate between resistance and defenses. Resistance may be under specific circumstances, attacked directly, but not the patient's defenses. In the instance cited, the therapist attacked the woman's defenses.

said to the therapist: "I think you would be a very good teacher." When asked why, she said: "Because you are kind." The others said that they felt that, if necessary, the therapist could discipline them, too. The latter asked whether that meant they really wanted someone to discipline them. Yes, they did. In the experience of each of the girls their mothers never knew what discipline really was; their mothers were either too good to them, or beat them. They just didn't know how to control by disciplinary measures.

Comment: In this episode, we have not only a demonstration of positive transference, but also the fact is fairly well established that mothers, teachers, and therapists are identified in the girls' minds.

Transference phenomena in groups are complicated. The sibling and identification transferences and the many attitudes of love and hate, rivalry, jealousy, domination, and submission are ever present. Though these are evident in the patients' attitudes toward one another, they reflect in a large part attitudes toward the therapist. Likes and dislikes of members of a group are important because they determine the fundamental group atmosphere, and such initial feelings are influenced and modified by the role of the therapist. Initial antipathy and antagonisms do not deter development of positive transference among members in later stages of treatment if the transference to the therapist is positive. The very fact that patients overcome ambivalence, hostilities and antipathies toward each other indicates emotional growth. It means that narcissistic and infantile characteristics have been overcome, that projection has been diminished, and that aggressions had been brought under control. These are all indications of ego strength and improved capacity for object relations.

Because of this empathy and commonness of unconscious pressures and strivings, interchange in groups are significant, even though they may not plumb so deeply as do other types of psychotherapy. This may, as well, be the cause for the acceleration of the therapeutic process in groups. The *collective experience* derived from identification, mutual support, reduction of ego defenses, sibling transferences, and other dynamics involved increase productivity through catalysis.[5]

The collective experience is based upon the integration of the

[5] See pp. 42, 96.

individual into the group, and is itself derived from the effect groups have upon ego-defenses. The acceleration of regression may be a result of the same dynamics as the catalytic process. It is further aided by the sibling identifications and the activation of the infantile aggressions toward the parent and early infantile memories of the family. This means that the group weakens the ego defenses. Inner impulses that had been kept in check gain some precedence and the individuation already achieved is partially, at least, given up. In the collective experience the individual gives up some of his autonomy; he comes under the domination of the group, a process that is most clearly seen in mobs, where regression is at its highest.

Through his awareness of the two processes—collective experience and associative thinking (see p. 58)—the group therapist steers his course. In dealing with the first phenomenon, collective experience, he has to counteract as far as possible the tendency of submerging the individuality of the members, who may readily submit as an escape from autonomy and responsibility. These patients need to be guided to assert themselves, and in this the therapist's help may be necessary. He must recognize ready agreement and compliance, for example, as mechanisms of escape or hostility that should be brought to the surface. Compliance may be a form of resistance and is frequently observed also in individual treatment.

The aim of therapy is to strengthen the patient's ego to be able to express his aggressions. The therapeutic experience itself serves to strengthen the ego and in the submissive, diffident, and withdrawn, removes the blocking toward emotional growth. The aggressive and domineering members, on the other hand, constitute more of a problem. They are brought under control through the restraining pressure of the other members of the group, and the narcissistically assertive may in all probability not return for treatment as a result. It is, therefore, necessary to evaluate thoroughly and in advance the psychodynamics of each patient to determine his suitability for group treatment.

One of the elements that facilitate positive transference toward the therapist in groups is *multipolarity*. In individual treatment, the therapist is the sole center of focus of the transference. In the group, there are others, as well, who have various emotional meaning to each member. They are sources of fear, support, reinforcement of hostility, of sadism and masochism, of sexual attraction and repulsion. The presence of these positive and negative interpatient attitudes changes the centrality of the transference. Even though the therapist is the source of many feelings in the group and at the apex of its emotional network, he is not the sole focus. The network of transference, both quantitatively and qualitatively, involves all the members of the group, including the therapist. Thus its polarity is distributed and must be understood in terms of each patient. As can be expected, each member of the group is at once a focus or pole toward which feelings are directed by others, and he in turn directs his feelings to or dispenses them upon some of his fellow group members. This phenomenon in the dynamic of transference where the transference cathexis is invested in more than one person we designate as multipolarity.

Mrs. E., a psychoneurotic, acted out intense sibling rivalry in the group interviews. She dominated the group and monopolized the therapist. The group provided her with an opportunity for acting out rivalry without fear of punishment and as a result she became more communicative. In the past she had not been able to accept individual treatment, but had become less resistive and more accessible because of the transference dilution in the group through multipolarity. She accepted individual treatment by the group therapist concurrently with the group sessions.

Rivalry in a group has value for only children and for those who had been in conflict with siblings. Sharing the therapist brings out a variety of reactions of antagonism, submission, and ingratiation. Some of the more fearful band together for support. Others expect the therapist to protect them, and when he fails to do so, they either express their hostile feelings toward him directly or displace them on one another. This may create conflict in the group.

Patients reinforce one another in their hostility toward the therapist. Such support is very valuable for it renders them less fearful to make feelings known by acts or words. The therapist has to help the patients individually or as a group to bring out their feelings toward him and interpret these transference attitudes. An instance of this is given in the following incident taken from the record of a group of nine-year-old boys.

After a considerable struggle, Richard took the saw away from Larry. Then, Stephen (a very aggressive boy) teased Richard. He threw pieces of wood at Richard, went through the motions of piercing his eyes with a pair of scissors, threw objects into his face, and struck him. Richard continued working with the saw, but seemed quite uncomfortable and looked helplessly at Stephen. Stephen abruptly and without any relation to what he was doing, threw a piece of wood at the therapist, who worked quite a distance away in another part of the room. The therapist covered his face with his hand and the wood struck it. Stephen pretended to be frightened, derisively shivered with feigned fear, but instantly turned to Richard, shook hands with him and said: "Now we are friends." From then on until the end of the session there was harmony between the two. Richard was cheerful and happy for the remainder of the session.

Interpretation: Since Richard vanquished Larry, it behooved Stephen to vanquish Richard. This established his superiority over the group and he became stronger than the therapist (the father). When he threw a piece of wood at the therapist he further proved his strength, especially since he was not punished. Because his attack was accepted by the father (therapist), Stephen no longer needed to attack Richard (sibling). Stephen's competitiveness with the therapist had been demonstrated in many other ways throughout the treatment sessions, which were a continuation of his Oedipal struggle with his father.

Hostility is seldom expressed as overtly as in the above example, except by very young children. Adolescents and adults employ more subtle techniques. They may shuffle their feet to the extreme annoyance of all present, sniffle in a very obvious and disturbing way, interrupt the interview, suggest that the session end prematurely, complain about the uselessness of attending sessions, or make sarcastic and derogatory remarks about fellow group members, the clinic, or the therapist. In a state of strong negative transference, an adolescent girl once characterized the therapist as a dissolute old hag. When, despite these exacerbations of hostility, patients continue to attend sessions, the outburst must be viewed as transitory negative phases in the transference. Since improvement can be achieved only when patients discharge hostility toward a parent figure, such as the therapist, it should be encouraged and even activated.

At the eleventh session of a group of adolescent girls the therapist was unavoidably delayed for about ten minutes. When the therapist came in, she found the girls sitting very quietly and did not react to her entrance. She asked what they were talking about before she came in. Ella remarked they were relaxing; the others remained mute. The studied quiet of the girls masked an evident resentment that was to come out later when the therapist was again delayed at the fifteenth session. At this session she was met with an angry outcry. She waited until the outburst subsided and then told the girls that they had a right to be angry, she should not have been late. Were they angry because they thought she really wanted to come late? All talked at once. They knew that the therapist must have been busy. Ella remarked: "Why shouldn't you be late? You have the privilege, if you want to."

However, at the next session, Ella was particularly hostile toward the therapist. The latter asked if she was angry at her. Ella admitted that she was very angry, and she might "as well come out with it now." The therapist encouraged her. Ella said that she did not think the therapist had a right to keep them waiting. Anne asked Ella why she had concealed this until now. In fact, Anne said, she had noticed that Betty also concealed her feelings. The therapist asked how she knew this. Anne and Ella both pointed to Betty's drawings. She had not really drawn what she wanted to. At this, Betty seemed a little confused and vehemently scrawled over her drawing.

Interpretation: This episode demonstrates also the principle of target multiplicity. We see how Anne, growing anxious by Ella's attack on the therapist, deflects it on Betty. The therapist falls into this trap and becomes a party to it, instead of helping the girls to plumb more deeply into the nature of their hostilities toward her.

Sometimes patients are drawn together in the face of the anxiety that negative feelings provoke. They seek protection in one another, become more friendly, agree with one another's statements, and on the way home leave the room together. Thus, hostile feelings toward a common target—in this case the therapist—intensify mutual acceptance among members of a group. It can, therefore, be said, that negative transference toward the therapist augments the positive transference among patients. The libido withdrawn from the therapist is transmuted into sibling transference.

At the twenty-eighth session, the therapist made a point, during a discussion, of the effect emotions can have on physical health, saying that they occasionally interfere with the regularity of the menstrual period and that they effect muscles, as in Georgia's case, by twitching. As the therapist said this, Georgia's face twitched considerably. The therapist called it to her attention, saying that whenever Georgia is angry she begins to twitch. Reva, in her excitement, stood up in her chair, pointed accusingly at the therapist and exclaimed: "I'm glad you brought that up." Why? She can now tell for the first time (apparently because of the girls presence) how angry she had been when, in the individual interviews, the therapist urged her to speak her mind. In a piercing voice, she shouted, "You're always saying I'm angry at you!" Well, isn't she? And aren't the others occasionally angry?

Sandra and Georgia both remembered getting very angry when the therapist asked them some questions. Why can't they admit it when they are angry? Lydia and Paula had never been angry at the therapist, they declared. The therapist questioned Lydia about this, saying that Paula did not know her except for the short period in the group. Yes, Lydia said, she had been angry at the therapist when she first came and did not want to go to school. She expressed her feelings by refusing to talk and staring straight ahead. The therapist remarked that different people express their anger differently. Paula said that was really true, and giggled.

Interpretation: This process occurs at periods of disturbed transitory transferences. When the fundamental transference is negative and the basic feelings hostile, the resultant emotional frustrations set up permanent discord and recrimination among the group members.

Harmony in any group can be achieved only through the emotional growth and adaptation of its members and is nearly always preceded by conflict and struggle. However, when this struggle is prolonged and too intense, the various transferences may become permanently impaired and the group disintegrated.[6] This usually occurs when the therapist develops negative countertransference. In such circumstances, members of the group reinforce one another's hostility, emotional intensity mounts, and, without leadership (transference) control, negative outcomes are inevitable. This aberrant behavior is possible because members of any group are, to various degrees, de-egotized. They give up part of their autonomy and self-control; super-ego restraints in each are weakened and what resembles a "mob spirit" emerges. When the therapist shows displeasure, annoyance, or anger, his role as the strong and loving parent figure is destroyed; he is no longer the tolerant, accepting person, no longer the source of security, or a suitable ego ideal. The natural hostility toward the parent is at once activated and mobilized. The transference controls disappear and the therapist (or others who serve as targets) may become the victims of the group's wrath. When the controls are thus removed, the likelihood is that early Oedipal hostility will assert itself and will be directed toward anyone in authority or any representative of it. Such reactions are rather common experience in institutions where these struggles are near the surface, as well as in society generally.

There is considerable doubt whether transference in the strict

[6] See also S. R. Slavson, "Some Elements in Activity Group Therapy," (section on Phenomenon of Nodal Behavior), *American Journal of Orthopsychiatry*, October, 1944.

Freudian sense is present in children of pre-school age. Observation of young children in individual and group treatment seems to indicate that they do not develop transference attitudes of the same nature as do older children and adults. The adult patient redirects emotions to the therapist, *as though* he were the parent. He is fully aware, however, that the therapist *is not* his parent, and that he is not actually *like* him. The phases of positive and negative feelings are attached to an image of the parent in effigy, as it were.[7] There is always the awareness of the difference in identity of the two persons. In cathexis displacement [8] which occurs in transference, the two foci are not confused. The individual is clearly aware of both of them: it is rather a *transfer of emotions* from one to the other that occurs, but the different entity of each persists in the patient's awareness.

This ability to detach and transfer emotions (cathexis) is still not a part of the equipment of the young child. Because of his narcissistic state, objects and his feelings about them form a unitary complex: he perceives them as one, much as primitive man does. Objects—things, toys, and people—are not entities, they are rather a part and extension of himself, or his feelings about them. He is still in the stage of oral incorporation. Individuation or autonomy has not begun or is only partially achieved. This narcissistic identification eliminates, or certainly limits, object relations and transference. Another reason for the young child's inability to develop transference relations is that he still has the original love-object, the parent. This and the child's pre-verbal state and his still undeveloped ideation make interview therapy unsuitable to his needs. The small child has means of communication other than language, that is, action.

When the young child acts out his love or hate toward the therapist, he does not do so *as though* the therapist were the parent, but rather with the therapist *as* the parent. What the child would like to do to the parent, he does to objects and pets, and to persons in his environment, such as siblings, nurses, relatives, the therapist. If he

[7] In fact, burning, hanging, or mutilating an effigy is based on infantile identification of the object and its representation. The effigy takes on magically the attributes of the original, who suffers the pain inflicted on it. This imagery is rooted in primitive narcissistic, omnipotent feelings.

[8] See p. 76.

is restrained from such action, or when these targets are not accessible, he creates others as objects of love or hate, in phantasy. Whatever these manifest substitutes may be, the real targets are the parents, but because the child fears losing them or being punished, he either represses his aggressions or displaces them.

In the light of these facts, "acting out" by the child can be better understood and its importance more appreciated. The earliest targets of the child's aggressions are, of course, parents. These aggressions are freely expressed in the pre-Oedipal period, but are repressed later, during the Oedipal conflict. If early aggressions are not dealt with appropriately, one of the several results is resentment. Accumulated resentment is one of the foundations for reactive or primary behavior disorders. Infantile aggression also represents the patient's effort to control the environment in accordance with his narcissistic strivings, and his regressive wishes to reestablish conditions that gave him the greatest satisfactions, namely, freedom of action, ready indulgences, and feelings of omnipotence characteristic of the pre-Oedipal phase of development. These strivings for control are evidenced in the play and phantasy of children and frequently in their verbalizations. The child's play is replete with desires for unrestrained freedom, unlimited powers, and pleasure urges. He creates a world in which these wishes are satisfied through phantasy as well as through his aggressive effort. Thus, the aim of aggression here is to recapture a narcissistic way of life.[9]

Because of the existence of these narcissistic cravings and his dependence upon his mother, who satisfies them, the small child is unable to transfer his emotions to others and to establish a true transference.

"The infant and young child is very much a part of the mother, both from the point of view of his own feelings toward the mother and from the mother's feelings toward him. This relationship can be described as symbiotic [10] and whenever it is in any way pathogenic, treatment of both the infant and the mother is essential. The most effective results can be obtained where this procedure is followed. Since the child's personality is still weak, he cannot retain

[9] For a fuller discussion of this subject see p. 115.

[10] S. R. Slavson, "Types of Relationship and Their Application to Psychotherapy," *American Journal of Orthopsychiatry,* April, 1945.

improvement against the pressures of his relationship with the mother. Treatment of mothers of young children is nearly always indicated, and in many instances treatment of the mother alone is adequate to correct whatever problems the child may have. This is true of the treatment of children at all ages, but is especially in point where infants and young children are concerned."[11]

In one of our groups of five-to-six year-old boys and girls, the children have happily accepted a newcomer from the very start. This is not common. Ordinarily, young children display jealousy, reject newcomers and isolate them. The readiness with which the new child was accepted can be explained by the fact that the therapist was an accepting and kindly person, who did not frustrate the children and, therefore, their hostility was not activated. Had they felt hostile toward her, they would probably have redirected it toward the new member. This reaction, however, has also another element. Since the mother occupies so important a role in the psychological economy of the young child, other adults are not highly important. The children in the group were, therefore, not too disturbed by the therapist's acceptance of another member. The mother is still the most significant person in the young child's life and no one can take her place until separation (individuation) has been achieved. Still another factor that may explain the children's ready acceptance of a newcomer is that the group was small, and since the avidity for playmates at this age is rather intense, they were glad to receive another playmate into their midst.

Some evidences among young children of the substitution mechanism as differentiated from transference follow:

A six-year-old boy who behaved in the presence of the other children in the group in a boisterous, careless and destructive manner, acted demure, punctilious, and subdued when he happened to be alone with the therapist. He seemed uncomfortable and kept asking when the other children would come. In the anamnesis of this case we find that the boy was an only child of a very rigid, and tyrannical mother (who was treated in a group at the same time that the boy was). It was evident that the discomfort he felt with his mother was reactivated by the presence of the woman therapist when he was alone with her.

[11] S. R. Slavson, "Differential Methods of Group Therapy in Relation to Age Levels," *The Nervous Child,* April, 1945.

A very aggressive girl of five who seriously disturbed the group and was hostile to the therapist, was particularly destructive at one of the sessions. The therapist was aware of the fact that the child was to undergo a tonsillectomy the next day (against our advice). During the course of the session, the little girl struck children, destroyed their projects, hit the therapist with a hammer and kicked her in the abdomen while the latter was leaning over trying to pacify her. She called the therapist vile names. The therapist firmly removed the child to an adjoining room and told her gently that her behavior was probably due to the fact that she was to have an operation the next day. Was she afraid of the operation? In response the girl said: "I am frightened," then interrupting herself said, "No, I am mad." She added: "I am not mad at you, but I want to kick you and I want to spit in your face, you dumbbell, you big horse." After acting out in this manner our little patient grew calm by the end of the session and on leaving shouted to the therapist: "Goodbye, Liar" (the therapist's name being Lia.) However, as she was leaving and the elevator door was about to close, she suddenly jumped out, embraced the therapist and ran back into the elevator.

Interpretation: The episode clearly reveals the child's displacement of her resentment toward her mother upon the therapist. The following incidents are further illustrations of this process.

A woman therapist took a group of three boys and two girls between the ages of five and six to have refreshments at a corner drugstore. The moment the children entered the restaurant they began calling her names. One said: "You are a crook"; another added: "You stole the money" (for refreshments). All continued baiting her along these lines. One of the boys later said "You are my mother," whereas both girls said, "You are my father."

Interpretation: Being fed by an adult recalled to the children family relations and their associative feelings were reactivated. The parent who presented the greatest problem to each child came to mind first. Thus, the preoccupation of the boy was with the mother and of the girls with their fathers.

The essentiality of authority in the therapy and education of young children (more fully described in Chapter VII) is emphasized by this substitutive mechanism. Self-control and self-discipline that result in ego strength are incorporated first through fear of parents and later through identification with them. A home that permits unbridled expression of anarchic impulses and self-indulgence weakens the ego, deters development of object relations, and results in general maladjustment. It is through the parents' wise authority that the child is helped to bring his narcissistic impulses under control and affect integration of his personality.[12] Inconsistent treatment of the child by parents results in anxiety, regressive behavior and a weak ego. Since the young child in a therapy group substitutes the therapist for the parent, he expects from him the restraints and guidance supplied by the former. When he does not receive these, he feels the therapist is not interested in him and does not love him. At the same time, in the absence of outer restraints aggressive impulses come to the fore and because his own system of inhibitions (ego) is still unformed, he becomes prey to primitive impulses beyond his control. Thus, his ego boundaries are extended beyond socially acceptable limits.

The important contribution of the group therapist at this point is to reeducate the child's attitudes toward authority, without the undesirable features that characterized the parents' role in this respect. Since the therapist is devoid of countertransference so characteristic of parent-child relations—irritation, anger, annoyance, disapproval, or maudlin enthusiasm—he can exert restraint with an even, quiet, and objective mien. He can serve as the source of inexorable, uncompromising, and unyielding response to the child's behavior, which the child soon learns to accept and respect. Needless to say, these reactions, despite consistency and firmness, must be founded in genuine interest and regard for the child. This is well illustrated in the incident of the girl with the pre-operative disturbance. The therapist's firmness gave the child the security that maudlin sympathy could not have done, and her understanding of the child's anxiety assured her of affection. She, therefore, embraced the therapist. We trust those who understand us.[13]

Among the chief therapeutic experiences which are related to the transference relation in activity groups is the refreshment period. The family setting is most realistically reproduced at such times

[12] This is the reason why a permissive environment and overtolerant relations essential in psychotherapy are not recommended for education in the home, school, or resident institutions.

[13] In the analysis of the etiology and treatment of primary behavior disorders in older children, we have come to the conclusion that there is a striking similarity in these and the treatment of the very young child. The "acting out" pattern of the former is in nearly all respects similar to that of the latter, except that in older children feelings of guilt, fear, and shame are more easily aroused.

and face-to-face situations occur more directly and more consistently than during the work period of the sessions. Whether food should be supplied to the analytic groups as well has been a matter of considerable study and observation. Our conclusions favor supplying refreshments to play groups of preschool children and withholding them from older children, adolescents, and adults, because giving food may deter them in their expression of hostility toward the therapist; they would find it difficult to be negativistic and aggressive toward a person who feeds them. The therapist-patient relation in these groups should be the same as in individual treatment. It needs to be free of any social or other involvements. However, we have found that in the early stages of treatment a small dish of hard candies or nuts left on the table during the sessions with adults and adolescents is helpful. Although most often the candy or nuts are ignored, a patient who grows particularly anxious or disturbed turns to eating and offers food to the others. This discharge for oral anxiety, however, can be eliminated after treatment has proceeded for eight or ten sessions.

Young children differ in their attitudes toward food. Since they are motivated by substitution rather than transference, reproducing the family setting is advantageous. It helps them to relive and reactivate their feelings toward their parents in a therapeutic setting and relationship.

As in individual psychotherapy, the factor of countertransference must be taken into consideration. The therapist may develop, often quite unconsciously, attitudes of countertransference which may manifest themselves in three distinct channels: *negative*, *positive*, and *aim-attachment*.

The first is characterized by feelings of irritation, displeasure, anxiety, or disapproval on the part of the therapist. Through these feelings the ego-support the therapist gives the patient by his objectivity and relaxed attention is removed. This in turn results in interference or blocking of catharsis and regression, and either direct resentment (negative transference) or submission on the part of the patient to the therapist occurs. All of these militate against progress in the treatment interviews and relations.

Positive countertransference manifests itself in the therapist's pleasure in or approval of the patient's therapeutic activity or progress, or in his preference for one patient over the others, a situation of which the therapist may not even be aware.

The third type of countertransference may be termed aim-attachment. By this is meant that the therapist himself has definite aims for the group or for individuals in it. Such aims may be a particular objective toward which he is working but for which the patients may not be ready and do not reach through their own free association. When the therapist sets up an aim rather than permitting the group to evolve its own purpose (or treatment foci) through free association or associative thinking, he prevents regression and development of insight.

Another aim a therapist may attach to his patients is a desire on his part that they improve. This desire is likely to be frustrated by the patients during the phases of negative transference when they would unconsciously fight off any improvement. Of greater disadvantage is when some of the patients play into the therapist's plans and in their effort to please him slough off their symptoms. This may result in symptom improvement or pseudo-recovery.

The therapist must always be on guard as to his own attitudes toward the group and individuals in it. He must make certain that he does not attach aims beyond the patients' readiness. This does not mean that the therapist should not help evolve treatment aims as the interviews proceed, but rather that these aims must be related to the immediate needs and must be psychologically continuous with the existing preoccupations of the patients. In the latter instance the patients are helped in their free association along channels in which they are thinking and feeling, instead of being countered or diverted.

CHAPTER THREE

CATHARSIS, REGRESSION, AND ANXIETY

WE NOW come to the second of the basic elements of psychotherapy, catharsis. Because catharsis, regression, and anxiety are dynamically related in the therapeutic process, we shall deal with them as a unit.

It was Freud who first recognized that psychoneurotic symptom formation is a compromise between the id and the superego in conflict with which the ego is unable to deal. He also found that free association ultimately leads to the source of the unconscious conflicts and to the early traumata in which they originate. He has suggested it as a technique for resolution of inner tensions and consequent elimination of symptoms. This regressive free association Freud and his associates designated as catharsis.

Freud also pointed out that catharsis can occur only in a transference relation. If catharsis is to bring to consciousness repressed, guilt evoking and anxiety-inducing feelings, thoughts, and strivings, the emotional setting in the treatment relation must favor it.

One of the sources of resistance to uncovering repressed earlier feelings is the warding off, by the patient, of any regression to infantile cravings, interests, and preoccupations. Because these are chiefly of a hostile and sexual nature, they tend to arouse shame, guilt, and anxiety. The fear of regression is also one of the causes of negative transference, and catharsis cannot occur unless a patient has the security which a positive transference assures. The value of catharsis, whether by verbalization or activity, lies in the fact that it induces regression to stages at which arrest in emotional development (fixation) occurred. It is necessary for the patient to be freed of fear and misgivings before he can allow himself to regress. In addition to the deeper psychological elements in this resistance to regression, there is also present the factor of self-regard or pride. Thus a "self-respecting" individual who occupies an influential position in the community may find himself confessing to "hideous" impulses which make him feel debased, immoral, and anxious. The self-esteem (ego ideal) that he had built up receives a severe jolt. It is very difficult to face these truths within oneself, and much more difficult to impart them to others. To facilitate revelation one has to give up some of one's ego defenses. One also needs to be sure that one's guilt will not be further intensified through disdain, criticism, or punishment from the therapist (parent figure). The therapist's attitude has to be such that the patient is assured of this, for the therapist symbolizes not only the parent, but also society, whose mores must be temporarily revoked during treatment. In this sense also, the therapeutic situation is a social situation in which the sensorious societal values are for the time being suspended. To be able to achieve this against his own fears and anxieties, the patient must feel the acceptance, if not the approval, of the therapist. This is the ego or narcissistic aspect of the transference relation.

Despite this favorable transference relation, psychotherapists very frequently come upon narcissistic defenses or the narcissistic core of patients that frequently defy their most skillful efforts. At this juncture the patient mobilizes all his protective defenses. These take the form of either subtle resistances or of defiance, and the therapeutic process may be blocked for long periods. In such instances, it may be necessary to go beyond the analysis of defenses, which often proves to be ineffective, and to attack them directly. This is, however, a risky procedure and should be undertaken with great care.

In groups the narcissistic defenses and resistance to regression are diminished through identification transferences and because the members support [1] each other, catalyze [2] one another and sanction aggression, especially toward the therapist (parent). Identification [3] and universalization [4] reduce guilt and the friendly atmosphere of the group makes it possible for patients to discharge hitherto hidden feelings and to break the dams that blocked the flow of their psychic energies. Resentment and hostility that had to

[1] See p. 20. [2] See p. 42. [3] See p. 18. [4] See p. 96.

be held in abeyance can now be expressed with impunity. Egress of emotions under such favorable conditions relieves inner tensions that had caused much of the disturbance.

Resolution of conflict is as important for children as it is for adolescents and adults, though the channels through which this is achieved are different. What young children gain through therapeutic play and "acting out," adolescents and adults accomplish by verbal communication and insight. At a group session of boys five to six years old, Eli urinated into a pan of water-color paint. He and the others referred to the mixture as feces and used other anal appellations. Similarly, the mothers of these children talked in their own group sessions about frequency of urination, defacation, pregnancy, and sexual intercourse. As they were freed of their repressions, mothers and children alike, reacted in almost the same manner. Both groups regressed to the pre-Oedipal level when they could talk about and do whatever they wished. Although the form of expression differed in the two groups, the meaning of the regression was the same for both.

Catharsis and regression in adolescents and adults occur largely, though not entirely, on a verbal level. The advantage of the group is that it facilitates the process for reasons already outlined but also because it offers opportunities for acting out as well. Patients in groups reenact their attitudes toward parents, siblings, husbands, wives, and other persons in relation to one another and toward the therapist. To many with weak egos, this is particularly valuable, since it helps them overcome resistances and serves as a reality testing situation. Many a patient with a weak ego finds it easier to act out than to verbalize his difficulties. Acting out by such means as anger, aggression, rivalry, and hostility also serves to detense the total organism (body-mind), with a consequent equilibrating effect. Draining off emotions through the vasomotor channels helps reduce tensions in the neuroendocrine system.

As is to be expected, the interviews in analytic group psychotherapy are not always friendly or placid. Members grow tense, attack one another, violently disagree, project attitudes upon others in the group and upon the therapist. These are forms of acting out analogous to the cathartic physical activity of children, who are supplied with appropriate materials and situations for this purpose.

Acting out as such probably has several values and significances, the understanding of which would also help understanding the therapeutic process generally. Primarily it is a means by which the patient seeks mastery over his life situations. It also serves patients to whom other means for emotional discharge are unavailable, which is particularly true of young children. Children are handicapped by the fact that their language facilities are incommensurate with their emotions and they resort to action.[5] Most frequently however, acting out is a result of weak ego development. Where the ego is unable to deal with impulse, the id takes precedence and finds egress in direct action. By these means the burden the ego has to bear is reduced. Frequently when one is unable to reveal his unconscious to his own gaze and to that of the others, one becomes defensively aggressive, or wards off depression through hilarity and hyperactivity.

Acting out, as a preliminary to verbalization, is of great advantage for eliciting catharsis and establishing a positive transference. Because it tends to diminish anxiety and resistance, it is valuable in the treatment of adults as well as children. As a patient succeeds in strengthening his ego and his need for group acceptance is enhanced, he curbs his aggression and gives up bizarre and unsocial behavior.

We found that in both activity and analytic groups diffuse acting out gradually becomes canalized and the members more purposeful and self-disciplined. Children grow less aimless, work on definite projects, and improve in their relations with one another. Instead of continuing along general lines and lacking direction, the interviews in adolescent and adult groups, as well, lead toward their difficulties. These improvements occur through the inner integration which follows on the wake of a strengthened ego, and also through improved attitudes on the part of each toward the others in regard to antagonisms, dependencies, ambivalences, tolerance, and cooperation, the changing role of the therapist, the changed nature of the transferences and libido reorganization.

It must always be kept in mind, however, that regression is a

[5] This is also true of mentally retarded persons, whose reaction to frustration may at times be quite violent.

source of anxiety in group as well as in other types of psychotherapy. Both children and adults struggle against revealing themselves. They are afraid of the punishment and stigma associated with undermature behavior and regressive cravings. During the Oedipal conflict the child had striven to be worthy of acceptance by the parent of the opposite sex and was chagrined when made to feel small and weak. This feeling of stigma and worthlessness is associated with regression throughout life and is resisted by all patients. To help the patient to regress is one of the important tasks of psychotherapy and is achieved through transference.

Fear and anxiety are usually differentiated by the fact that in the former the threat originates outside of the individual, it is exogenic, while the latter is endogenic. Anxiety is usually the result of the conflict of the id and superego, though it may also stem from ego defenses. Whatever the theoretic source, the empirical fact is that in all human relations there is present latent and manifest anxiety with which one has to deal in everyday life. The therapeutic relation is particularly fraught with anxiety because of the patient's hostile or ambivalent feelings in the transference relation and the fear the patient associates with the parent figure. The patient's need to reveal himself is another source of anxiety, because, in addition to other outcomes, he sustains thereby an injury to his self-esteem (ego-ideal). Still other sources are the fear of punishment and the possible loss of the therapist for being "bad" and, in a group, the reaction of the other members.

In group psychotherapy, especially, the factor of anxiety must receive the therapist's special attention. Since each patient is preoccupied in the presence of strangers with such subjects as unresolved Oedipal conflicts, infantile sexuality, destructive drives, and other types of infantile impulses and cravings, a great deal of anxiety is inevitably generated. One of the important, as well as complicated, tasks of the therapist is to deal with it. Even where the patient fully trusts the group therapist, he still fears other members, and the reaction of the group-as-a-whole. He is afraid of being unmasked, stripped naked as it were, before a group of people. Despite all this, patients must feel free to speak of whatever comes to their minds at the moment, for in this therapy lies.

At the 34th session of the group, Bertha interrupted the discussion by saying she wanted to speak of something that was not related to the subject at hand, but that had bothered her greatly. Without any trace of self-consciousness she asked if a boy or girl was "so hard up that their emotion and feelings are more than they could bear, would they die if they can't get it (sexual intercourse)." Up to this point the girls listened to the speaker attentively, but at this there was a faint stirring among them. Bertha, however, went on and said, among other things: "Shouldn't they go and get it [intercourse], for instance, if that person is nearly driven crazy." Bertha was tense and pale and it was quite evident that she spoke about herself. Sandra said seriously that such a person "should go to a psychiatrist." Georgia questioned whether a person could have such strong sexual urges unless he had had sexual experiences before. Vehemently, Bertha denied it: "No, the person is just curious and needs it." Georgia, with an air of finality, said: "It can be overcome;" and Sandra added, "You need a psychiatrist." Rose asked whether kissing is a substitute for sex, to which Lydia laughingly responded that she knew a slightly off-color saying about it. When encouraged to go on she said that she heard it said that "a kiss is an upper persuasion for a lower invasion."

One may expect anxiety to diminish as relationships in the group become more firmly established. With the resulting ease there is a concomitant freedom of communication. The reserve and caution observable at early stages in discussions disappear, and the members enter into a relation of considerable intimacy. They confide in one another intimate details of their lives and communicate facts and phantasies that had been locked in secrecy for many years. The timing for such communication varies as different members become ready for it. After the initial stage of taciturnity and fear, the cathartic process in groups is greatly accelerated by those patients who are less conflicted and less inhibited. They serve as *catalytic agents.*

After the initial period, anxiety in groups is seldom as intense as it is in individual treatment. As already indicated, the transference, which is a major source of anxiety, is diluted. The therapist is not the exclusive source of libido gratification, nor is he the only target of hostility. Others in the group also serve these ends. The phases of negative transference are usually periods when anxiety is strong and the hostility toward the therapist is a displacement of the hostility toward parents. This is bound to create some tension, which is greatly diminished in the group because of the support each receives from the others. Here it is not one patient against the therapist, but the group, a fact that diminishes fear, anxiety, and guilt in each. One feels justified when the group approves. One is less threatened, and punishment, if any, will be shared by all.

Our observations lead us to the conclusion that, in groups where there is acting out, there is an unmistakable diminution in anxiety. In analytic groups, for example, anxiety is much more intense than in activity groups; since activity catharsis is the pattern of the latter, patients are not prone to arouse the same amount of tension. In interview groups, a revealing statement by one member or an interpretation by the therapist may activate severe anxiety in patients. No matter how skillful and cautious a therapist is, he cannot avoid this, and brief individual interviews immediately following the group sessions are necessary to allay anxiety in a particularly disturbed group member.

Other factors also operate in the direction of increasing anxiety in groups. One of these is homosexuality. It is quite understandable that homosexual trends, which may otherwise be latent or in repression, would tend to be activated in groups of such emotional density as are therapy groups. Patients in need of psychotherapy are more likely to be disturbed in the sexual area than is the average person. In addition, the transferences among membersof a therapy group must of necessity enhance the sexual component of their relation. Thus we found in groups of married women that some "made a play" for the others. A woman with strong masculine drives exhibits her social prowess or intellectual powers and asserts herself in a manner that is transparently charged with sexual content. Usually her behavior toward one of the group members is particularly tinged with an erogenous quality. Some of the abstracts from the records of adolescent girls' groups included in this volume unmistakably reveal this. In an adult men's group, the request by patients that women be added to the group was an evident defense against the anxiety arising from homosexual impulses toward one another.

Another manifestation that adds to the anxiety content in groups is *rivalry*. In every group there are always individuals who are rivalrous of one another, seek to keep the center of attention, or to monopolize or displace the therapist. This is a source of tension in the group. For this reason it is suggested that persons who are excessively narcissistic and rivalrous, for whatever reason, are unready for multilateral relations and should not be included in groups. Certain types of compulsive patients, particularly, have a deleterious effect upon the therapeutic process because of their uncontrollable need to speak so that they give others little chance to participate and thereby raise the anxiety index.

Because the total effect of the group is to diminish anxiety, and to dilute the transference,[6] the treatment is as a result never as deep as in psychoanalysis, for example. In the latter, the analysis of transference and resistance is the focal means of therapy which intensifies rather than diminishes anxiety. The analyst's aim is not to spare the patient from the resultant anxiety. It is through the analysis of resistance and transference (in which the patient's libido strivings are involved) that the basic conflicts of the psychoneurotic are reached. For reasons already delineated this cannot be done with the same thoroughness and intensity in groups, and it can be expected that recovery will never be as complete as in a thoroughgoing psychoanalysis.[7] However, there are many evidences that improvement in nearly all patients under our observation is sufficiently great and permanent to justify further work and investigation in the field of analytic group psychotherapy and the following are just a few of the reactions from patients and others in this regard. Other evidence of improvement in patients can be found in many of the extracts from the records in this volume.

Anne suddenly said, "What goes on here?" All looked at her questioningly for no one knew to what she was alluding. Since no one spoke, the therapist asked Anne what she meant. Anne speaking directly to the therapist with an accusing air, said: "You cured Yolanda." "Of what?" "Of her self-consciousness. Yolanda now walks straight, is much more friendly and free than she was before she came to the group." She, Anne, often wonders just what she gets out of coming here. The therapist asked Anne if she was angry at the therapist for not curing her as well. Anne said it is not entirely clear in her mind. She does not feel herself improving, yet, her mother (who was very rejecting and cruel to Anne) said that she has improved. At this point Yolanda interrupted and said that she agrees with Anne. Formerly she, Yolanda, really did not stand erect; she always tried to make herself look as small

[6] See p. 20. [7] For a further discussion on this subject see p. 237.

as possible, because nobody that she goes with is as tall as she, and she felt ashamed. Here in this group, no one is as tall as she, but she can now straighten herself up and stand erect. For sometime now, nobody has said anything about her posture. She generally feels much happier than she used to.

Perhaps an even more conclusive reaction is one that comes from an outside person, as occurred when the therapist after the 26th session was told spontaneously by the elevator man, who regularly took the girls to and from the interviews, that "those girls are certainly different from what they used to be when they first came. It's like taking down altogether a different bunch of girls. They certainly are different."

A number of points raised in the foregoing pages, especially with reference to regression, are illustrated by the following abstracts from group interviews with adolescent girls.

Paula said she always imagines that New York is being bombed and that people are running away from it (this was during the war). Betty laughingly responded by saying that she dreams of sex.[8] Sandra, also dreams of sex. Bertha looked significantly at Sandra and said that she also dreamed that she was married and had "millions of kids." Sandra interrupted her to say she dreamed her friend Anne (see p. 178) had a baby and that Sandra was present when the baby was being born. Almost as though she tried to outdo Betty, Sandra told of a dream in which her mother was masturbating very violently. (Sandra actually did witness her mother masturbating.) Betty asked whether watching her mother "do it made you hot," and whether it caused her to masturbate too, and while masturbating did she think it was someone else's hand "doing it" to her. Sandra was not sure of this; her mother did masturbate "but not all the time," and so does Sandra. Lydia said: "Consciously I don't." She later added that maybe unconsciously she might be doing it. Sandra wondered whether the girls felt any embarrassment at talking so openly about such things and Lydia said why should one be embarrassed? "You talk about things with a fellow when you're in the dark, don't you?" Sandra said that was different

Lydia spoke of her pubic hair. She was impressed by the fact that the hair on her head was black and thick, while her body hair light and thin. Rose laughingly said that her pubic hair is "like an ape's." Paula said hers is too. Sandra thought it was queer to have a lot of hair on her head when her pubic hair was very sparse. Georgia's is very black and thick. It seemed, however, that as the girls were talking their anxiety mounted, for Lydia suddenly changed the subject and said she heard Sandra's song called "Relaxing" sung over the radio. (About a year

[8] Of special interest is Betty's association of bombing and sex, i.e., bombing is equated with a sexual attack.

later, the same girls frankly talked about their passion and uncontrollable desire for sexual intercourse. At times they were so passionate, they said, that they almost could ask the first man they met to gratify them. On a number of occasions, the girls openly talked about their masturbatory activities.)

In another group of seventeen-year-olds, one of the girls spoke of her poor appetite which, she said, had been better that week. She quite suddenly said: "I didn't menstruate yet this month." The others pricked up their ears. The therapist asked: "Are you worried?" "No, I am not worried," the girl said. By way of consolation, one of the girls stated: "When I once had a lot of trouble, my menstruation was delayed more than two weeks." Another (who, unknown to the others was having sexual relations with her boy friend) said: "I never missed a month. I am always right on the dot!" Another said that she is never prompt; while still another attested to being always on time.

Interpretation: Although there is quite apparent homosexual interest in these conversations, the permissive attitude of the therapist and the total group atmosphere temporarily suspended the restraints of the superego (shame). The girls make the transference to the therapist and each other on a pre-Oedipal level, namely, the stage where restraint is minimal and permissiveness is the rule of life.

The following interesting excerpt from a group record demonstrates catharsis, free-association, identification, Oedipal conflict, castration fears, and other mechanisms.

Reva, much of whose behavior is infantile, narrated a very early experience. Lydia told the girls of her mother's illness and Reva recalled a tonsillectomy she had had. Before coming to the session, she had a tooth drawn and though she had no pain, thought she looked pale. (Actually she looked quite well.) The other girls also told of their tonsillectomies. They all remembered them, but the conversation did not seem to stimulate further discussion. Reva said she could recall vividly the week during which her mother was in the hospital when she gave birth to Louis (Reva's younger brother). She and Charles (another brother) had always been in rivalry. She explained that there is very little difference in their ages, and though she is older, actually she always felt younger and wanted more attention than Charles was getting. When her mother went to the hospital, a housekeeper was sent to take care of the family. Reva, who was about six years old, remembered distinctly how jealous she was of the housekeeper and how enraged she was at her father for "having taken another woman into the house so soon after my mother was out of it." During the period when the housekeeper was there, Charles was not the one who misbehaved or screamed. With much feeling Reva said, "It was I. I was the trouble in the family." The therapist asked Reva if she felt she should have taken over the mother's duties, and she said she remembers distinctly that when the mother was out of the house, she "felt very big." At this she giggled.

She had a clear memory of the day when her mother returned with the baby. She had a "queer feeling" when she saw the child placed in one room and her mother in another. She couldn't conceive of the baby being separated from the mother. Reva went into the room where the baby had been placed on the bed and she, though a very little girl, removed the baby's hat. She said she could still recall the hair on the baby's head and laughingly remarked that he had a lot of hair for a newborn baby.

Rose also remembered well when her brother was born. There was a very bitter note in her voice as she told how friends and relatives teased her and told her that she would now no longer be wanted or needed because her mother had a new baby. Her father, too, impressed it upon her that she would have to give up everything for the little brother. The therapist remarked: "And you still do?" With considerable bitterness, she said: "That's right, I do."

Activity catharsis for young children requires a special setting. Their play and activity materials must be varied in accordance with the age of the children and should be designed to stimulate catharsis and regression. Clay, water, fire, paints, brushes, dolls, mannikins, guns, soldiers, rubber darts, dollhouses, and furniture—including beds and toilet fittings—are among the equipment suitable for young children. These are among the essentials, and such secondary equipment as wood, tools, airplane models may be added for older children. The equipment should be used spontaneously and phantasies about play and games should be elicited by the therapist. An occasional question and interpretation is necessary.[9]

Dollhouses that have a number of rooms with bedroom and bathroom furnishings are particularly valuable for children below school age. In play each reconstructs and refurnishes the "house" in a manner that reflects individual preoccupations.[10] One may place both parents in a bed, and the child in another room; another beds the child and the mother together with the father in another room or bed. The latter is often left out altogether. Still another child places the father outside the house trying hard, but unable to get in. Some children push father and child dolls out a window. One

[9] See Chapter VII, p. 98. [10] See Chapter VIII, p. 124 and Chapter IX, p. 138.

places the bedroom on an upper floor, while another locates it as the first room upon entrance into the house. The bathroom receives similar diversity of treatment, with the toilet bowl being the center of attention.

Other materials provided are also used variously and the uses they are put to reflect preoccupations with basic organic functions and phantasies about them. Water and fire are employed to discharge urethral, sexual, and sadistic phantasies; clay and paints sublimate anal drives; chewing, shouting and eating assuage oral cravings.[11]

Young children at first act in a very uncontrolled manner. They rush about helter-skelter, fight with one another, make demands, are provocative and unreasonable. As their anxiety is lessened, behavior becomes more controlled and more mature. Conversations in interview groups of adolescents and adults are also of a regressive nature. They are concerned with childhood grudges and urges, and matters taboo under ordinary circumstances. In young children such unrestraint takes the form of hilarity and diffuse active aggression. There is regression to an infantile (pre-Oedipal) level.

Explosive behavior, which may become violent at times, may also serve the same purpose.[12] Such acts on the part of one stimulates the others to hilarity and destructiveness. There is little therapeutic value in such acting out. In individual therapy, behavior is more likely to be related to the child's central problem than it is in groups. In the latter aggressiveness may be initiated by one of the children and taken on by the others through suggestion, infection, or social hunger, quite unrelated to the central problem of each. It therefore has no meaning in terms of the child's basic difficulties. Free acting out, the same as verbal free-association, has value only when

11 Materials supplied to children of different ages should not be too varied or too difficult for them to understand or manipulate. Materials of greatest value are those of low resistivity and low degree of complexity. For the young child they need to be soft and pliable, such as clay, plasticene, paints, and water. For older children they can be more resistive, such as wood and metals. Gradation of resistivity aids in the development of power, improved self-regard, and in appropriate catharsis. The materials listed in the above paragraphs can be described as *libido-evoking* materials and the activities resulting fıom them as *libido-revealing* in contrast to the *libido-binding* activities in activity group therapy. The former can be permitted because in analytic group psychotherapy interpretation is employed; it is not in activity groups.

12 Such behavior is anal in nature and is in fact frequently accompanied by passing of flaetus. It has been shown that passing of flaetus and belching are used as aggression.

it stems from and is related to the patient's psychological difficulties. When it becomes diffuse, it may have an effect opposite to the desired one, namely, it may disorganize personality, weaken ego, and prevent general integration.

It must be expected that after the initial insecurity is overcome in the early stages of treatment, there will be considerable diffuse hilarity and "wild" behavior. This is the preliminary stage in acclimatization, a testing of reality and of the therapist. In a sense, this is the most trying period for the latter, for not only does he have to withstand aggression and frustration, but he also has to convince the children of his basic acceptance of them and at the same time prevent disorganization in the group. Frequently, hilarity is suggested by activating materials.[13] Some of the devices used to prevent group disorganization are shortening the treatment hour, introducing food at a high point in hyperactivity, a walk outdoors, or story-telling. When hyperactivity continues, it may be advisable to reexamine the personnel of the group. There may be one or more children not as yet ready for group treatment, or the grouping may be wrong.

The following situation is an example of the effect of over-stimulating material upon group disorganization.

In one group water in pails was made accessible to children four and one-half to five and one-half years old. Because this gave them an opportunity to splash, pour it back and forth and throw it at each other, the children were soon in a state of near-panic. They threw paints, water colors, clay and other materials into the water and onto the floor, trampled on the mess, screaming at the top of their voices, pushed each other around. The children became quite uncontrollable and the therapist, unable to check them, had to resort to arbitrary restraint, thereby jeopardizing her role. This was the outcome of the therapist's unwise encouragement that the children carry water in large pails and then pour it into basins. Because they were physically unable to manage this satisfactorily, some water was spilled on the floor, which in turn activated them to hilarity. It was necessary later to limit the use of water to a small pitcher.

[13] See S. R. Slavson, *An Introduction to Group Therapy* (New York, Commonwealth Fund, 1943), pp. 191 ff.

CHAPTER FOUR

DIRECT AND DERIVATIVE INSIGHT

CATHARSIS may give the patient temporary relief, but emotional maturity is achieved through insight. Adults, especially, must come to understand—and emotionally accept—their mechanisms and their behavior, before personality changes can be affected. In group psychotherapy limited levels of insight are attained, but this in no way diminishes its importance. One of the difficulties in groups is that members become ready to gain from interpretation at different times, a fact the therapist must always keep in mind. Not only do the members differ from one another in this respect, but variation also occurs in an individual himself. He may be ready and able to deal with one problem but becomes seriously disturbed when another is brought forth by someone in the group. This disharmony demands the therapist's utmost care and attention and he must possess a high degree of skill to deal with it.

Patients induce insight in each other partly because the group provides a realistic background against which the individual's activity and views are mirrored. In this setting they can be viewed more objectively than in any other emotionally charged group such as a family. The presentation of common problems and the spontaneous interpretations of each other's motives help each member to understand himself and his fellow patients. The fact that problems and preoccupations prove to be universal eliminates or at least reduces the anxiety and concomitant guilt that ordinarily strengthen the ego defenses and resistance.

The following, a rather lengthy report of a group discussion, illustrates some of these points.

At the 27th session the girls talked about marriage between persons of different religious faiths. One of the girls brought forth the topic of petty annoyances. A considerable period of silence followed as the girls seemed to be engrossed in thought. When the conversation was resumed it took an entirely different turn. All said that they often got very mad at their parents. Georgia said she takes about two hours to get ready for school. She does little things in her room, such as picking up her wardrobe and books; then she has to wait to get into the bathroom. There is a good deal of nagging in her home. First one, then the other nags at her because she takes too long in the bathroom, or eats too slowly. She gets furious.

Sandra said she takes about an hour to get ready for school. She likes to be alone, then she can do things as she pleases. But when she is alone, she becomes unhappy, but this is not as bad now as it used to be. Neither Rose nor Georgia like their families around, either. Georgia said that on Saturdays, her mother nags her older sister, telling her that she is lazy. Her sister gets terribly angry, but she cannot express her anger toward the mother and "goes into hysterics." Sandra said she can easily understand this. Once she was reading something that was very interesting. Her father kept calling her and she hated to stop, but after he had repeated his call many times, she got so angry that she almost tore her book.

Reva looked compassionately at Sandra and said she "hates" to have her mother in the house, because she always makes her talk in a subdued voice. Sandra and Lydia asked whether that is why she always talks so low that it is difficult to hear her. Reva said "yes." But she has still another problem which is a little different from the other girls'. She is generally late to school, for appointments, and even for work. The reason for this is that it doesn't occur to her to gage time. In the beginning, she does things slowly, then suddenly becomes aware of how little time there is left and begins to hurry, but then it is already too late. She takes only half an hour to get ready for school in the morning, but to hear her mother talk, you would think it takes her all day. The therapist asked Reva whether she was not always late to school. Reva admitted simply that she was. The therapist asked whether the difficulty could be avoided by looking at the clock more often to help her gradually judge how long each operation takes.

Georgia laughingly said that the preceding evening her home was a "madhouse." Her mother, who is hard of hearing, likes to listen to a certain program. She turns the radio on very loud, but her father prefers another program. Each turned the radio on loud enough to drown out the other, until there was bedlam in the house. Georgia hates it when her parents are at home; yes, she has genuine angry feelings. But, when all is quiet in the house, she grows restless. Lydia does not mind what goes on, whether it is noisy or quiet. "I can shut myself out," she added. One of the girls questioned whether this was not bad for Lydia. When the therapist asked why, she said, "Maybe Lydia is too much in herself." Lydia did not agree; she has a very good time. She shuts out only the things she does not like. As soon as something happens that arrests her interest, she at once becomes aware of it.[1]

Reva asked the therapist directly: "Would you think me silly if I asked what is the sense of being born, for you only die in the end? All your life you're waiting just to die." When asked for an elaboration, she said: "Well, you are born, you grow up, you marry, you have children, you die." The girls did not pursue this and did not give the therapist a chance to answer. Later in the session when the girls talked again about Reva's annoying habit of being late, the therapist asked Reva how she understood her own lateness. Reva replied that there is something in the way you do it. She really is not interested. She is only going to die in the end, so why be on time; why do anything? Sandra and Rose seemed to go out of their way to impress Reva and almost pleadingly, speaking together, told her how good it feels when one accomplishes things. They want to help her, because "talking here helps." Reva said she knows it helps. All day today, she felt that something unpleasant would happen and just didn't feel like doing anything because there was this feeling in back of her mind. Sandra said she thinks that Reva wants to be punished for something. Reva says, "Maybe you're right. Maybe if someone would punish me, it would be better." Sandra pointed out to Reva that, with her attitude holding her back the way it does, she will never accomplish anything. "What if your mother was sick and needed you?" she asked. Defensively, Reva recalled that when she was four or five years old, her mother had a hemorrhage. She described the situation in great detail and then added that she called a neighbor after she helped her mother to a chair.

Interpretation: Through universalization [2] and identification,[3] catharsis is accelerated and intensified and thus leads to a veiled confession of incestuous strivings and death wishes against the mother. These in turn are punishable by death. The girls help one another bring out this repressed material through catalysis and positive sibling transference. These aid reintegration and object relationships. However, our special interest in this abstract is the way in which insight is derived or given directly in this group. All the girls are now aware of the irregularity of their behavior: the length of time they take in getting ready for school, lateness, dawdling, and spite. They see themselves either as causes of the conflicts in their families or, certainly, as contributory factors. They no longer put the entire blame on other mem-

[1] Lydia's statements are rather significant, since she is a latent schizophrene. We must also note the insight of the girl who makes the comment on her withdrawal.

[2] See p. 96.

[3] See pp. 18, 96.

bers of the family as they did in the past; they, too, play a part in these conflicts. The value of such objectivity toward social adjustment is evident. Reva recognizes that she is improving and the therapist suggests a practical way of dealing with her lateness by timing herself.

The girls help one another to understand themselves and their part in their problem. It is evident that each is on the threshold of doing something to remedy her situation as well as correct her attitudes. It must also be noted that at least twice is direct interpretation offered by one member to another. This occurs when Lydia makes a statement about her withdrawal and when Sandra tells Reva she is seeking punishment (for her incestuous striving toward her father and death wishes toward her mother). At a later session Reva is told by the girls directly that she is too strongly attached to her father.

It is also noteworthy that the discussion opens with a consideration of intermarriage (defense against incest), leads into family relations, and ends with death wishes toward the mothers (incest strivings). The excerpt also demonstrates free association in analytic group discussions.

The capacity for self-confrontation is one of the very important outcomes of understanding one's self and one's problems, especially when this understanding is buttressed by emotional flexibility.

Leah's monologue and Ella's remark well illustrate this:

During the group interview, Leah asked: "Isn't it hard when you have been a little girl for so long to suddenly find yourself growing up and yet having so many things still hanging on to you that you carried with you all along—the only things you have ever known?" The therapist asked: "What things?" Leah said it is hard for her to explain. She can see herself as having been pretty dependent on her mother, often turning away from things that she should be doing at home to help. It is so much easier to have one's mother do things for one. Then, one wants to know about sex, and yet has the feeling that it is bad. She broke off suddenly, seemed quite disturbed and asked in a choking voice: "Why are we born?" The therapist said Leah must have been thinking about it and could she elaborate on it? What she really was thinking about, Leah answered very self-consciously, was that she has often wondered why her sister was born. There has been such an age difference between her sister and herself. Her sister is eleven years younger than she. If her brother hadn't died, the sister might never have been born.

Ella said that her mother always wanted a male child and tried many times to have a boy, five times in fact. Finally, when Ella, the fifth girl was born, her mother was so disappointed that she gave her a boy's name.

At the 48th session, Georgia said she did not like New York and was planning to get a job in another city when she graduated from high school. Lydia wondered if Georgia was not really running away from her family. Georgia denied it. Rose agreed with Lydia that Georgia was only covering up a deep need and wish to get away from her family and wanted "to run away from something unpleasant." Paula said she could understand why Georgia denied it, she may not even be aware of the fact that she is running away from her mother. Georgia said that it could be so, for she is much more attached to her father than to her mother. The therapist said that it is as though Georgia and her mother were in competition. Georgia said she would like to be married and have a house of her own, "and not have to climb four flights of stairs." She described the kind of home she would like to have. Lydia said that she was thinking still about Georgia. It is her belief that she was jealous of her mother. At this Georgia giggled and said: "Girls, you'll talk me into it."

At this point, Lydia asked for pencil and paper and said she would like to doodle. Everybody except Rose and Paula took up pencils and began doodling. Paula said that Georgia wanted to leave home and apparently did not worry about being lonely, and yet it was her impression that Georgia was more sexy than Lilly, who openly states that she wants a husband and a home of her own. Georgia has the same wish, but hides it.

Interpretation: In this interlude considerable insight is displayed by the girls in the matter of Georgia's motivation for leaving home. They help Georgia recognize it without pressure, in a natural and easy way that makes it acceptable to her. She does not overtly acquiesce in their interpretation, but apparently perceives it to be true as shown by her giggling and her half-hearted acceptance when she says the girls will talk her into it. Note also Lydia's anxiety at this when she turns to doodling. Apparently her own problem was touched here. This is identification therapy (see p. 95).

When a psychotherapist speaks of interpretation, he differentiates it from explanation. The latter is an ideational process to establish the relation between cause and effect and give intellectual meaning to a phenomenon. Explanations deal largely with manifest phenomena and involve the emotional factors to a minimum. In psychotherapy, however, the emotional elements are predominant; it concerns itself largely with the latent content of what a patient says rather than with the manifest. It is not enough for a patient to analyze his problems and reactions intellectually. In fact every therapist knows that this is often one of the most tenacious forms of resistance. Patients are prone to use lucid verbalization (rationalization) as a means of warding off therapy. Volubility is used as a defense against the therapist's effort to penetrate the patient's inner world; it may also be employed to prevent anxiety. The therapist's technique in dealing with this will, of course, vary in accordance with the patient's psychodynamics. While he may press a patient who is psychopathic or one with a character disorder, he will deal more cautiously with the anxiety hysteric, for example.

Mere "understanding" cannot be relied upon in psychotherapy. The intellect is a subsidiary factor in the therapeutic process, which consists essentially of emotional activity. It is important that we do not overvalue "understanding" at the cost of the emotional freedom and flexibility which are the aims of the therapeutic process. Members of a group of adult women once complained that their feelings and attitudes had not been altered, despite the fact that they came to understand the reasons for their destructive treatment of their children. One of them said: "I know that it is wrong after it is all over, but I can't stop myself while I am in the midst of it. My feelings get the best of my reason."

This is a perspicacious remark and correctly describes the ascendancy of emotions over reason in behavior and therapy. The statement was really intended as a veiled complaint against the therapist who had repeatedly emphasized the mothers' "understanding" of their own role in their children's problems. Instead of activating their background emotions and using them in the process of emotional growth, she limited the interviews to educational discussions. The woman's remark reemphasizes the fact that ideas determine attitudes only little and do not control behavior. On the contrary, one is led to believe that there is very slight, if any, carry-over. Personality changes occur through emotional experience in transference and not through teaching and learning. Mere understanding may serve rather to increase rigidity.

Through well-timed interpretation the patient is helped to recognize the unconscious drives and strivings that motivate his behavior. This postulates a *readiness* on the part of the patient not only to accept what is said by the therapist and the other members of the group, but also to recognize its *relevance*. To do this, some resistances have to be overcome first and a transference relation established; for, without these, interpretation is rejected or not understood. The ability to develop insight and accept interpretation postulates a degree of emotional maturity and ego strength that the patient must first attain.

Because of this, the factor of timing is of utmost importance. Freud said that interpretation should be given only when the patient is at the point where he can almost formulate it himself. When interpretation is forthcoming at an appropriate stage in treatment, it has meaning and relevance, but when it is proffered too early, it is either not understood or rejected. On the other hand, when the therapist fails to recognize the point of readiness for insight on the part of the patient, the latter may repeatedly return to the same topic or dream. It is as though the patient wishes by repetition to inform the therapist that his needs have not been met.[4]

Interpretation in groups presents some difficulties not encountered in individual treatment. Among these are the differential in readiness and the varying reactions to a problem in different members of the group. The latter dilemma is partially solved by the grouping of patients with common psychological syndromes. Because the members of the group have the same problems and preoccupations, interpretation given to one may apply to a number and even to all present. There usually is enough identification among a group of patients to enable them to accept or, at least, to understand it. The more difficult factor, however, is readiness. One cannot assume that all patients have worked through repressions and have overcome resistances at the same rate, and, as already indicated, an interpretation that is well timed for one may be out of place for others.

In such circumstances it may be necessary for the therapist to turn his attention to the one member, leaving the others to remain as spectators. This is a *treatment in a group* which I have differentiated from *treatment through the group*,[5] and should be resorted to as little as possible. One finds in practice that when the therapist becomes so involved with one of the members, others, because of sibling rivalry, will soon enter into the discussion, or they may interrupt or change the subject. The reader will find illustrations of this in the various extracts from records included in this volume.

Interpretation given by one of the group members is much more

[4] See "Stereotypy" p. 114.
[5] See S. R. Slavson, "Group Therapy," *Mental Hygiene*, January, 1940.

acceptable than that proffered by the therapist. This is partly due to the transference relation (in which the therapist is the parent figure), but is largely determined also by the fact that the intuitive perceptions and identifications are frequently sharper among the patients than between them and the therapist. The following passage from a record illustrates the profundity both in identification and insight among group members:

At the fifty-fourth session the group talked about Rose's absence. Leah and Georgia thought Rose would come back to the group. Leah said maybe Rose was trying to make up her mind. When asked by the therapist about what, Leah said she did not know, but that Rose may be now at a crossroad trying to make up her mind whether to remain dependent upon her parents or grow up and become independent. The therapist wondered why she thought so, and Leah referred to the statement Rose once made that, after a long talk, she and her father had come to an understanding and that she had felt content and happy. Leah thought that actually Rose seemed confused. Didn't she say that analyzing the things she says and does only starts a tumult in her all over again? The therapist asked Leah to elaborate on this. Leah said that it seemed to her as though Rose, who is fairly content now, is sort of trying to let well enough alone. Georgia's opinion was that it was not a bad idea to have a rest from treatment for awhile. Sometimes a rest does not mean that you are finished, "rather that you are thinking about it." She knows this to be true of herself. She has been going along for a long time now without individual treatment, but when the family situation got beyond her once, she came back to discuss it again. Was there anything particular that she was thinking of at the time? She said she was not clear as to how much she should inject herself into the family situation. This gave rise to group discussion, as a result of which she came to the conclusion that she could do very little. The problem was between her parents.

An example of clever interpretation is supplied by the following:

At the seventeenth session Betty again spoke of her unfathomable hatred of her sister and mother and almost uncontrollable impulse to kill them both. At one time she was fond of her sister, but now she hates her. Betty was very intense and very emotional, and as she spoke she doodled. Ella said that Betty ought to try to recapture some of the friendly feelings she formerly had for her sister. Betty flashed angrily, saying that Ella does not realize how terrible her sister is: she wants a great deal of attention, she never helps anybody, and is selfish. Ella, looking at Betty's doodling, commented that Betty hides her real thoughts, because whenever she draws she starts out making geometrical designs but immediately criss-crosses over them so that no one can see what she was trying to draw. Betty threw a glance of surprise at Ella as though she had been discovered at something she was concealing. Betty turned to the therapist and asked what the meaning of her drawing was. The therapist asked what it meant to her. Betty replied that she did not know, that's why she had asked. Ella said, "I already told you. You are trying to hide something." Betty clamped her lips tightly and said nothing.

In group therapy the therapist will do well to allow full reign to the members' perceptiveness and intuition. Experience with such group discussions is convincing in this respect. Because of the similarity of problems among the members, the resulting identifications and empathy of their unconscious, they frequently perceive the latencies of each other's statements and strivings more unerringly and more quickly than can even the most skillful therapist. The perceptiveness and intuition even of very young children—four and five years of age—frequently amaze the uninitiated adult. Children have an uncanny capacity to speak directly to the unconscious of their group-mates and sense the hidden and unrecognized motivations and conflicts.

In group therapy, and perhaps also in other therapies, there is need to differentiate between *free association* and *associative thinking*. In free association the patient brings forth emotions and thoughts in a vertical direction, as it were, leading toward earlier traumata. The free flow of thoughts and feelings, however, may not always take such direction; it is likely to be more lateral. In associative thinking, as we employ the term, correlative and contemporaneous events come to mind because of their bearing on the event or situation with which the patient is concerned at the moment. This may or may not always lead him back to the past; rather, he may deal with the situations and emotions in the present as they relate to the problem at hand.

It cannot be assumed that free association and associative thinking are entirely separate and mutually exclusive. Both are present in all types of sound psychotherapy. Experience with interview groups, and this is amply illustrated in the record material, shows that both occur during a treatment session. However, one must recognize that free association is more safeguarded in individual treatment than in a group. This is due partly to the nature of the transference and partly because in a group there is diffusion engendered by the remarks of other members. In individual treatment, especially in psychoanalysis, the therapist, through his interpretations, activates childhood memories and the discharge of unconscious and repressed material which are not diluted and diverted by the reactions of others as it occurs in groups. It should be kept in mind, however, that neither free association nor associative thinking is absent from any type of sound psychotherapy. The difference lies in the frequency of occurrence rather than in the exclusiveness of one or the other.

The early interviews in therapy groups are usually of the associative type. They concern themselves with the problems and the circumstances that relate to the immediate lives of the patients. Later these discussions are likely to become more of the free association type, though even in the earlier phase there are frequently flashbacks, as it were, to the earlier causes of difficulties. Compulsive and hysterical patients usually either omit or greatly abbreviate the preliminary stage and plunge directly into their life histories.

The therapist who is acquainted with the nuclear or core problems of each of the group members, their symptoms and behavior, can readily recognize when they use associative thinking as resistance. While one cannot pursue a patient or press him beyond his readiness to advance, the therapist's awareness alone helps the cathartic process, especially when he can subtly convey his understanding by an indirect remark, a nod, or a smile. One method is to use the generalization technique, namely, make a general impersonal statement that has relevance to the problem at hand. A patient may not respond at the first trial (patients usually do, especially when therapy is well under way), but he is likely to do so after several trials, particularly when other group members participate. The supportive and catalytic effect of the group weaken ego defenses and resistance.

Sometimes a direct question aimed at helping a resistive patient to acquire deeper insight in his problems is helpful. Before using this method, the therapist must be aware of the state of the transference relation, and must not overstep its bounds. One cannot play havoc with a patient's defenses before he is ready to give them up. In one group of adult male patients, the penetrating interpretations of basic motives so distressed a psychoneurotic member that he withdrew from the group. On occasion, patients became greatly distressed and some did not return for treatment because of the tactless use of interpretation—actually it was explanation—by the therapist. In fact I once came upon a psychiatrist who believed in what he called "forced therapy."

As already stated, interpretation leading to insight should be given at the point where the patient is almost ready to perceive the meaning of his behavior and its causes. It is always best when the patient comes on it by himself. In this respect a group is very valuable because other members, frequently quite unawares, help each other in this respect.

During group interviews, a patient may ask the therapist's advice for dealing with situations or for solving some problem. Generally speaking, seeking advice can be construed as resistance. Through it the patient wishes to find short cuts to his difficulties and at the same time to remain psychologically unchanged. Seeking advice can also be a sign of fear, dependence, a weak ego, or a way of expressing hostility. Patients often disagree with the advice given, attempt to prove it wrong, and thus defeat the therapist.[6]

If the query represents hostility or resistance, the therapist must prevent becoming involved. He can turn the question on the patient by asking what he thinks about the matter. If the transference is solidly established, the therapist can suggest or indicate the patient's motive. He can go even further and interpret the latent resistance represented by it. In case of hostility, the therapist cannot be as direct, but here, too, he should convey to the patient the fact that he understands the underlying attitude.

In the matter of a dependent patient with a weak ego, it is sometimes advisable to support him by appropriate suggestion and advice. The value in this is not only that the patient is helped to resolve his conflict and vacillation, which is in itself important, but more significant is the fact that the therapist demonstrates interest in him. The ego-strengthening effect of this is quite obvious. In

[6] See S. R. Slavson, *Introduction to Group Therapy* (New York, Commonwealth Fund, 1943), p. 147.

group, as in all forms of psychotherapy, the burdens we ask patients to carry should be commensurate with their strength. Like children, through appropriate help and support they grow strong.

When the transference is positive and patients feel close and friendly toward the therapist, they may ask advice in an earnest desire really to deal with a problem. Seeking advice is then not a subterfuge, an escape mechanism, or a tool for negative aims. It is the realistic and understandable wish on the part of a younger (or less mature) person to profit from the maturity—and objectivity—of the therapist. When this is the true motive, giving advice is not counterindicated and can be considered as a graduated movement toward reality, a process that is an integral part of psychotherapy. It may be advisable in most such instances to see the patient individually and explore with him the attitudes, fears, and misgivings surrounding the situation at hand. More often the group can be drawn in so that the others can participate in arriving at a solution.

I have described the concept of *derivative insight* elsewhere.[7] The phrase is intended to designate the understanding of oneself and one's own behavior and impulses acquired through the spontaneous psychologic evolvement of the individual rather than from direct interpretation by the therapist or other members of the group. We have found that even in activity groups where no discussions are held and no interpretation given, youngsters become aware of the changes within themselves as compared to earlier reactions and attitudes.

Derivative insight occurs also in interview groups, manifested by the various extracts from the records included in this volume. Even very young children are prone to derive insight as a result of changes that they perceive within themselves. Patients begin to see themselves as stronger, more capable, less afraid and better able to relate to others. These changes manifest ego strength as well as changes in libido organization.

Interpretation and insight given to young children is graded to their level. Much insight is acquired by the patients themselves through their own perceptions and through the spontaneous conversations that arise among the members of a group. The princi-

[7] S. R. Slavson, "Differential Dynamics of Activity and Interview Group Therapy," *American Journal of Orthopsychiatry,* April, 1947.

ple of derivative insight operates here as it does in activity groups. Observation indicates that a considerable amount of insight arises spontaneously, proceeding from the awareness of inner change and from improved facilities to deal with impulses and the outer world. The children may compare present with past attitudes and recognize in themselves greater powers for dealing with reality.

A very interesting illustration of such derivative insight is provided by Beatrice, five and a half years old, who came for treatment because she had been very shy, inhibited, uncommunicative, and unable to play with children or talk to adults. At the twenty-third session she held forth as follows:

"My drawing isn't very good but I can draw. Would anybody like to see how I used to draw when I was three years old?" The other children walked over to watch her. Beatrice criticized six-year-old Murray's drawing of a house and demonstrated that her drawing was better than his. She said she now draws better than when she was three years old. "I used to draw fast but not so good. I used to draw when I was two years old. Of course, when I was a month old I didn't draw. My little sister thinks that she draws but she doesn't. I'll show you how I drew when I was two years old and how my sister draws now."

Interpretation: In this monologue she is displaying insight into her growth within the last several months. She tells us that she no longer behaves as a two or three-year-old. She now is beyond that stage. Her little sister is a baby (as she herself has been until recently) but she is no longer a baby.

Another example of such insight is displayed by a six-year-old boy in the same group. He was an only child of a strict and dominating mother and was not able to adjust in any of his relations.

When the mother called for Mike after the thirty-sixth session he accidentally dropped something to the floor. In her customary peremptory manner the mother ordered him to pick it up. Mike replies: "You ought to see what we do in this room. The trouble is you want me to be different from everybody, but I want to be like other children."

Interpretation: Having experienced the free, unrestrained behavior in the group, he now recognizes his mother's attitudes.[8]

[8] Although it does not have a direct bearing upon our present discussion, it must be pointed out that both children have moved in a centrifugal direction. Beatrice has separated herself from her little sister, with whom she was identified in order to enjoy the mother's love, and the boy separated himself from his mother who used him as an extension of herself. This movement toward autonomy or emotional separa-

Other examples of insight into their problems that young children attain through a therapeutic situation follow.

In the group of the nine to ten-year-olds, there was some discussion about Richard's excessive thumb sucking. Sylvia complimented him on his improvement. James (nine) said, "Isn't it funny. Now I get more angry than I used to." The therapist asked why. "Because I don't get my way and I want my way," said James. The therapist asked him to give an example of what brings on his anger. He said there had been some wrangling at home over his refusal to go to a Religious School and he is still insisting on not going because he wants to listen to his favorite radio program, or go to the movies. His mother used to hit him when he did not do his homework. Now she does not hit him for it. She merely tells him: "Do it if you want to." (This change was affected by the mother's caseworker. In the past the mother used to punish the boy very severely because of his resistance to doing homework.)

Alice said if people just wouldn't fight, if all the people individually would refuse to fight, there would never be a war. James said: "That's the way it was with my tics. I never think about them and I never have them any more."

Interpretation: He had seen the apparent relation of the outer struggle as represented by war to his own inner struggle which was resolved by his tics. An even more striking example is the following:

"While working on his plan, James asked whether the girls knew that he had brought in some felt which he thought they would enjoy working with. The girls said they were delighted with it. They all had projects in which they used the material and almost a half hour passed as everyone worked quietly with hardly a word said. Finally Richard said: "Even if we don't say much, we are all being helped." In a lower voice, he said to the therapist: "You know, I stopped stealing." When the therapist asked him what made him stop, Sylvia said: "You should know. We talked about it, didn't we?" Alice said: "It isn't only that we talked about it; we thought about it and we realized we shouldn't steal."

Derivative insight also occurs in groups of adolescents and adults. In evaluating her improvement through the group, Rose said that she felt happier generally, as well as at home. Her dreams (which used to be nightmares) were also changing. They are "less frightening and are no longer in a maze of confusion." She said that since the group had a discussion about fathers, which she reviewed as she

tion (weaning) is one of the major results of satisfying and therapeutic group relations. See also Cathexis displacement, p. 76.

spoke, (showing excellent understanding of the Oedipal conflict), she felt much less restless, was able to concentrate better on what she was doing; and she now sleeps more peacefully. She repeated that her dreams at the present time consisted of short isolated scenes which no longer frighten her.

At the same session, the fifty-first, from which the preceding episode was taken, a session that the girls chose to devote to "self-evaluation," Reva displayed insight into the mechanisms of her being late, as the following clearly shows.

Reva said that she had been coming for treatment not nearly as long as Paula and yet she feels she has made a great deal of progress. Formerly, she had not been aware of time. Wherever she went, she was always late; she felt no responsibility for keeping appointments. As she looked back on it, she could see also how silly she was for staying away from school as much as she did. All of these things she had now given up. When the girls mentioned how unsophisticated she was, Reva responded by saying that she feels she is rapidly growing up and feels much older. She is no longer afraid of the responsibility that goes with being grown up. Reva continued to say that she feels she also does things more thoroughly and better. "And I have given up biting my nails too," she added, displaying her nails.

That this development was gradual, can be seen from the following extract from the twenty-second interview:

The girls had been critical of Reva's dilatory behavior on a number of occasions. When she came in to this session late, she at once said she had telephoned to say that she would not be able to come on time. The girls quickly observed that she was now wearing powder and rouge and that her lipstick was attractively applied. Reva seemed embarrassed but also happy over the compliments and modestly said that she had been getting many compliments lately. Paula told Reva that her handwriting was very poor. Reva laughed gaily and quite freely admitted it. It seemed the two girls had written to each other. (There was a freedom and spontaneity in Reva's manner that contrasted sharply when compared with her fearful, retiring manner in the past. The use of cosmetics was entirely a new development. Reva was really very neatly dressed.)

Equally good insight is displayed in the following conversation:

Paula (whose membership in the group was being terminated as part of a treatment plan) behaved annoyingly throughout the session. For the second time, the therapist told her that she was acting as she did because she was angry. Paula admitted that she was angry. She was angry because, against her wishes, she must leave the group. Again, the girls discussed it. The most articulate was Rose, who said that Paula ought not to be angry; she should feel glad that she is being sent into the world. But she understands how Paula feels—she is afraid to go out on her own. By being disturbing she is sort of going back to being a little girl again. Rose went on to say tenderly: "Paula, it is not only the group: the group is only a small part of it. You gained a lot from your caseworker and from this group. You should be on your own now." All the girls agreed to this.

Georgia reminded Paula how, in the early group sessions, she had been very noisy and had screamed at the top of her voice. Now she is quite different; she gets along well with people. Lydia remarked that, to annoy the group, Paula had taken an endless amount of time to describe some relative's wedding. Yes, Paula remembered. Lydia recalled how Paula used to chew her gum so loud that everybody was annoyed and despite all protestations Paula would not stop. She also used to scrape her feet across the floor, making an ugly sound like scratching chalk, which drove the girls mad. (See p. 71, Chapter V) Paula laughed good-naturedly, and the girls laughed with her. (It was the therapist's impression that Paula got the feeling that everyone here considered her greatly improved and that they understood that she was behaving as she did because she was unhappy about leaving.)

Reva told about a boy she had met at her place of business. When he accompanied her once on an errand, he told her of a dream he had had. He dreamed that he saw his "dream girl" in a negligee. She was sitting in a chair opposite him and they stared at each other. In the second part of his dream, he suckled at her breast. Reva interpreted the dream to the boy. She said that on the one hand he phantasied about marriage and, on the other, he was still a baby at his mother's breast.

During many of the group interviews adolescent and adult patients discuss ideologies, criteria for living, personal and social values, and sometimes social problems and current events. The latter two receive consideration only very infrequently. The topics center on those aspects of ideological criteria that are closer to the problem of managing one's life: God, religion, intermarriage, jobs, boy-girl relations, husband and wife conflicts, the family, the place of the individual in the scheme of life.

The place of ideologies in the therapy of neurotic patients and other personality malformations has not been adequately evaluated. In therapy of the revivalist type, lectures and discussions are planned by the therapist to stimulate the auditors or participants, to help guide their lives by principles considered helpful and valuable, and to inculcate desirable attitudes; but such efforts have seldom been made in the more intensive group psychotherapy.

Lydia, the only girl at this point who had left school and had taken a job (in which she was quite successful) expressed some nostalgia about returning to the past and the days when she was younger. The girls discussed this and decided that once one has taken steps toward a more mature life, one cannot be happy as a "bobby-sockser" again. "Things happen to you," they said. A few weeks later, Paula, in discussing her own attitudes, said: "As in Lydia's case, I don't think I could catch again the happy feelings I had when I ran around with a group of bobby-sock kids, with their funny clothes and crazy paint on their faces."

When Reva mentioned that thoughts of death recur to her, Sandra interrupted and asked Reva if she thought she was the only one who had such thoughts. Sandra, for one, has them too, but she doesn't really want to think about death because "death is so final. To think of finality makes it sort of awful."

Patients are greatly preoccupied with thoughts of death and clarification of them is rather an important consideration in psychotherapy.[9] While one can assume, a priori, the value of ideas and philosophical concepts that bear upon one's problem, the therapist must utilize these with great caution. It may be helpful to mobilize intellectual understanding in support of the therapeutic process. Even in so thorough a psychotherapeutic method as psychoanalysis, when indicated, educational techniques are employed. Intellectual exploration and understanding of ideas aid and buttress the changes in the patient's perspective and establish a *raison d'être* to emotivity.

The danger of emphasizing ideology in psychotherapy is that it may serve as an escape from the effort necessary for affecting change in the emotional structure. To accomplish the latter, the patient must be willing to make the effort and submit to the pain and unpleasantness that it entails. Every patient is resistive to this, and only because of his own suffering and the transference relation does he continue in treatment. To supply him with a ready and easy escape into ideas that on the surface appear like treatment would

[9] Paul Schilder, "The Analysis of Ideologies as a Psychotherapeutic Method, Especially Group Treatment," *American Journal of Psychiatry*, November, 1936.

serve to strengthen and abet resistance. However, discussions of ideologies are of value as guides to living when they follow a prolonged and thoroughgoing psychotherapy and emotional reeducation. Discussion of ideologies that the patients bring forth spontaneously are more suitable at the end rather than at the beginning of treatment. The therapist should not introduce such discussions, but rather follow through on them after they have been initiated by the patients.

CHAPTER FIVE

EGO STRENGTHENING, CATHEXIS DISPLACEMENT, SUBLIMATION, AND REALITY TESTING

A LARGE number of patients who come for psychologic help are persons whose self-esteem has been deflated; others are unable to mobilize power to hold in check their impulses (id) and to deal with outer stresses. Because of these conditions they have adopted either withdrawal or defensive aggression as a pattern of life, or have found a compromise solution in neurotic symptoms and behavior. Positive experiences in interpersonal relations have been found to have a good effect on persons with weak ego development and with deflated self-esteem. This is especially true of children, when the libido organization is in its formative stages and the ego is fluid, still possessing little autonomy. In view of the fact that the controlling and regulative mechanism of the human psyche is the ego, strengthening of it is one of the major aims of psychotherapy.[1]

In the psychic economy of the individual, the ego's function is to hold in check undesirable impulses and to deal with outer pressures and demands. The patterning and strength of these executive functions are derived from early experiences and from identifications with significant adults in the child's life, the most important of whom are the parents or parent surrogates.

Of the three dynamic forces of the psyche—id, ego, and superego—the ego is the more complex both in constitution and function. For the purpose of our discussion here it need only be recognized

[1] In activity group therapy, where no insight is activated beyond limited levels of derivative insight on the part of the patient, ego strengthening is the major dynamic involved.

that the ego deals with reality to a greater extent than do the others. One of its two main functions is to deal with reality by selecting permissible channels for expressing urges, for pleasure, and instinct gratifications, and repressing or blocking those that are not acceptable to the internalized superego or are not in conformity with social demands. When conflict of the outer and inner forces occurs, it is the ego that finds compromise solutions or acceptable gratifications. It is also the ego that accepts or rejects the stimuli from the outside in accordance with the dictates of the superego. The constitution and strength of the ego determines to a large extent the character of the individual in his multitudinous adaptations in daily living, for it is also within the province of the ego to mobilize power for carrying out one's aims.

The structure of the ego is complicated. The ego is a product of the ways in which earliest primary cravings were dealt with during the oral incorporation (narcissistic) and the individuation (autonomy) phases in development. Either extended infancy (dependency) or overstrict, overrigid and overdemanding treatment of the young child weakens the ego. Both extremes in treatment by parents and educators renders the ego incapable of mobilizing forces. Parents who allow ascendancy of the child's impulses beyond a permissible age and stage in his development prevent the orderly and normal ego organization; the ego remains weak. The child is prey of tyrannical and anarchic instincts and impulses which extend into his later life. The power of discrimination, that is, selective capacity, which is one of the functions of the ego, is impaired when there is either too much leniency or too much restraint.

Perhaps one more point should be made in this connection, though only briefly. This is that the presence of neurotic symptoms does not necessarily posit a weak ego. The intensity of the conflict that underlies the symptom may be too strong for the ego to deal with, but this does not mean that the ego itself is weak. The fundamental structure of the ego can be strong, yet it may not be able to resolve a particular unconscious conflict. We all know neurotic persons who manage social relations acceptably and mobilize powers necessary to achieve aims. In fact, psychotherapy can be effective only with persons whose ego strengths are at least minimal. Patients whose ego is weak beyond a certain point cannot be rehabilitated by psychotherapy, for patients with too defective an ego formation, may be unsuitable for any type of psychotherapy.

The foundations of the ego are laid chronologically before the neurosis. The ego is structured by the manner with which the infant's earliest impulses are treated, while a neuroses is a product of the Oedipal conflict. Thus a psychoneurosis can be overlaid upon a fairly strong ego, which comes into its own when the neurotic conflict is eliminated or diminished. In the self-evaluative statements of the girls on pp. 64 f. this fact is made clear. As their neurotic conflicts diminished, they themselves became aware of their growing ability to accomplish their aims and to deal with their impulses.

In addition to the controls that adults implant in the child, through teaching and discipline, ego development is also affected by identifications. When identification models are lacking, or are inadequate or weak, or when the child does not incorporate adequate regulative powers (self-control) from the parents, his ego is unable to cope with inner and outer forces. One of the major processes through which the ego is built is through the child's giving up self-indulgent, narcissistic preoccupations, self-centeredness and feelings of omnipotence and acquiring instead inner controls and a sense of reality with parents as models. Parents whose own egos are strong demonstrate through their behavior adequate means for dealing with problems that the child at first unconsciously imitates and later integrates into his own psychic structure. These are some of the reasons why regression is so important in psychotherapy. The patient has to return to the early egocentric state before he can give it up, in this case for the therapist, who is the parent substitute. The patient also incorporates the therapist's values, attitudes, and patterns which he should have done in relation to his parents.

To gain the normal love of the parent is the chief motive for the self-inhibition and self-discipline that result in ego strengthening. In individual psychotherapy the transference relation has the same effect, but in group psychotherapy there is the added dynamic, *social hunger*. Acceptance by the group (and by the therapist) is the motive for emotional growth, but growth cannot occur unless regression is permitted and accepted. In ordinary social and professional groups, regressive acts are at once challenged, disapproved, or punished. The offending individual is discriminated against or is excluded, which further weakens his ego, increases guilt, and deflates his feelings of self-esteem. A therapy group must be planned and organized so that everyone is fundamentally accepted, his opinions treated with respect and his behavior tolerated or accepted.[2] Because of these conditions and relations, the patient perceives himself as worthy, and having achieved status—his self-image improves. He gradually incorporates into his psychic structure the newly acquired sense of security and self-esteem, and he no longer needs to overassert himself or withdraw.

At one of the earlier sessions of the group, Lydia and Sandra agreed that Rose is not one to be much affected by her surroundings. Reva said directly to Rose that she had not become any more Americanized than when Reva first met her three years before, but she had grown stouter. Rose blushed but made no comment. Paula was chewing gum very noisily. Rose showed annoyance at the clicking sound and angrily told Paula to stop. Lydia at once pointed out to Rose that she is intolerant; no one likes the way Paula chews gum, but no one else has shown any outward annoyance. Paula defiantly continued to chew noisily and to crack the gum. Rose grew quite angry and stamped her foot in anger as she told Paula to stop. Paula laughed, but chewed her gum less noisily.[3] At the end of the session, Paula stayed behind and voluntarily helped the therapist set the room in order, attempting to draw her into conversation by saying that she had not kept her appointment with her caseworker and that she would like to postpone the next scheduled appointment as well. The caseworker, she said, talked about things that she is not eager to discuss. The therapist recognized in this Paula's bid for becoming her child, exclusively, and as resistance to therapy; she therefore did not respond. After setting the room aright both left together.

Interpretation: This incident shows how through their need to be accepted by the group, Paula and Rose curbed their undesirable behavior. Rose repressed her anger against Lydia and Sandra in order not to arouse too much hostility toward herself and Paula used infantile and annoying means to attract the therapist's attention and to take revenge on the other members who are more favored (having no other therapist). However, the girls are able to exercise control only after they have fitted comfortably into the group. This they have done successfully, as other quotations from the records amply demonstrate.

This incident illustrates several other interesting interpersonal dynam-

[2] See S. R. Slavson, "Some Elements in Activity Group Therapy," *American Journal of Orthopsychiatry*, October, 1944.

[3] See quotation from record on p. 65.

ics. There is the hostility felt against one of an out-group (Rose, a visitor, is a German refugee with a foreign accent). Another is Rose's displacement of hostility against Lydia and Sandra upon Paula and indirectly against the therapist for not protecting her. Still another is Paula's resentment for being a "stepchild," (as she described it later in group treatment) and her attack upon the group as a displacement of her anger against the therapist for whose love she later makes a bid (cleaning of the room and disclaiming the caseworker); also her identification with another "underdog," Rose, when she stops clicking her gum to please her. In this there is also the element of fear of redirecting hostility from Rose to herself, if she continued to click her gum.

Another illustration of the strengthening of the ego through group psychotherapy of a different order is presented by Betty, who had been an invalid for some nine years. Psychogenic factors were suspected by the hospital staff where she had been under treatment. Several months of analytic group psychotherapy, exclusively, had enabled her to go to school instead of having the teacher come to her house as a "shut-in." (See also p. 155.)

At the sixteenth session, Ella mentioned that Betty looked much better than when she, Ella, first came to the group. Anne said that Betty looked even thinner last year than she did when Ella first saw her. She used to be "pale as anything." Betty blushed. Yolanda and Anne turned to Betty and told her how nice she looked now. Betty responded to this praise, but seemed self-conscious. Betty was again impeccably attired, well-groomed and much healthier looking. There was slight coloring in her transparent skin that was not there before and which made her look quite attractive. Betty herself made the rather significant statement during the session to the effect that since she had been going to school and was kept busier, she does not feel as tired as she used to be. Anne said this is probably because she was not as bored.

Betty complained about how annoyed she was with her home, she said she knew it was so because she did not get out more than she did. If she could only get out more, she would not be so bored and irritated. She commented again that she had not felt as tired since she began going to school every day. Yolanda warmly invited her to come to her house Saturday evening, where Betty would meet very nice friends of hers. Betty was hesitant and Yolanda added that she knew Betty was interested in interior decorating and one of the girls who would be at the party was also interested in the subject. Betty seemed to perk up at this and accepted the invitation. (Yolanda displayed good insight in dealing with Betty's fear of people because she, too, had been a "shut-in" for about eight years.)

In this connection it should be noted that the term ego is used in more than one sense. The ego as the regulative and executive dynamic has been briefly outlined in foregoing pages. Ego, however, also conveys the concept of self, the self-image and self-esteem, which is part of the inner reality with which the ego deals. Thus the recognition of self as an entity, and the attitudes toward that self, are part and parcel of the ego structure, as well as its function. Feelings of unworthiness and the need for self-debasement and humiliation are both the result and a cause of ego-inadequacy. Psychotherapy helps the individual overcome his feelings of worthlessness and weakness by strengthening his ego through changes in the self-image and improved self-esteem.

One of the results of a strengthened ego is that the patient gives up some of his defenses, attains greater objectivity and self-acceptance. The need to protect oneself against injury to self-esteem is diminished, and, since these defenses are one of the major sources of resistance, therapy is aided. It is understandable that a person would feel uncomfortable in confessing to tabooed desires and thoughts against which a whole system of associative guilt attitudes had been built up. It is equally understandable that an individual would be loath to admit to himself, and to others, that his parents and relatives fall short of the ideal or that they do not compare well with members of other people's families. One of the tasks of psychotherapy is to eliminate these protections so as to enable the patient to communicate freely. When he succeeds in this, the therapeutic process is aided and he establishes a better relation to reality, for much of one's phantasy is a defense against self-confrontation and revelatory activity.

Establishing a transference is in itself an indirect admission of weakness and dependence, the existence of which the ego does not wish to admit, for, by and large, the ego is unwilling to let one see one's weaknesses, failures, and foibles, preferring to keep one in a fool's paradise of phantasy and imagination. Fear of failure prevents many from undertaking an enterprise or testing themselves against the world. Some patients can mobilize powers for situations in which they are secure and in which failure is either impossible or only a remote possibility, but they are blocked when difficulties arise, or when there is actual threat of failure. In such circumstances the ego is not strong enough to permit uncovering its weakness. To prevent this, the individual may remain inactive or find even more injurious escapes from reality.

Thus ego defenses are in many respects pivotal in the psychotherapeutic scheme. Not only do they interfere with its basic dynamics, but they also serve to increase anxiety. It is the function of the ego to deal with all these inner stresses. This being the case, the more constricted the ego is, the less is it able to permit repressed material to come through to find either direct expression or sublimation. In such circumstances it also interferes with catharsis.

One of the major values of group therapy is the effect it has in lessening superego restraints and ego defenses. The fact that other members of the group have similar problems and are similarly handicapped (universalization) is one of the strongest agents in weakening one's self-protectiveness. The fact that one is not unique in his peculiarities reduces guilt and shame, buttresses self-esteem, corrects the self-image, and reduces feelings of inadequacy. The relief resulting from all this is reflected in enthusiasm for the group, direct expression of pleasure, and regularity in attendance at group sessions. Added to this are the satisfactions derived from the positive attitudes of the therapist and the other members of the group.

A few brief manifestations of ego defenses as described will suffice at this point.

Sandra said she would like to make "a confession." She thinks that she is quite unstable, and her instability is manifested by her "show-off" behavior. Lydia said we all have something about us that is a little different from the next person. She herself is a "fanatic" about cleanliness; everything has to be "just so." Unanimously, the girls agreed that Lydia was by far the best-dressed among them. Sandra became provoked when Rose and Paula told her that she did not dress carefully and was sloppy. Because of this display of anger, Paula countered, "Look at your spotted skirt"; Rose added, "And your sleeves are rolled up." Sandra finally admitted that she does not dress too carefully, but called attention to the fact that she was no longer bleaching her hair (which she used to do in a bizarre way) and that she fixed it in less striking fashion. She said she was honestly trying to look neater. The girls agreed that she was achieving this.

At the 52d session Reva (who, as we recall, had been extremely infantile and dependent) told the group why she came for treatment and what had happened since. She said she is now growing into maturity, living at her own age level, and she is much happier. She does many things for herself she never thought of doing before. She is no longer afraid of responsibilities. She is on time for appointments and at school, and no longer truants. Lydia laughed at this and said she was still waiting for the day when Reva would be able to go into a store and buy her own panties. Reva laughed and said she thought that day, too, would come.

At the 17th session Betty asked whether there are any good people in the world: she has not seen very many good people in her life. She said she was particularly thinking of her family. There isn't a single member in her family to whom she feels close. Before Betty went away to a convalescent home, she was devoted to her sister. They were very much attached to one another. Now, she despises her sister. She never dreamt she could despise anybody so. The only other person she despises like that is her mother. As Betty spoke, she displayed intense hostility and was so carried away with emotions that she repeated her statements several times. (At one session she spoke of her desire to kill her mother and sister and inquired whether she would be electrocuted for it. Perhaps it should be noted that she had tried to commit suicide as a reaction to this homicidal drive.)

Many adolescent and adult patients at first attempt to conceal the true state of affairs in their homes. Sandra, for example, pictured her father as an ideal person and her family as pleasant. Later she revealed him as a narcissistic, immature, and irresponsible man and the home as poverty-stricken, conflict-ridden, and depressing. Betty similarly described her family as a devoted and loving group of people, though later in treatment she openly spoke of her impelling desire to kill her mother and one of her sisters. The need to describe relatives as persons other than what they really are arises partly from a desire to make a good impression (ego defenses), and also because these persons have special meaning in the libido economy of the patients. They are the most significant and important persons in their lives and are, therefore, afraid to weaken these sources of security.

One of the values of transference is that the libido of the patient is redirected from primary persons such as parents and siblings to the therapist and the other members of the group. Ego defenses are diminished when the libido is detached from its earlier anchorages. These anchorages may be one's own ego or persons close to one.

When these earlier foci become less important, that is, less cathexized, the patient grows freer, more objective, and either through catharsis or through sublimation is able to rid himself of the quantum of love and therefore also of hostility and aggression against them. While the libido remains anchored in the parents, other members of one's family, or one's own ego, resistances to therapy persist. When the cathexis is lessened or displaced, emotional change can occur, but as long as a patient clings to the original infantile love objects there is little chance for emotional growth. It is suggested that the process of substituting one emotional focus or anchor for another be termed *cathexis displacement*.

Cathexis displacement is inherent in the transference relation in which the therapist becomes the center of the patient's emotions (as his parents had been). In group psychotherapy, we have found from the patients' own statements, as well as through their behavior, that attachment to the group and to the members in it forms a major inducement for attending sessions. Enthusiasm for the group, which is freely verbalized, and consistent attendance clearly indicate that there has occurred a transfer of emotional focus. As the discussions continue, the intensity of the preoccupation with parents, siblings, and mates greatly diminishes. The group members talk about them with less disturbance and tension, as though the latter were no longer so meaningful to them. Such emotional detachment is a part of maturation and occurs when substitute sources of satisfaction are offered to the patient to take the place of the earlier ones. Patients in a group grow more homoerotic. They become preoccupied with one another, and with the group as a whole.

A therapy group, as does a family, becomes a focus of cathexis. The group becomes a source of comfort, satisfaction, and substitute gratifications which the patient, fixed at an infantile level, sought from his parents and other members of his family. These dynamics are probably at the foundation of the psychologic process emphasized by some child psychotherapists and termed "separation." The child, however, cannot separate from the cathexized person without the aid of a substitute (transference object) as a supportive emotional relation.

The meaning of the group to its members is illustrated by the following rather typical incident.

Because of a holiday the following Monday (the regular time for the next session), another day had to be set. The girls insisted that they did not want to miss an entire week and suggested that the group meet on Wednesday. The therapist asked whether that was not too close to the regular day, but the girls insisted they wanted to meet on Wednesday anyway.

It is of singular significance to analytic group psychotherapy that some patients can attach themselves to a group more readily than to an individual. While they cannot develop a therapeutically adequate transference upon an individual therapist, they more easily relate to a group, sometimes under the same therapist. In some instances of specially resistive patients, individual treatment was successfully reinitiated after a period of group treatment. Other patients feel disloyal to mothers, husbands, or wives when they develop positive feelings toward another adult of an intensity such as a transference relation entails. Guilt feelings thus aroused prevent their venturing into a new relationship, and various types of resistances spring up. Still others have an unconscious fear that they will lose their parents' or mates' love if they become emotionally involved with the therapist. There are also patients in whom distrust is so intense as to render them emotionally inaccessible; they grow anxious and build up a resistive wall against a transference relation. Because of the transference dilution in a group, these and similar reservations, resistances and fears are greatly diminished.

Patients are sometimes so competitive or rebellious that they are unable to subordinate their ego-drives as is necessary for individual therapy. Resentment and hostility toward adults in authority are also greatly diminished and diluted in a group. However, there are patients who feel so antagonistic to the therapist, as a parent substitute, that they challenge him, seek to dominate and provoke him, and generally resist treatment. Frequently such patients withdraw from group treatment as well.

We have found also that some patients cannot develop a transference relation (or effect cathexis displacement) because of an unconscious fear of homosexual impulses toward the therapist. In psychotherapy, other than psychoanalysis, this situation cannot be dealt with adequately; transfer to another therapist or termination is, therefore, indicated. In groups, the fear of homosexuality is less likely to be activated, because the transference is diluted and distributed. The other members of the group serve as protection against homosexual impulses, thereby making it possible for the patient to continue in treatment and displace cathexis on the group instead of the therapist.

When cathexis in relation to a parent or mate is diminished or displaced, the patient is more tolerant of the latter. He can accept the fact that the parent, sibling, or mate is himself a product of circumstances and, therefore, unable to be different or act differently. The patient can accept the fact that some acts are beyond one's control; they result from conditions in the making of which one has had no part. Since the parent, sibling, or mate is no longer charged with the same emotional significance (cathexis) the patient can be more detached and can view him more objectively. In this process the discussion and interpretations of the other members contribute greatly, both because they engender insight and because an ideology emerges to foster better understanding. Especially is this helpful in cases of projection. A group member is helped to overcome his tendency to project by the repeated corrective analyses and discussions of attitudes among the members. Through these discussions, his perspectives are widened, distortions due to emotivity corrected, and hostilities diminished.

Betty said her mother often told the family that when she was a child her mother never gave the children candy, decent clothes, toys, or anything they longed to have; Betty's mother was deprived of all these. Anne said that her father, too, was terribly frustrated as a little boy; he never got any gifts, and never gave any, and her mother also did not, for the same reason. She proceeded to defend her father, but at first did not justify her mother. (The father had been in the First World War and suffered a great deal, which may have made him bitter.) However, after some discussion in which all the girls participated Anne finally said that there was a reason why her mother, too, is not a giving person. When her mother was twelve years old, she lost all of her hair (universal alopecia). She had no eyebrows or lashes and had to wear a covering over her head for four years. Anne described the intense suffering her mother had undergone. She was teased by everybody, and her teachers did not understand her. When the mother reached her fifteenth year, her hair grew back, but it had changed from a beautiful auburn to black.

Interpretation: The objectivity on the part of the two girls is in itself striking. What is even more remarkable is that Betty, who had had such intense hatred of her mother and had harbored homicidal phantasies and impulses, gave them up through group treatment to such an extent that she was now able to find extenuating circumstances for her mother's really harsh and rejecting behavior. Similarly, Anne's resentment of her mother has also decreased. Both girls not only understand their parents now, but also forgive them—a direct result of cathexis displacement and a diminishing tie to them. At first both girls were defensive about their families; they pictured them as ideal. As a next step, they freely expressed hostile feelings and complaints. They finally reached a stage when they could see their parents realistically.

The awareness of the dynamics of cathexis displacement is revealed in a conversation of sixteen-year-old Negro girls in analytic group psychotherapy:

Winnie repeated again "Mrs. G., is it right that a woman should not love a man before she knows that the man loves her?" Bee said: "You're a coward." Winnie: "Maybe I am." Bee: "You must not think that the man will not love you. Maybe he will, maybe not; but don't think." Jennifer here stated that she also thinks that no man would love her. Winnie then said that she does not know, perhaps the man might love her, but she is afraid he would not; if she did fall in love, it would be awful. And so it would be better if she didn't even start to get near a man. The therapist asked: "You are afraid of loving a man?" "Yes," said Winnie. "And why shouldn't I? You know, Mrs. G., my father doesn't love me." "That's too bad," said Bee, "If your father didn't love you, then you think a man can't love you, either. My father is a stinker, but I guess he did like me. It is good if you love." Winnie said: "It must be good, but I don't dare. You see, I am afraid to love a man and yet at the same time I would like to try it out." "Oh," said Greta, "they sure will love you. Why shouldn't they?"

At this point, Winnie, Jennifer, and Bee spoke simultaneously. Jennifer and Winnie were elaborating on the fact that in their homes nobody was good to them or loved them. This is why they feel that nobody else will love them and why they are so afraid of meeting someone with whom they might fall in love—they think he would not love them. "Yes," said Greta, "And then that makes you so afraid at night." Bee said: "This is very funny. In my home, too, there is nobody who loves me, but my grandmother lived with us, and she died two years ago. My grandmother loved me and now I am not afraid. I like to love."

Winnie said, with great feeling: "You mean your grandmother loved you and then *this is in you?*" Then she added, "I think my mother must have loved me but I was so small when she died, I don't remember her at all. Now I am with my grandmother and she does not love me. She said she wants to send me to reform school."

Caroline, 14, a colored girl in a racially mixed activity therapy group, had made several references to her father. On one occasion she said that until her father died, she never thought of boys, "He was the man in my life, but now that he's dead, oh boy!" She said that her mother eats everything. "But there are a lot of things I don't like. My father was like that, too," she added. On another occasion Caroline revealed her guilt feelings while narrating a dream in which her father came to her and told her he wanted her with him. "I woke up scared because I thought I was going to die, too!" she exclaimed.

As a further illustration of the effect of cathexis displacement upon attitudes toward parents, we are reproducing in full an interview by a six-year-old boy. The boy was alone with the therapist.

Mike [4] came to the therapist's room as she was leaving for the group room. He asked about airplane models and was shown the boxes the therapist was carrying. Mike said he was glad. On the way he asked whether Judah or John were coming. Then he said would the therapist please invite Noah again because he, Mike, wants "to adjust him." When asked why he wanted to do this, Mike said: "You can't do it. You don't help each of the children. Instead, you let the kids help each other." At this point the group room was reached and Mike took out parts of his plane, looked them over, and began talking. "Lola," (previous group therapist) he said, "used to help each of us." When asked what he meant, he said: "Well, I'll tell you. Lola and my mother are the same, both are strict. Your way is different. You don't go over to each one and so they don't throw paint at you." The therapist said, "You like Lola and you don't like my way." Mike replied: "No, I like your way, but you see when I get home it is hard for me. My mother and father are different. You know something? My mother and father won't buy me toys. They don't want me to be a child. They want me to be a man. You know how when you walk along the streets, you see children playing with guns, wearing soldier or sailor suits, but my father doesn't believe in anything like that." The therapist said that he must be angry with his father. "Well," Mike went on, "you don't understand; no, you do; we are really talking about the same thing. Wait, I'll explain it to you."

Mike took the lock off the toy-closet door and put it down in front of him on the table and sat down. The therapist remained standing. He continued, pointing to the two sides of the lock successively: "Look,

[4] For case history see p. 124.

you are talking about this side and I am talking about that side." The therapist asked if he meant he also liked his father as well as being angry at him. Mike nodded his head: "Yes, my father and I are exactly alike. When I go out with my mother and father, I have to be quiet and not like a child." Therapist: "Yet sometimes boys feel like acting up." Mike replied: "Yes, but then I get punished. How? I punish myself. I don't know how it will happen, but it will happen. I can't give you an example." He then got up and walked toward the work table.

Up to this point Mike kept himself under control but now he burst into tears: "I am sick and tired of being mature. I want to be a child. I am a child." He then wandered over toward the therapist, picked up his plane parts, looked them over and sat down again, continuing to speak: "You see, I'll tell you how it is. I'm not supposed to tell you this because it is home matters." Did he feel he should not talk of his mother and father? He agreed. The therapist then said that his mother knew he was to tell her anything that she might need to help him. Mike then said that his mother had telephoned to say he wasn't coming any more (for treatment). It was because his father didn't want him to, but his mother does. He then hesitated and stopped. The therapist asked whether he was wondering if she would tell his mother what he told her. Mike said he thought she would. The therapist told Mike that she did not tell his mother what he told her. She could tell only people like the doctor or psychologist, if they were going to see him. In response Mike said: "Well then, how did my mother know I had three frankfurters?" The therapist did not know. He said: "John didn't tell her, and Judah didn't." The therapist said he didn't seem to trust her. Mike denied this and said: "All right. Well, my mother and father fight all the time. I can hear them talking sometimes when I am in the other room. They are thinking of getting a divorce. When they fight, I do all kinds of ceremonials." Was he worrying that he would not be able to live at home with them? Mike said that this was what he was thinking about. "You see," he said, "it isn't just that they fight, but my mother is tired of taking care of me. I tried to bring out to my mother that there is something the matter with her. Our house isn't like a house should be any more. She doesn't clean it up. You know: we don't even have handkerchiefs. Sunday, she gave me a rag. It is like this, my mother didn't have a mother and father to bring her up. She just had two sisters, so she doesn't think a child has to have a mother and a father. She had to be independent; my father too had to be independent. So you see they think I have to be independent, too."

Having said this, Mike turned to working on his airplane. He first examined the materials in his own carton then the contents of another and pointed out what he thought was missing from his. The therapist showed him the list for getting missing parts. Actually there was some glue missing. Mike knew it. He then sat down again and began to talk: "You know sometimes when I am home, I dream about being a very good pilot or a good businessman who makes a lot of money. You know the way a child does. Then when I get to school, it seems I can't do the work." Therapist: "It seems you want to do what much older people do and don't think you can do what boys your age do." Mike said: "I know I can do it, but I just don't. I'll tell you how you can help me. Will you get a big book and everytime I see you alone, I'll tell you my problems and then you can write them down. Then, when I get all through, you can put down what is the cause, then I'll be all right." The therapist said she would remember what he tells her, but he still did not seem to trust her much, since he made up his own ways for being helped. Mike then said: "All right, then you can do it your way. Would you do me a favor? My mother doesn't know how to bring up a child. If you help me, that's all right, but when I get home it is different. Would you write my mother a letter and explain to her how she should bring up a child?" The therapist said she didn't think a letter would help, but may be she could arrange for someone to see his mother, so she could help him more. Mike said that would be good.

He returned to working on his plane, asking for help. As is usual with him, he did not use enough glue. He soon asked if he could go to see Santa Claus. When the therapist answered in the affirmative, Mike put away his plane unfinished, looked over all the empty boxes left from used airplane models, and asked if he could have them. The therapist said that he could. The two then got ready to go to see Santa Claus at a near-by department store. As they were leaving the room, Mike said: "Shoo fly, get away from me, I belong to somebody." He seemed very happy.

On the way down he said his mother would not take him to see Santa Claus because she thinks he is too old a boy for that. Mike suggested going down by the back stairway and when he reached the street he took the therapist's hand and pulled her toward a stationery store. He said that the girls (members of the same group) would probably buy her a Christmas present. They had bought one for Lola. He thinks they will get her a slip and all the children put paint on it. In the stationery store, Mike picked out a Christmas card and asked the therapist to hold it for him.

The two continued to the department store, where Mike went over rather timidly to the Santa Claus. He received a present, which he opened immediately. It was a game. He studied it for awhile. He then asked permission to look at the toys. He pointed to a tool set and said that that was something he was going to get and that this year it was cheaper than last. He asked the therapist to read for him descriptions on other boxes. After doing this the therapist told Mike it was time to start back. He said in an off-hand manner: "Come on, dear." Outside he seemed very much interested in the window display and in the nativity scene. He wanted to know what the nativity scene was, and the therapist explained it to him.

When the two reached the corner leading to the clinic, Mike ran away, hid himself, and then came running toward the therapist, laughing hilariously. He took her hand and said, "Well, here we go to the gallows." When asked what he meant, he responded, "Well, I'm going home." Did he feel guilty about telling the therapist what he had? Mike answered: "I had to tell you so you could help me." When he entered the elevator, Mike in jaunty fashion, told the elevator man the floor at which he wanted to get off.

As the therapist and Mike entered the group room he said: "Oh boy, what the others missed today! We had such a good time!" Mike began collecting the empty boxes again, putting one into the other. The time was up, but, when the therapist told him this, Mike continued to putter with the boxes. The therapist said it looked as though he didn't want to leave today. Mike said, no, he did not and added in a soft voice, keeping his head down: "I like you." The therapist said she liked him too, but that the time was up today and he would be coming again next week. Mike took only one box cover, leaving the rest of the boxes behind, and went with the therapist downstairs where his mother was waiting. He seemed subdued, but also content.

Interpretation: The record has a variety of implications and demonstrates many points in child psychotherapy. We are, however, interested at this juncture in the process of cathexis displacement which makes it possible for little Mike to speak of his parents as he does and which he clearly conveys when he says: "Shoo, fly, get away from me. I belong to somebody." Perhaps the reader should know that Mike's characterization of his parents was entirely correct. There is no exaggeration in what he said about them.

Sublimation serves to redirect instinctive impulses into channels acceptable to the ego, to society and its mores. Sublimation as an alternative to repression is important in maintaining mental health and psychic equilibrium. One of the difficulties the neurotic experiences in this regard is that he is unable either to repress or sublimate adequately urges which he is not allowed or is afraid to express. He is, therefore, in a state of continuous conflict that prevents him from canalizing his drives into permissible aim-fulfillment. The child who has not brought his impulses under control (repression) can canalize them either through direct or sublimatory activities. Play and work with clay, water, paints, fire, hunting games, shooting, killing insects, sliding down banisters, see-sawing, and the numberless other play and creative activities supply him with suitable outlets which are less accessible to the adult.[5]

One of the aims of psychotherapy is to bring the patient to a point in his psychic development where he is able to accept or seek out for himself sublimatory occupations either in work or leisure-time interests. In clinics and hospitals, and in some instances, also in private practice, psychiatrists employ ancillary forms of treatment to achieve this. Occupational therapy, individual and group recreation, clubs, education, environmental manipulation, group discussions, dramatics, and other channels of a similar nature are employed to redirect and sublimate primitive drives and supply more evolved and mature ways of aim gratification. These strengthen the capacity to control impulses. In some of its forms, activity catharsis serves also as a channel for sublimation, and one of the main values of activity group therapy is that there are always opportunities at hand for it. In fact one of the criteria for placing children in such groups is their capacity to sublimate primary drives.

Frequently patients find for themselves interests and occupations in the community that serve as adequate fulfillment or as substitutes for more primary drives. Thus mothers who are too preoccupied with their children, to the detriment of the latter and to themselves, are encouraged to find interests and associations outside the home. One of the important functions of social workers in the treatment of mental patients is helping them find sublimatory interests and activities. Patients neurotically preoccupied with themselves are stabilized and taken out of their self-incapsulation by occupations particularly suitable for them.

Children, especially, are disposed to find sublimations of their primitive impulses in group activities. Individual work with materials, group play, fights and struggles serve these ends. The value of these as activity catharsis has already been discussed, but they must be viewed also as sublimation channels, and playing with fire, water, clay, and paint, hammering and shouting, are only a few other examples of these.

[5] See S. R. Slavson, *Recreation and the Total Personality* (New York, Association Press, 1947), for further discussion of unconscious roots for recreational activities.

As is evident from the record material, a number of sublimation channels are supplied by group discussions as well. In addition to the fact that speech itself is a form of sublimation, free discussion of sexual problems is helpful in this respect. Anger and hostility, when not acted out, are sublimated (as well as displaced) in conversations in the group. Doodling, drawing, and giggling serve the same ends. Adolescents and adults burst into laughter when their unconscious repressed and guilt-evoking thoughts and phantasies come through.

These and many other forms of sublimating emotions occur spontaneously in treatment, but often there is need for sublimation of particularly strong emotional drives, and this requires planned action by the therapist. The patient must be exposed to occupations that serve his psychological needs and through which he can express himself in socially acceptable patterns. Aggression and exhibitionism, for example, can be sublimated, respectively, through sports and dramatics.

The treatment of a girl between the ages of fifteen and seventeen years through individual and analytic group psychotherapy resulted in striking improvement in adaptive capacities and personality traits. This was noticed not only by the girl's therapist but also by her mother, schoolteachers, and friends. A Rorschach Test confirmed their observations, but the nuclear problem, that of an overwhelming, though unconscious, desire to displace her mother, persisted. Because of this drive, the patient protected her younger brother, (who was later removed from the home because of a problem of his own) and fawned over neighbors' children. In her desire to be a mother, behavior that bid fair to lead to sex delinquency appeared. To sublimate her maternal drives, the girl was helped to get a part-time job to care for small children until this problem was worked out with her in the course of treatment.

In group therapy, as well as in individual treatment, it may be necessary to go outside the treatment situation itself to supply necessary sublimations. Patients are, therefore, referred to group work and recreational centers, music schools, and camps to find suitable expression of their needs and talents.

Patients themselves become aware of the value of sublimations as a result of their growing awareness and maturity through derivative insight.

Lydia said that she knows a girl who has had a disappointment in love and "is now only existing." The girl acts as though she had nothing more to live for. Sandra asked, "Why doesn't she get some interest in life, some new interest?"

Reva said she wanted "something to happen." When the therapist asked her to elaborate a little on what she meant, Reva tried to explain but seemed confused and began to look flustered. The therapist said, "I know it is hard to talk about it"; to which Sandra responded, "I would advise her to write." Georgia asked Reva whether she dreams. No, she doesn't. All the girls seemed to agree with Sandra that Reva should do as Sandra is doing: she should write, bring her writings to the "meetings," and the girls would help her express herself. Reva said that she had begun to write something but had lost the papers.

For the sake of brevity we shall give only a few examples of activities that served to sublimate impulses and cravings in a group of adolescent girls and in a group of younger boys and girls.

Reva said she had written the words to two songs and asked whether the group would like to hear them. Everybody expressed interest. Reva said she got the idea of writing them from the announcement of a contest on the radio. The ideas came to her very spontaneously. One song was titled "I Love You."

I love you more than I can say
I love you more than the breath of day;
Can't you say you love me too
Hoping you will make it true.
Day and night will pass me by like the moon;
Will you love me too, hoping, praying, you'll make it soon.

The next one was called "Maybe."

Maybe you and I could watch the stars above,
Maybe you and I may chance to fall in love;
It may be a thrill to have this fulfilled
on this beautiful warm April;
Maybe you and I with our love like this,
Could surely part or end in bliss;
Maybe you and I could love this way forever and a day.

Georgia seemed more impressed than the others and she sang along with Reva. In fact, she seemed so possessed with the words that she kept repeating them again and again. Rose commented that Reva is longing for love. Paula said: "It is love." Reva asked, "With whom, myself or with love?" The therapist asked what she thinks and she replied, "I'm in love with my ideal." Lynn said, rather sarcastically, "My little pin-up boy!"

The following week, Reva brought another poem to read to the group:

Where Are You Now

Where are you now
I've looked all over town
but still haven't found
the sweet little dear
who kissed me and said he'd care.

Where are you now
I've looked all around
since you went away.
I'm counting the days
but it seems there's no way
for us to meet again.

I've walked in the rain
down by the lane, hoping
to meet you there again.
Oh! Where are you now
it seems so long now
since we kissed and said goodbye
before God and the beautiful sky.

A nine-year-old girl brought in a play which is reproduced below and which she wished to have the group act out. The play is transparent in that it conveys her feelings of deprivation, phantasies of magic, attitudes toward her mother and the goodness of the group therapist. The activity that immediately preceded the writing of the play was the furnishing of a dollhouse with toy furniture consisting of various rooms, including bedrooms, bathroom, and kitchen. The group consisted of two boys and two girls, all severely disturbed and all diagnosed as psychoneurotic.

After the house was furnished at the second session of the group in the therapist's own room, the group went to the therapy room. Alice had brought a play which, she said, she had worked on and written for "the club." She thought it would be nice if the club could study and act it. Richard grabbed the papers from Alice and began to read it. Alice grabbed it back, saying that she had written it, and therefore wants to read it. All listened intently as she read.

At the top of the first sheet appeared, "Writer: A. Lazarus"

The Sad Christmas Tree

Characters are:
Teacher
Esther (schoolchildren)
Herbert (schoolchildren)
Abe (schoolchildren)
Place: A small schoolhouse
Time: Morning

Act I, Scene I

(In a classroom the teacher starts to ask a class a question)

Teacher:	Children, I think it is time we had a play.
Esther:	What kind of a play?
Abe:	Let's act out the play about "The Sad Christmas Tree."
Esther and Herbert:	That's a good idea.
Teacher:	I will start to make a plan for the play so we can start to practice it by tomorrow.
Herbert:	Next month would be a good time to have it because it really isn't a long play.

Act II, Scene I

[Some poor children have just found a tree in the woods which they took home and put in the living room. After the children went to sleep, some sleeping on the floor and some in the bed. The tree starts to weep. (Here Alice elaborated and said: "You see, they were very poor children. They didn't all have a bed and the tree feels sorry for them.")]

Tree:	Boo-hoo, boo-hoo, I have no candy and no lights for the children. I wish I could cheer them up. If only I had some candy sticks and lollipops for them to eat. I wish the fairy mother would come to see them.

Act II, Scene II

(A few minutes have passed and the fairy mother comes)

Fairymother:	Here I am, little tree. I heard your wish and I'll give you some lights, lollypops, candy sticks. I'll give you a silver star to shine for the children.
Tree:	Thank you, fairy mother. The children will like it, I'm sure.

Fairymother:	And you, tree, I'm proud of you for you are not selfish. For that, you shall not die for days and when you die, you will still look pretty, in fact, you will be the prettiest dead tree.
Tree:	Thank you fairy mother. You better go now. The children will be getting up.
Fairymother:	All right; but first I will make a breakfast for them to eat and put some food for them in a box. Goodbye tree.
Tree:	Goodbye, goodbye and thank you for what you did for me and the children. I am glad I have candy for the children. Oh, there they are; they're getting up.
1st child:	Look! Look!
All:	Food on the table and candy on the tree.
2nd child:	It must be a magic tree.
All:	Yes! Yes!
3rd child:	We are very lucky this Christmas.

Act III, Scene I

(Back in the classroom after the play)

Teacher:	You did very good in the play, children.
Children:	Thank you, we liked it too. Oh, there's the bell. See you tomorrow.

Interpretation: Evidently, the children in the play represent Alice's new siblings, the members of the group. The tree is her mother and the fairy mother, the therapist who in reality is giving them toys, a place to play in, freedom and food. It must be noted that all the four children had been in individual treatment with the same therapist for six to eighteen months, but Alice apparently tells the therapist "You must be good to your new family as the fairy mother was in the play. Be our fairy mother."

Reality testing is a major process in psychotherapy that should be used planfully. In fact everyone constantly tests himself against reality. It is an integral part of living.

The realities the infant perceives are limited to his inner cravings, desires, and feelings. As he grows older, the limitations that hamper incorporative drives appear to him as deprivations. During later stages, he has to accept the fact that the mother and others, who have appeared to him as extensions of himself, are really separate, autonomous persons. Later the limitations imposed by toilet training, food habits and routines bring home to him the pressures and demands of a world beyond his anarchic and narcissistic drives for instinct gratification. While the average person makes acceptable adaptations to these demands and limitations, those individuals who fail to make such adjustments need some form of reeducation, guidance, or psychotherapy.

As the patient's conflicts are diminished and his ego strengthened, he tests himself against the world, and, as he finds himself wanting, returns to the therapist for further support. When he finds himself adequate in dealing with reality, his image of himself grows more positive. He grows increasingly more satisfied with himself and moves further toward reality and hence also toward recovery from his emotional illness.

At the forty-eighth session, the girls discussed summer camp, which they had attended for several summers, but now they all wanted to get jobs and go to work instead. Rose said that she had improved in her work and her speed is much greater. Within the next few months, she should earn as much as fifty dollars a week. She has also sent for a prospectus and hopes to attend evening college next year. She feels that she will be pretty well oriented to her job and be able to spend several evenings at college. When she saw the group therapist individually, she said that her father was unfair when he only gave her two dollars a week from her earnings. She once waited until both parents were in the kitchen and spoke openly to her father about it. She was surprised to find her mother supporting her. She pointed out to her father that she is aware of the fact that he wants to keep her like a little girl, but if she is grown up enough to work, she is grown up enough to handle some of her earnings in her own way; she asked for five dollars a week. Her father tried to bargain with her but she did not wish to enter into any bargaining. She felt that there was no point in arguing the matter too much, and they settled on four dollars a week. She said she had mastered something within herself—a fear of her father—and she thinks she will never again let him get away with anything like that.

At the thirtieth session, Sandra described how during the preceding week-end, she, Helen, and Don picked up several unusually fine young army officers, who took the girls to a well-known night club of the less expensive caliber. After the group responded to this, the therapist asked how many had ever been in the Greenwich Village section of the city. Lydia and Sandra were the only ones who had. The others seemed afraid to go there. They knew it had some connection with Chinatown and fear was registered about going to that part of the city. When probed further, it came through that though intrigued by the idea of going to new places, the girls actually have not traveled outside their immediate neighborhoods. It also came out that they all feared new situations. After these generalizations, Rose came out with a blanket statement: "What you all want and yet are afraid of is an (sexual) affair." This statement caused loud laughter among the girls. (The therapist later arranged for the girls to visit as a group both Greenwich Village and Chinatown, which are actually distant and distinct from each other.)

The group represents an important reality situation in therapy, though I do not hold that social reality is essential to the treatment process itself; rather, the latter is a preparation for dealing with social realities which may or may not be involved in the treatment situation. Patients in individual therapy can, and usually do, test themselves against the realities of everyday life. Living and therapy thus always go hand in hand whether or not we plan it so.

The therapeutic group supplies a reality, graded in complexity so that the patient can himself incorporate it as part of the total treatment process. This fact is both an advantage and a limiting factor. It is an advantage because the pressures and complexities of reality can be graded and controlled. The environment is conditioned in accordance with the patients' existing capacities, but these very conditions exclude many patients who are not ready for the stress and relationships inherent in group therapy. Thus we can assign to groups only persons who are able to utilize multiple relations beneficially and must exclude those who cannot.

Young children, especially, require experience with reality as a part of treatment. Action, not language, is the natural form of child expression. In many instances even with adults, direct action is more effective than explanation. The child can accept direct impedment to his behavior, whereas he may not understand the reasons for it. Controls are particularly telling when they come from his peer culture; there is less resentment than when controls are imposed by adults. In play therapy groups and activity-interview groups, the setting is so designed that reality is graded. Each child is free to utilize it in whatever way he wishes. He can participate with or shun the others; he can work or play or be idle. In this way, the child has an opportunity to test himself in the therapeutic setting and as he finds himself not wanting in dealing with it, he is strengthened and enters into more active relation with his environment.

An interview group for grownups supplies a rather intensive emotional reality. Reactions to the emotions of the individuals constituting the group is difficult to escape. Here, too, one can act out and react to others, but this is of necessity more restricted than in the case of children. Only rarely is acting out in these groups of a physical nature; feelings are expressed rather through language. Anger, love, resentment, hatred, dependence, are conveyed verbally, rather than by actual physical acts, and these communications are utilized by the therapist in interpretation and evoking insight, or are analyzed and elaborated by other members of the group.

The therapist supports his patients by allying himself with their impulses (id) as against their superego. In doing this, he encourages free catharsis, reduces guilt, and allays anxiety. But the important realistic factors are the reactions of the other members of the group, their encouragement or displeasure, their approval or disapproval, and the interpretations they give to actions and statements. Groups are a significant reality in the lives of people, whether in treatment or living, and all therapy groups provide such reality. But it must be always kept in mind that testing of reality is not limited to the group; it is carried on in the outside world as well.

Reva (who had been shy, very infantile and withdrawn) said that she is continuing to work as a messenger for a telegraph company and enjoys it, because she feels that she is learning a great deal. She is getting accustomed to going about the city by herself and likes to listen to people and see how they act and talk. She is learning from all this.

CHAPTER SIX

SOME SPECIFIC DYNAMICS IN ANALYTIC GROUP THERAPY

TRANSFERENCE DILUTION, TARGET MULTIPLICITY, DISPLACEMENT, ESCAPE, DEFLECTION, CATALYSIS, MUTUAL SUPPORT, IDENTIFICATION, AND UNIVERSALIZATION

THE reader has at this point probably become aware of the difficulty and the inappropriateness of breaking down the structure of psychotherapy into component elements. The psychotherapeutic process, like all important life processes, occurs as a whole and is not a piecemeal phenomenon. It is difficult, therefore, to convey the total process by merely describing its constituent parts. Integration of these is essential in the actual practice of psychotherapy. The psychotherapist faces and deals with numberless dynamics simultaneously and uses his psychotherapeutic armamentarium as a totality to meet the variety of situations presented by a patient. This is especially true of group psychotherapy in which the dynamics are even more varied and are complicated by the network of interpersonal and group interaction.

In the preceding chapters, an effort has been made to describe separately some of the various elements that go into the total therapeutic process. It is, however, evident that such fragmentation is at best artificial and organismically inadequate.

The universal observation by all group therapists is that patients are incomparably more productive in groups than in individual treatment, and that the therapeutic process is greatly accelerated. To a considerable extent these phenomena can be understood through a perusal of the dynamics already discussed, especially those that allay anxiety. A number of other dynamics that facilitate therapy in groups will be briefly indicated in this chapter. These are Transference Dilution, Target Multiplicity, Deflection, Escape,

Catalysis, Mutual Support, Identification, and Universalization.

Transference dilution occurs in therapy groups through the transference relations among the members; it reduces the anxiety activated by hostile and aggressive feelings toward the therapist. We have already discussed the processes by which this occurs, describing them as sibling transference and identification transference (p. 18).

Another dynamic that facilitates psychotherapy in groups which has been only briefly mentioned before is *target multiplicity.* The hostility inherent in the transference relation toward the therapist as a parent figure, especially during its negative phases, is divided among the members of the group, thereby considerably reducing fear and anxiety. When in individual therapy the patient's ego is unable to deal with these aggressive impulses, they are repressed, thus blocking catharsis. This is treated as resistance. In the group, however, patients can redirect or deflect this hostility toward fellow members, that is, make them the targets of hostility. For this we suggest the term target multiplicity, and because it diminishes the fear of punishment or retaliation by the therapist, the result is lowered resistance to treatment and accelerated catharsis.

Mutual support that occurs in groups is in many respects related to the phenomenon of target multiplicity. What the individual may be afraid to reveal or express when alone with a therapist, he may easily release in a group. This is particularly valuable in discharging hostility and aggressive feelings toward the therapist and other persons of importance. Mutual support is tantamount to group sanction and, therefore, the superego is to a greater or lesser degree suspended. Mutual support is also a factor in group morale, although it differs from it in a number of important respects. In view of the fact that a therapy group seldom, if ever, becomes a group in the ordinary sense of the term, morale as commonly understood is absent, though mutual support is always present.

The dynamic of *displacement* involved in this process is one that occurs constantly in groups as the record material throughout these pages demonstrates. Various emotions felt by the patient toward the therapist, which he may be afraid to express, are displaced on other members, who are less threatening, or upon persons who, though not present, are important in the emotional economy of the patient. Such persons are siblings, parents, mates, and employers. One is impressed with the frequency with which the stratagem of displacement is used by patients in group interviews. In terms of therapeutic dynamics, displacement is a form of resistance, and although it serves to reduce anxiety, it may, if used too frequently, vitiate or block therapeutic progress. The therapist may have to deal directly with displacement and interpret it as a form of resistance, for it may be used to evade free association and serve as a means for defeating the therapist.

In a similar manner *escape* is employed by patients in groups. Such escape is frequently achieved by the patient's selective silence during group interviews or when he changes the subject as he feels the onset of anxiety. Lydia, for example, changed the subject when pubic hair was under discussion.[1] Reva employs the same strategy in the following abstract.

Sandra was reminded of a song, "A Man Ain't Nothing but a Little Boy." Georgia remarked, with a chuckle, "My father is in his second childhood." Rose commented, "That's why you go with boys younger than yourself, even though you always talk about liking older boys." Reva (who has a strong father fixation) apologetically and self-consciously changed the subject. She said she knew she had been absent for a few weeks, but even during her absences she was still preoccupied with the question she had asked the group, but which was not answered.

The strategies of escape and displacement can also be employed by the therapist for constructive purposes, as when he becomes aware of rising anxiety in the group members, which may be contraindicated at a given time. Still another escape for patients is provided when they focus attention on another member and thus redirect it from themselves. This is the process of *deflection;* it has therapeutic value, for, as the problems of another person are discussed, a particular patient can venture much further in the exploration than when he himself is under consideration. He may be strengthened through identification [2] until he is able to admit the relevance of the discussion to himself. Sometimes a patient presses an especially painful subject with a fellow member because he really seeks to clarify it within himself. Thus each can use the others

[1] See p. 45.
[2] This can be described as *identification therapy.*

in the grist of his own therapy. Such strategies are among the major advantages of a group, for, through exploring the difficulty of another and identifying with him, each evolves insight into his own.

Still another element that accelerates the therapeutic process in groups is *catalysis*. Each person present activates all the others to expression and action. It would take us too far afield to discuss the psychodynamics of suggestion, induction, and interstimulation that occur in groups beyond the point of saying that the effect of the least conflicted person has a releasing effect upon the others.[3] Thus the least inhibited and the least frightened individual tests the ground for the others. When the latter find it safe to enter upon ordinarily prohibited areas, they too venture out. It has been found that patients who have been unable to express their problems, phantasies, and preoccupations in any other relations, are enabled to do so in group interviews. The catalytic effect is undoubtedly charged with sexual libido and the catalyzing influence occurs on a self-selective basis. One member of a group may activate some and have a lesser effect on others.

The element of *identification,* to which reference has been made on a number of occasions, is of immense importance in group treatment. Identification, being a basic and fundamental process in developing relationships from early infancy, is one of the important dynamics in the development of human personality. It is the source of both superego and ego development and for overcoming the narcissistic state of the infant and child. It has been rightly said that the power of identification is the mark of a civilized person for it is through identification that social attitudes and values are evolved and it is of no small value in the therapeutic process as well.

Universalization, also, has the effect of reducing anxiety and guilt which in turn favors catharsis in groups. When patients discover that other people have problems similar to their own, entertain the same forbidden thoughts, and are given to unacceptable impulses, their guilts are greatly reduced. The emotional burden of each member of the group is lightened thereby, and his self-esteem is raised. Because other members of the group have the same phantasies and strivings of which a given patient is ashamed and afraid,

[3] See S. R. Slavson, *Character Education in a Democracy* (New York, Association Press, 1939), Chapter IV, "Group Dynamics."

he no longer needs to employ defensive disguises, subterfuges, amenities, and façades. One no longer needs to appear as a paragon of righteousness, and thus the burden of the ego is lessened, since it no longer has to hold in repression impulses and maintain disguises. This leads to a greater equilibrium in the psychological economy of the individual and to a better integration of his personality. Universalization, therefore, must be viewed as one of the major contributing factors in activating catharsis, acquiring insight and generally accelerating the therapeutic process in groups.

I have already indicated that because of the several dynamics present in analytic group psychotherapy which reduce anxiety and modify transference, the depth and thoroughness of this treatment does not reach those of an individual psychoanalysis.[4] This does not, however, in any degree detract from its clinical and social value, for not all patients need, and even fewer can avail themselves of, so thorough a form of treatment.

It is also an error to expect similar results from widely varying treatment methods. I have suggested elsewhere [5] that each method of treatment has its specific levels and limitations, and that it is unsound to apply the criteria of one to the other. The aim of all psychotherapy is to correct personality and increase human adaptability and happiness, but there is considerable variance in the levels of treatment and, accordingly, in the methods employed to achieve them. An evaluation of any type of psychotherapy must be made in relation to its special field and defined objectives, as well as in terms of the patients treated. Group psychotherapy deals with selected patients only, but among them are some that would be inaccessible to any other type of treatment.

[4] For further discussion of this subject see p. 237.

[5] S. R. Slavson, "Group Therapy," *American Journal of Orthopsychiatry,* October, 1943.

CHAPTER SEVEN

FUNCTIONS OF THE GROUP THERAPIST

THE PRACTICE of psychotherapy is more an art than it is a science, but the art is rooted in the science. Psychopathology and psychodynamics can be taught and described, but the practice must be acquired, as is any other skill, under the direction of experienced supervisors and teachers who sensitize the prospective therapist to his manifold functions in the dynamic process of therapy. By and large the role of the therapist in analytic group psychotherapy is in many respects the same as in individual psychotherapy. It is based upon transference, catharsis, and insight even though these are modified through the multiple relations in the group. Effective practice depends upon perceptiveness, skill, tact, the insights of the therapist, and the proper selection and grouping of patients.[1] In this chapter, it is intended to deal briefly with the theoretic and practical aspects of the function of the therapist.

In the first place, the therapist must have full information of the psychodynamics and psychopathology of each patient in the group and must know the *nuclear problem* of each. This is necessary so that the therapist may direct the interviews, when indicated, and may better understand each patient's production. The therapist cannot rely entirely on clinical and diagnostic categories. It is not enough to know, for example, that a patient suffers from a psychoneurosis or from neurotic anxiety, without knowing more about the nature and intensity of the symptoms and the contributing factors in the etiology. Clinical categories may indicate the general direction the therapist is to follow, but he cannot deal with a specific

[1] Perhaps humility and caution should be added to the list of the indispensable qualifications of a therapist.

patient unless he knows a great deal more about him. It is essential to know, for example, whether the father or the mother is the central figure in the emotional constellation and to what extent siblings, grandparents, and others have contributed to the onset and development of the difficulties. It is also necessary to know what form the symptoms take and the patient's general social adjustment.

This information is obtained through the anamnesis prepared in advance; it can also be adduced from and supplemented by the statements the patient makes in the course of the group interviews.[2] Whatever the method employed, the therapist must have sufficient information to determine what course of treatment he is to follow with *each* of the patients and the "depth of treatment" necessary, that is, whether he will deal with basic conflicts or behavioral and attitudinal manifestations.

In planning treatment—and there must be a plan for each of the members of the group, even if it later has to be changed or abandoned—it is necessary to set general goals. It is also essential to know something about each patient's own perception of himself, his own goals and aims, his ideals and identifications, awareness of power or weaknesses, his feelings of worthlessness or his self-maximation. All of these factors, and many others, are essential to understanding and planning the direction of treatment.

Secondly, the therapist should always be aware that he is dealing with transference relations and emotional attitudes toward himself even if these are not apparent. When the patient comes for treatment he tests the therapist against his ego ideals, acquired during the Oedipal struggle and modified in later life. The patient may desire a therapist who fully or partially resembles his parent, or is the very opposite. This preference is determined by how successfully he has repressed his drives toward the father or mother, and whether he has built up in later life supplementary, confirmatory or negative images. To his images of the real parents he may have added others that he had for some reason found desirable; he may have continued to "worship" his early ego ideals and have patterned his own life in accordance with them, or he may have rejected every-

[2] It is, however, rather important that enough of the patients' problems be known in advance to determine their suitability for group treatment and for effective grouping.

thing that reminded him of his parents. It is with such factors that the therapist deals in the transference situation and it is such factors that determine the ready response of a patient to one therapist while he may reject another. Such rapport and antagonisms stem from the resemblance of the therapist to earlier images which the patient unconsciously recognizes. The initial and automatic response is an instantaneous reliving of emotions experienced in the past. These early experiences also determine the nature of object relations generally.

It is important to be aware of the fact that members of a group come with a variety of feelings, but, by and large, all have basic attitudes which are the latent and covert strivings associated with parents. The therapist, therefore, becomes the recipient of love and hate, and at once the libidinal object and the frustrating agent. If the therapist is of the opposite sex, the neurotic patient, especially, wishes to make him the sexual object and, possibly have a child by him. If of the same sex, the therapist is perceived as the impediment to fulfilling the libidinal strivings toward the parent of the opposite sex, and, therefore, hostility is likely to appear.

At the sixteenth session Betty said she wished the girls would discuss boys. (Betty had been confined to her home most of her life because of illness.) Ella guffawed, but Betty went on to say that in her opinion, all boys are bums. Yolanda emphatically took exception to this. She admitted that some boys do not act right, but "a boy is the way the girl is, generally." Anne agreed with Yolanda and proceeded to elaborate on this. She herself is usually pretty wild with boys. When she plays with them on the street, the boys react to her in a rather loud and boisterous manner, but if she ever has a date, and that happens occasionally, she behaves much more sedately and the boys take the cue from her behavior. At this point, Ella held up a pencil pretending that she was smoking. The therapist, who was smoking at the time, asked Ella if she was imitating her. Ella laughed and said, "A guilty person needs no accuser." Anne denounced smoking as a "rotten habit." The girls all dislike smoking. The therapist wondered if the girls were angry at her not only because she smoked but probably also because of other things. Yolanda laughingly recalled how angry Ella was the preceding week because the therapist came late to the session.

Interpretation: The hostility toward the therapist is evoked by the fact that, like their mothers, she prevents them from having boys. There are no boys in the group, and the therapist (mother) is to blame. If they cannot have boys, they will at least talk about them. Hostility against the therapist is further intensified when she fails to recognize the symbolism of Ella's putting the pencil into her mouth. Ella is a tomboy, has strong masculine identifications and wears boys' clothes (see p. 105).

At the first session the therapist states directly the purpose of the group, saying that the members have come for treatment of their personal problems and the group has been formed so that they can be helped by the therapist and by one another. The therapist further tells them that they can talk at the "meetings" about anything they wish. There are no programs or plans in advance; conversations are free; since the talks will relate to personal and intimate matters, they are confidential and nothing that transpires in the group should be discussed with anyone outside; if something is troubling the members which they would rather discuss with the therapist alone, they will be able to do so occasionally.

Such a statement sets a pattern, but the pattern is not a rigid one. It suggests that the patients are free agents and that help will come to each from the others. The statement also sets the *primary group code:* [3] the members now understand that it is not a "social club" or a gathering "for fun." A further value is that the responsibility for treatment is placed squarely upon the patients. This has at least two beneficial effects: dependent trends are discouraged, and resistance is diminished. The patients are reassured that they will not have to submit to the power or control of the therapist, and this prevents mobilization of resistance. That such a *contrat social* is effective is demonstrated by the following incident in one group.

One of the adolescent girls wished to rediscuss in the therapy group the concept of God. She had participated, she said, in a similar discussion in another club which she now attends, but felt dissatisfied. She felt that the members of that club had not plumbed the question deeply enough. In the therapy group, significant associations emerged. One of the girls, for example, perceived God "as an eye who watches everyone in everything he does."

Interpretation: One of the reasons the discussion of God was a superficial one at the "other club" may have been an untrained leader, but

[3] See S. R. Slavson, *An Introduction to Group Therapy* (New York, Commonwealth Fund, 1943), p. 153.

the more likely reason is that the primary code as understood by the members of the two groups were different. One was a gathering for fun and intellectual discussions, while the purpose of the therapy group was treatment. However, a more important reason is that in the therapy group the members feel safe to express reactions as they come to them, which is not the case in ordinary clubs. There the members are afraid of criticism which is not the case in therapy groups.

In the early stages of analytic group psychotherapy, the therapist plays a passive role, which, as far as possible, he also maintains later in treatment. He must allow for a period of acclimitization, or warm-up. Assertiveness on his part would set the plan of treatment and increase suspiciousness. His actions and role must accord with the patients' readiness. Interpretation, for example, can be given only when the emotional setting is appropriate, that is, when suspicion and distrust have worn off and positive transference has been established.

Lydia talked at the twenty-sixth session about how hard she works on her school assignments. She is never angry because she has to study hard, but she is angry at her mother who never appreciates her efforts and makes more and more demands on her. The therapist said that what Lydia wanted to do was to return to the time when she was a little girl so that she could win her mother's love all over again. The girls listened intently as the therapist went on to say that Lydia would be unhappy if she returned to her childhood as she is thinking of doing, because the answer to her problem is in her present relationship with her mother. Paula said that she feels the same way: Lydia would not be happy to return to an earlier stage in her relationship to her mother.

Lydia (who is a latent schizophrene) said she had been thinking about her attitude toward school and had decided that one thing she cannot tolerate is being dominated. She loves to cooperate with people and would do anything for anyone, but she cannot do anything when she is ordered around; she can't bear the "authoritative approach." Rose said: "But half of your life is like that: you're being told to do this or that." The therapist then talked at length about society in general, how all require discipline to assure law and order, but she can understand how some people resent certain attitudes they have toward one another. Very often people resent the approach made to them in school, and even at work, because it is similar to the treatment they have received at home.

Lydia said this is what she likes about this group. Here one can get something that one cannot get other places. What is it that one can get here? Lydia was the most articulate. She said, "It is intangible. You can't put your finger on it," pointing with her finger. She recalled well the first session: "We were all uncomfortable in the beginning." Paula said that she felt like a stepchild; now she feels so differently. What was the turning point? She will never forget the time the girls and the therapist wrote her a letter when she was sick once; she still has that letter; she will always keep it.

Interpretation: Note that Lydia changes the subject when the therapist plunges into an analysis of her relation to her mother and again when the therapist delivers the rather long sermon on discipline and the social order. They are both unacceptable. Lydia employs the escape stratagem by changing the subject, but uses ingratiation the second time by telling the therapist how much she likes the group. Instead of identifying with Lydia and thus supporting her, the therapist unwittingly allies herself with the authority Lydia resents. The girls are also unready for the interpretation of authority as manifested at home and school and become resistive. This they express by agreeing with Lydia's opinion of the group. They are unanimous in this, because they are also unanimous in their rejection of the therapist. *It must be kept clearly in mind that whenever there is unanimity in a therapy group, there is hostility to the therapist.* The therapist falls into the trap, however, and seems pleased by the praise, which is a manifestation of counter transference. Had the therapist perceived that actually the group was being described in the light of home and school, it would have been better to bring the girls' feelings into the open by asking them: "But what is wrong with this group?"

The aim of therapy is to prepare the individual to accept reality, and the therapist is part of that reality. He cannot reveal himself immediately for what he is, with all his lacks and defects. The patients may need to idealize him at first and can accept him only on that basis. At the beginning, the therapist represents the symbol of the all-giving mother or the protective, security-giving father. But as the patients become emotionally stronger, he has to relinquish the role of a pre-Oedipal parent and the patients must accept him in a more realistic light. Dissolution of the transference in this manner is an integral part of good psychotherapy, but takes a long time. The change occurs through the automatic maturity of the patients, which eliminates their cravings for protection and infantile love. As treatment proceeds, the therapist explains, restrains, criticizes, as well as interprets, the patients' behavior and attitudes.[4]

Expanding reality is a major aim of psychotherapy and the group

[4] See also the discussion of advice-giving on p. 60.

therapist systematically helps his patients to achieve it, both through interpretation and through actual experiences such as trips, visits, concerts, community contacts, and similar means. Trips are particularly important for children, but is also useful in the treatment of adolescents.

The value of the therapist is illustrated in a group of adolescent girls sixteen to seventeen years old. They had been in interview group treatment for about a year and a half during which period they talked very freely about many intimate problems on personal matters—hostilities toward parents and siblings, fixations on their fathers, genitals, sex urges, masturbation. The therapist found that she would have to be absent from one of the sessions, but too late to cancel it, and the group met without her. The girls reported later that they sang songs, gossiped a little, and had refreshments. They did not discuss anything, although there were a number of topics pending from previous sessions. Though the therapist participated very little in the group interviews, her very presence facilitated communication and gave it direction and meaning. Without her sanction and support the girls seemed afraid to free themselves from their superego restraints. The factor of homosexuality needs also to be taken into account here. Without the protective presence of the therapist, the fear of their homoerotic drives, asserted itself. There is every evidence that homosexual tendencies are intensified in these groups, as shown by the following episodes:

At the third session all the girls doodled as they talked. Anne drew a very voluptuous-looking girl. As she did this she said that whenever she doodles it always ends up by her making the picture of a voluptuous girl. Celia said: "It's queer how different people are." Whenever she doodles or draws she always draws legs. Betty giggled at this and said that she always draws a house or makes a diagram for a house.

At the eleventh session Ella commented that Anne was a voluptuous girl. At another session—the tenth—Ella announced that she does not like boys. When the girls sang a song she asked Anne to dance with her.

At the seventeenth session Ella remarked that her brother has been beating her, and with consternation on her face, said that he kicks her in the stomach. She thinks her brother is crazy. The therapist asked her why she thinks so. Ella said he is athletically inclined, and described him as a tall, well-built, robust young fellow and very vain. He constantly looks at himself in the mirror and flexes his biceps so that she would see how strong he is. She wished he would die. "Yes, and I could kill my mother, too," she added impetuously. The night before Ella threw a knife at her brother and barely missed him. She wants to leave home and has about made up her mind that if her mother gets married again she will do it. She just cannot stand the fights any longer.

Interpretation: Ella's envy of her brother's masculinity and her strong attraction for her mother are quite transparent. Her homosexual trends were manifested by the masculine clothes, the fact that she carried in her purse a boy-scout knife and a large pin to prick "would-be mashers."

The improved attitude of patients toward parents, mates, and other relatives through psychotherapy was attributed to the draining off of psychic energy and cathexis displacement (see p. 76). Another reason may be the gradual acceptance of the therapist as a real, rather than idealized, person, an attitude that the patients transfer to others as well. This is *transference in reverse,* as it were. Just as the patient first makes the therapist the recipient of the same feelings he had formerly had toward his parents, he now in turn discovers characteristics in his parents and others that he sees in the therapist. These feelings had been obscured earlier by resentment and hostility. The tolerance and permissiveness of the therapist at first surprise the patients. The surprise changes into an appreciation of the fact that adults can be good. As a result of this, the badness and unfriendliness of parents and others in one's family undergo a change. As the patients can view the therapist more realistically they can also appreciate parents and other relatives as being both good and bad, friendly and hostile, giving and denying. In other words, they have ordinary human attributes.

As patients give up the infantile need for protection and love antedating traumatic occurrences, they come to realize that before repressions and frustrations were imposed on them, parents were sources of pleasure, comfort, and love.[5] To recognize the fact that they and siblings can be a source of satisfaction is important in the therapeutic process and the first step in this direction is the therapist's permissive and tolerant role.

But these are only the first steps in treatment. The therapist's role changes with the unfolding powers of the patients. In group therapy as well as in other forms of psychotherapy, the therapist plays a con-

[5] It is interesting to note in this connection that Ella advised Betty to recapture some of her former friendly feelings toward her sister (p. 57).

stantly changing role to accord with the maturity of the patients. His is, not a static, but rather a dynamic and changing function.

When the patients complain against persons in authority, such as parents, teachers, employers, they are accusing by implication the therapist who, being in a position of authority, is also a target of their hostility. The negative feelings toward him are implicit also in the complaints against the hospital, clinic, agency, or institution with which he is associated. The therapist has to stand ready to accept expression of these feelings unperturbed and even encourage them.

When the therapist cannot be attacked or criticized, the repressed hostility and resentments are displaced by the members on one another,[6] which is one of the outstanding characteristics of repressive group life.[7] The symbolic role of the therapist is quite clear. It is also equally clear how he can generate through his attitudes positive fundamental transferences among the group members to himself and to each other. Intense hostility and rampant expression of it in a group may become disturbing to all concerned and even vitiate the therapeutic setting. To make this clear it is necessary to digress briefly for a description of the general character of therapeutic groups.

Elsewhere,[8] I described the behavior of groups as having two phases: nodal and anti-nodal. The nodal phase is one during which the peak of hyperactivity is reached, which is always followed by a period of equilibrium, quiet and constructive activity. The therapeutic process occurs at the point where hyperactivity is transformed into a state of equilibrium, where self-control, compromise, mutual understanding, and other neutralizing forces emerge. It is at this point of transition from the nodal to the anti-nodal state that integration, maturity, and emotional growth occur in the individuals participating. In groups where there is constant or too frequent

[6] See case of Stephen on p. 26.

[7] Cruelty, for example, is more prevalent among the populations of autocratic countries where the state (father) is repressive than it is in democratic nations where the state can be attacked and governments periodically changed, i. e., the father killed off. Where one cannot be aggressive against the parent surrogate, hostility and cruelty become diffuse and are displaced on fellow citizens (siblings). For the same reason autocratic nations can be more easily mobilized for aggression, such as war.

[8] S. R. Slavson, "Some Elements of Activity Group Therapy," *American Journal of Orthopsychiatry*, 1944.

eruption of aggression with inadequate or infrequent transition to equilibrium, little improvement can be expected.

The therapist in analytic group psychotherapy has to deal with hostilities as they arise. He must help patients interpret and understand their latent and manifest negative feelings toward him; that is, he must interpret the transference. But the entire therapeutic process may bog down when the patients do not feel free to display negative feelings.

The group therapist needs to be constantly aware of the latent content and the direction of the group interviews. His knowledge of each patient's psychodynamics and of the principles of psychopathology and psychotherapy need at all times be poised for action. A well-placed and well-timed question opens the sluices of the unconscious and of free association, which is further aided by the catalytic effect of the other group members. The therapist must also be aware of the periods when fear, anxiety, and resistance appear. At these points he needs to help the patients overcome their differences and fear through the appropriate use of the transference and by giving support. He may, according to the indications, analyze the resistance of the group, facilitate expression of hostility to himself, or reassure the members of his acceptance of them. The direction to be taken is indicated by the nature of the blocking, the manifest and latent content of the discussion, and the anticipated anxiety sources inherent in the situation.

In one group the adolescent girls repeatedly returned to the same topic of conversation. The group seemed blocked. A study of the records of the preceding interviews showed that the girls were unable to proceed because they repressed their hostilities toward the therapist as a result of her consistent pleasantness and benign manner. The group reached a point when they needed to discharge some of their resentment against her, but could not because of their "admiration and love" for her. She was advised to encourage expression of hostility toward herself, and when she did this successfully there was a dramatic change in the content of the group sessions. During this change the transitory transferences became negative and the girls expressed considerable hostility toward the therapist and dissatisfaction with the group (really the therapist).

To help release expressions of hostile feelings toward the therapist no food is supplied to groups of adolescent and adult patients as is done with children in activity, activity-interview, or play groups. It is difficult to display aggression against a person who feeds one; it blocks catharsis. Small children, on the other hand, act out aggression toward the therapist as freely as they do toward their parents (substitution).

Rivalry for the attention of the therapist is as common in groups of adults and adolescents as it is among children. Patients in a state of rivalry mobilize a great deal of pseudo-positive attitudes toward the therapist [9] to outdo one another and the therapist becomes the center of an undesirable network of conflicting emotions. The manifest attitudes toward him are positive, but the underlying feelings are more or less hostile. In addition, the rivals develop strong antipathy to one another, which infects everyone in the group. This situation needs direct handling, as it may lead to the deterioration of the group and cause some of the members to drop out. The therapist should call attention to what is going on by saying to the patient something like: "You don't like me to pay attention to Bill. You would like me to give all my time to you." This or a similar remark brings the patient's unconscious feelings to awareness. The very fact that the therapist understands him, but does not punish him for it, reduces his tensions and assures him, as well as the others present, of acceptance.

The therapist also plays an important part in making the group interviews fruitful. As evidenced in the record material, he can remain comparatively inactive after the initial period of warm-up. The patients carry on the interviews on their own, interpret each other's statements, and in other ways manage the therapeutic situation. But, as already indicated, this process is made possible only because the therapist is present, and is made more valuable when at important and critical points he gives the interviews direction and meaning. As far as it is possible to classify the therapist's functions in group interviews, it can be said that they are fourfold: *directional, stimulative, extensional,* and *interpretive.*

In the first, the therapist helps the group and the individuals in it to direct their statements toward a central problem which may be the source of disturbance. However, we have already seen that

[9] As reported in the extract from the record on p. 23.

when this is not done appropriately the patients either block or change the subject. The therapist recognizes this sudden change as resistance. At first he does not pursue the matter, but as treatment proceeds he may find it advisable to continue to explore emotions and attitudes involved and help the patients bring forth the associative memories and feelings. In the treatment of adolescents and adults (and even of children), we cannot rely entirely upon the "living nature of the experience," as is suggested by some therapists. Experience may perhaps be adequate to the average young child, but it is not enough for the patient, young or old, who is selected for group treatment.

Group interviews may grow undirected or desultory at times. Changes in topics may occur too frequently, and the conversations lag. The therapist understands this as either blocking, resistance, confusion, or lack of a therapeutic aim. The therapist has to deal with the situation according to the needs of the group by supplying information, giving suggestions, or exploring latent emotional content. But before he can do this adequately he must be clear not only as to the state of the group, but also of the direction the group is ready or is attempting to take. Even though he cannot press the group into a special discussion, he can suggest a question upon which, in his judgment, either the group or some members in it are seeking clarification. The therapist's recognition of direction is of utmost importance. Such directional orientation is necessary for individual patients as well as for the group as a whole. All psychotherapy has to be focused. It is usual for patients to be preoccupied with their attitudes toward themselves, parents, boy friends, wives, husbands, children, siblings, school, sex, even though discussions of these topics may be veiled and intertwined with numerous others. The therapist needs to be aware of the focal and peripheral preoccupations at a given moment and prevent the group from digressing too far from the central aim. To do this he must possess the perspicacity for recognizing hidden meanings, as the following illustrates.

At the eighth session of the institutional group (see p. 210, below) Marian seemed depressed and sullen. She took her seat very quietly. Clara was a little more cheerful and friendly. At this point, Myrna reported that Rhoda would not come to the session because she had to leave the campus for the day. The girls were quiet and the therapist asked what the girls would like to talk about. At first there was no response, but soon Myrna suggested that she would like to continue the discussion about clothes. She began by describing the various styles published in teen-age magazines (which she constantly reads). She discussed styles in a rather technical fashion and the conversation was confined to her and Marian, with some comments from the therapist. During this discussion, Mary was scribbling violently on the cover of a magazine she had brought with her. The therapist tried to broaden the discussion from clothes and magazines to some of the emotional problems of teen-agers. Myrna expostulated on the pleasures to which adolescents are entitled and which are denied at the School. This set Mary off into a violent outburst of recrimination against the School. She expressed hatred for everything in it and registered her protest against having to be deprived of many things just because she had to live there.

Interpretation: The therapist forced the situation by suggesting a line of discussion other than the one the girls were following. Instead of sensing what it was that the girls were trying to say, the therapist had something definite in her own mind. When Myrna spoke about the fact that magazines were giving so much space to teen-agers and styles for them, she was saying that adolescents are important people and that the world is giving them much attention. The girls sought to build up their self-esteem and self-worth or rebuke the therapist for not giving them more attention. Instead of asking them why they think so much attention is being given to teen-agers, which would be following the line of their own thoughts, the therapist had attempted to divert them to a discussion of psychological content. She turned the discussion away from what the girls were attempting to say to her.

On the other hand, just as the therapist has to be careful not to divert the group from material that is therapeutically valid, he has to change the course of conversation when, in his judgment, it may lead to distress to some of the members (or the group as a whole) beyond a point of their tolerance at a given time. Confessions that affect the patients too deeply may sometimes have to be prevented. In one instance, for example, Lydia related how in a fit of anger at her boy-friend she slashed a cat's abdomen with a knife. This disturbed the other girls so deeply that they all asked to see the therapist individually. The anxiety set up was too intense for them to deal with on their own and they sought the protective intimacy of the therapist (mother). Similarly, in a group of non-psychotics, direct revelation of incestuous drives and activity and psychotic behavior are unsuitable for general group interviews, and as far as possible the therapist has to find some means for preventing conversations of this nature.

Reference has already been made on several occasions to the need in some instances for individual interviews as supplementation to group treatment. The group therapist should, therefore, make himself available for individual interviews as in the case cited above. These may be regular or occasional, frequent or infrequent, brief or prolonged as needs may indicate. Treatment plans would have to be made in accordance with the needs of each patient. There are times of stress in the lives of patients that must be dealt with only through individual interviews and the therapist must be ready to meet this need when it arises. Such occasions are when a member receives rather rough handling from the others or a topic under discussion generates particular stress for him.

Whenever concurrent individual and group treatment are indicated, it is preferable, though there may be some exceptions to this rule, that the same therapist conduct both. It is difficult and undesirable for patients to carry simultaneously two separate transference relations. Transference in therapy needs to be concentrated. This unitary approach also makes for integration of the two treatment experiences. The insights the patient evolves in the group are rediscussed and reevaluated in individual interviews, and vice versa. Paula, the only patient in divided treatment, once expressed the dichotomy that arises from such a division when she said: "My caseworker told me this too, but I didn't believe her. Now that I heard the girls (in the group) say the same thing, I know it's true." There is a distinct advantage in investing the two therapeutic relations in one therapist.

The question of multiple therapists for non-psychotic patients repeatedly comes up both in practice and in the literature. Whether more than one therapist should participate in treatment of groups, such as a male and female therapist to reproduce the family setting, needs further clarification. From the theoretical point of view, this practice can be considered as undesirable. Since group psychotherapy, as all other forms of psychotherapy, is based on transference, the latter should not be diluted or confused. It is our conviction that adolescent and adult patients who are otherwise suited for group treatment do not require the duplication of a setting similar to that of their early childhood. The multiple transference relations need not necessarily be an exact replica of the pattern in which trauma had occurred. The presence of a man and woman therapist may encourage abreaction rather than insight. In one activity group for children of about nine years of age, we experimented with a man and woman therapist and found that the children were confused as to the roles of the two adults. They were hesitant as to whose help they should seek, uncertain as to whom they should become attached and against whom to work out hostilities. As a result of this experience, we have not employed multiple therapists in activity group therapy, and in our opinion this would be equally counterindicated, if not even more so, in group psychotherapy. However, as already stated, this is an area in which considerable experimentation and study would be necessary.

The therapist's stimulative function consists in helping the group find content for the interviews. Because of resistance or lack of awareness of a therapeutic aim, members of the group become absorbed in trivial matters and superficialities. This occurs among adolescents and sometimes also among adults. In a sense, preoccupation with trivia is more or less inevitable. The daily life of nearly all patients that come for treatment are filled with trifling matters that disturb them. The average person as well is preoccupied with details of living. It, therefore, becomes a habit to talk about them, which is naturally carried over into all social intercourse, including the therapy group. To pry a group away from this is no easy matter, and the therapist must find an opening for redirecting the course of the interviews so as to give them therapeutic content. One such situation was already described in the case of stereotypy (p. 107). There the therapist stimulated the group by activating hostility toward herself. We shall presently have an opportunity to further elaborate on stereotypy in group interviews.

The statement to the group at the outset of the interview sessions (p. 101) sets the general aims and intent; it is particularly effective when the therapist has treated all or some of the members individually before assigning them to a group. It is recommended that the therapist see the prospective group members three or four times individually in order to establish a relation and set a therapeutic attitude. This is not essential, however. A group can start cold, as it were, but the process is accelerated and the warm-up period shortened if each member has already made the acquaintance of the therapist.

Usually the immediate response to the rules of group interviews is that one or more members at once speak about their problems, thereby stimulating others to do so. But during the life of the group there are periods when the content of the interviews becomes unproductive. The patients either talk away from their problems or turn them into social conversations. The therapist has to deal with this situation by reminding the group of the rules for interviews, or interpret it as resistance.

Frequently the interviews may have direction and content, but the therapist may feel that the patients are ready to plumb deeper into their problems than they do. A statement or a well-placed question will help them to extend their communication into areas hitherto evaded or overlooked. This technique is closely akin to interpretation, and everything that has been said on that score applies to the extensional function of the therapist in group interviews. It is rather important that the therapist make statements and frame questions so that the direction of the interview is *extended rather than diverted.* The therapist's own set ideas as to what a patient needs to have clarified may cause him to introduce material extraneous at a specific juncture, even though it may belong in the total therapeutic plan. The therapist should at all times follow the associative thinking and the free association of the members in the group. In all conversation, as in dreams, there is manifest and latent content. Much of what is being said may be a disguise for what the patients would like to say, or for something of which they are still unaware. The therapist's perceptiveness of these is important in helping them find solutions for their deeper problems and concerns.

Adult and adolescent patients (the psychoneurotic especially) eventually need to understand their past in the context of their total development. They must also see the past in terms of their evolving present, before they can move toward a growing capacity for reality tolerance. The therapist has to help each member make this transition.

The management of the group interviews is a multiferous skill that requires the therapist's most cautious and tactful handling. He cannot press or accelerate it; nor should he overlook opportunities for furthering the effectiveness of the group interviews. Because it occurs so frequently and the damaging effect it has on interviews, a somewhat detailed discussion of *stereotypy* follows.

We have recorded a case of stereotypy in a group discussion that arose because the patients repressed their hostility toward the therapist (see p. 107). Stereotypy may also occur when patients do not gain emotional and intellectual clarity on some problem with which they are strongly concerned. Their preoccupation blocks movement; this can be overcome only after the pressing problem is solved or clarified. In nearly all our groups the members at times kept returning to the same topic, session after session, until the therapists were made aware of the fact that what the patients were attempting to achieve by the repetition was clarification. When patients are not understood they become blocked, and as the therapist helps them with the special problem he clears the way for further free association and the patients are then able to proceed. One of the by-products of such emotional blocking is weakening of the transference. The patient turns away from a therapist who does not understand him.

Stereotypy may also be an indication of resistance. When this is the case, it should be treated as is all resistance.

Because the interpretative role of the therapist has been referred to many times and described and demonstrated both in the text and the records in this volume, the discussion of it is omitted at this juncture both to prevent repetition and in the interests of space economy.

The delineation of the therapist's role in group interviews in the preceding pages is not intended to recommend excessive activity on his part. The rule that the therapy should be carried by the members themselves must always hold. The therapist is active only when the therapeutic process is either blocked or grows desultory. He should remain predominantly passive and at all costs avoid exhortation, preaching, and teaching. He must be aware at all times that improvement occurs through slow and gradual growth from within, and this principle must never leave his mind.

In psychotherapy we cannot rely on the *will* to improve and change, as though the will were an independent entity. The will without the withal fails. In the average person the capacity to mobilize powers emerges from a combination of favorable constitutional disposition, temperament, psychologic and physical health.

The role of the therapist varies also in relation to the age of the patients. The very important differences in the ego organization of children at different ages make differential treatment essential. The very young child of pre-nursery and nursery years has not as yet fully repressed primitive impulses and strivings. The taboos and social amenities that come later in life are as yet either non-existent or inadequately formed. The child is still able to act out his primitive drives directly and, when he is afraid to do so, resorts to phantasy and fiction.

As the infant grows into childhood he gives up some of his autism and narcissism, and his natural egocentricity is transformed into the ability to make contact with other persons and share with them. Though there is usually little actual cooperation among very young children, they are distinctly aware of one another. This awareness is revealed by imitation, manifest suggestibility, occasional struggles for possession of tools and materials and rivalry for the attention of the teacher or therapist. It is this awareness that is important, for through it the growing child breaks the confines of his incapsulation. This process can be characterized as *psycho-osmosis*—the interpenetration of one personality into the other without overt or observable action.

The skillful therapist is able to set situations in which some association takes place. The most common of these are the eating and the clean-up periods and the outdoor playtime. But one cannot expect too much sociability from very young children, though more of it appears at mealtime than at any other period. Contacts are at best fleeting and perfunctory, for the egocentric (autistic) trends are at all times predominant.

The therapist's role here is less permissive than with older children, adolescents, or adults, even though freedom is a primary condition for therapy, especially freedom to express agression and hostility. Freedom and restraint have to be balanced in the therapy of young children. The younger the child the more restraint is needed. We have already seen that self-restraint is derived from the child's internalizing the restraints from adults whom he accepts and trusts. The young child emerging from a state of nurture,[10] when all his wants and whims were unconditionally satisfied, needs time, strength, and maturity to internalize them. Discipline and authority acceptable to him and graded in intensity are necessary for personality integration, but they have to be applied with discrimination and care. The frightened and withdrawn do not need control; they rather need release. The overactive and aggressive need restraint. Their diffuse aggressiveness and pugnacious trends have to be impeded. Since the child had not as yet established controls within himself, these must come from the outside, namely, from

[10] We identify in the development of the child three stages: nurture, discipline, and education. The period of nurture is early infancy when the child lives a parasitic life, largely an extension of his intra-uteral existence when all his needs and wants are more or less instantaneously gratified through his peremptory demands, punctuated by crying and screaming. At this period the child is a completely dependent entity, but at the same time autonomous. He does not need to submit to external disciplines, routines, or the will of other people. The plan of his life is centered around his wants, needs and impulses. This is the period of incorporation.

As he grows older individuation occurs, that is, limitations upon his functioning are imposed. These usually begin with eating, when the nipple is denied him and other means of feeding are substituted. The new feeding methods involve greater participation and effort on his part to gain the sustenance he needs. This is followed by habit training in anal-urethral activity (toilet training). In some ways these limitations are even more difficult for the child to accept, for here he has to give up part of himself to the will of the person who does the training, the nurse or the mother. Just as he rebelled against giving up the nipple and refused to eat from a spoon, he now refuses to submit to the training in the second stage and only with great difficulty does he bring himself to it.

Education starts later in life—in our culture, around six years of age—when a definite regime of acquiring of skills, learning of facts and training in behavior begins. This stage can be described as reintegration.

One of the common observations of young children with psychological difficulties is that either nurture—namely, the stage of helplessness and self-indulgence—has been extended beyond the normal phase and into the phase of discipline, or discipline was begun too early—namely, it was substituted for nurture. Children in the first category, where nurture has been extended into the period of discipline, are usually the infantilized, pampered children who present problems of maladjustment because of weak egos. They are the overprotected persons who either adopt patterns of withdrawal or are weak and demanding. Children who had been controlled, frustrated, and whose behavior was managed and directed too early in life, develop behavior disorders, become aggressive, and sustain social maladjustments of various kinds. These are usually children who are fundamentally rejected. This rejection may be either direct (as in the case of restricted children) or may be indirect (as in the case of overprotected, infantilized children). Parents who basically love their children may either pamper or discipline them, but it can be expected that the presenting problem will be milder than in children where either disciplining or pampering are an outcome of basic rejection.

adults. It is for a kind, but firm, adult that the child will give up his egoistic and narcissistic characteristics. The therapist, therefore, needs to be more direct and more restraining than he would be with children who have already established inner controls and whose superego is better formed.

One of the characteristics of childhood is the surface nature of the unconscious. Repressions are still incomplete and in some areas have not as yet been achieved. Conscious and unconscious are closely related, and in the young child's psychic economy they often appear as one. The experience in actuality (reality) is, therefore, paramount in therapy here, and the therapist is part and parcel of that actuality. He, along with other adults, especially the mother, helps in the formation of the superego and the ego.

Physical combat among pre-school children is infrequent. It occurs most often among children between seven and twelve and is accompanied by intense anger, redness of face, screaming, and tears. There is probably less fear than anger in the fights of very young children. This seems to be reversed among older children, when fear accompanying fighting is a more evident element. It is of comparatively little value for the ordinary child of three or four to either win a combat or be vanquished, and the therapist should not permit the struggle to continue. It is advisable to stop fights between young children at once. This is less true of the frightened and inhibited child who has reached a stage, through the treatment situation, when he can mobilize power to fight. He should be encouraged to win a fight or two. Older children should be permitted to bring a struggle to a conclusion through their own efforts or those of the group.

The therapist has to help young children with their activities so that they will not be too greatly frustrated. He needs also to plan the activity setting carefully, so that tools and materials are not too difficult. In one group of five-year-olds the therapist failed to provide equipment appropriate in point of size and complexity, with the result that she was constantly in demand for help. This increased the children's dependence upon her. It also kept her very busy, which in turn made her tired. As a result she became peremptory and irritable, as shouts for help came from all sides. Removal of these overdifficult materials and tools helped greatly in stabilizing the group. It was also found that a period of an hour and a half indoors was too long for children so young; after about fifty minutes or an hour indoors, brief walks around the block or along the near-by river front reduced much of the tension. When the children became too hilarious, the therapist read to them, which quieted them down, and picture books that the children themselves could read were also helpful.

One therapist stimulated the children's activities into overmature channels by putting together jigsaw puzzles with the intention of interesting children of four or five in the same activity. This was evidently too difficult for them. The therapist who wishes to stimulate children in their activities might work with materials within their capacity and interest range rather than introduce occupations requiring help and direction. It was easier for the children to join in when the worker played with blocks.

Materials and tools should be laid out on the table rather than left in a cupboard out of sight or difficult to reach. This plan also utilizes *visual suggestion*. Plasticene, blocks, water, sand, a few simple tools, male and female dolls, animals, marionettes, large crayons, water colors, and large sheets of paper are the basic materials. Whenever possible free access to water should be provided. Because of the children's hyperactivity, paints, especially finger paints, may have to be temporarily eliminated.

For some of the older children, experience with fire is essential. With adequate precautions in setting and equipment, such as a large asbestos pad, it is possible to supply children with this activity. A less hazardous fire equipment is an electric stylus with which one can burn wood and paper and thus work through sexual aggressive trends. An electric stove should be part of the equipment, and cans of sterno placed on asbestos pads are helpful. The resistivity of materials should also be adjusted to suit age levels; the older the children, the tougher and more resistive the materials can be.[11]

Restraint can be either active or passive. Passive restraint derives from a situation or the manner of the therapist, as a result of which the child controls his own acts. In activity group therapy for children between the ages of eight and thirteen, restraint is almost entirely of a passive nature. The situation is so arranged that setting

[11] S. R. Slavson, *An Introduction to Group Therapy*, p. 36.

of the room, the materials and tools, as well as the group relations, exert a limiting influence upon the child. Only in rare instances does the therapist use direct controls. In the case of particularly aggressive children direct restraint may be employed, but only on rare occasions. With very young childen, however, restraint has to be direct and early because situational or passive restraint is not effective with them.

With older children the therapist is more permissive than with little ones. Much freedom must be given children between the ages of seven and twelve (latency period), so that they can find their own way in establishing relationships and evolving self-controls. We found this procedure suitable because at this age there already exists a degree of awareness of good and bad behavior, of right and wrong (superego). Having passed through the Oedipal stage and having identified to a degree with parents, the child has taken on some of their mannerisms, values, and attitudes. For further growth we must, therefore, utilize whatever inhibitions the child has already incorporated. At this period identifications are easily established and reactions from other children and of the therapist help build self-control (ego).

It is clear that the function of the therapist has to be graded to correspond to the evolving personalities of the patients, their readiness to form a group amalgam, and the ability to develop group controls. The younger the child the greater the activity of the therapist.

The setting of the situation is important in all types of therapy, though not enough attention is usually given it. Play therapists with young children are aware of it, as are occupational and activity group therapists, but those who employ the more verbal techniques usually do not give it the same consideration. But the setting and the atmosphere is as important as an awareness of aims and objectives, even though circumstances frequently make it impossible to obtain the environment that would produce maximum results. The choice is largely determined by what is available in the clinic or in the private office where analytic group psychotherapy is practiced. Sometimes group therapists sit at their desks and the patients sit in front of them, or the group and therapist sit around a fireplace. Both these settings are unsuitable for best results.

The atmosphere of intimacy and the complete relaxation induced and especially the intellectual and emotional preoccupation with the fire and its constantly changing patterns, forms, and shapes removes the patients too far from the inner problems they must face. Also, the fire has a narcotizing effect and is unfavorable for the active self-examination essential in psychotherapy. The patients' interests are directed toward the fire instead of toward themselves, and the induced lassitude is the very opposite of what is required for the necessary emotional and intellectual activity.

The separation of the therapist from the patients by a desk removes him from the group, and he becomes a different and therefore forbidding individual. The physical barrier renders him also emotionally inaccessible.

A group of adolescent girls chose to be crowded in the small office of their therapist, seated on hard chairs, in preference to a spacious conference room with comfortable chairs and attractive furnishings. For some months they spent from one and a half to two hours a week in these cramped quarters before they were ready to move to the larger room. It seemed that the intimacy of the small room, especially because it was the therapist's own, gave them a greater feeling of belonging and closeness. Only when they evolved a greater sense of security in the transferences did this situational element grow unimportant. We have had a similar experience also with a group of ten-year-old boys and girls in activity-interview therapy. They, too, insisted on remaining in the therapist's small office for some time before they were ready to move to another larger room that was specially designed and equipped for the purpose. The period of the resistivity to the change was very much shorter with the younger group.

The desirable arrangement for adolescents and adults is the circle around a table. A circle around an empty space renders patients insecure; it is as though they lack a solid foundation. Another threatening element is the easy physical accessibility of the patients to each other which may express itself in physical aggression. The solidity of a table is itself reassuring and serves to obviate these and other possible reactions. A circular table is better than a rectangular one, which has a head and a foot, and therefore presents the possibility of status, jealousy and resentment. The mere fact that certain individuals are opposite (opposed to) certain others in this arrangement may intensify aggression or submission among some of the patients. A circular table eliminates these problems.

Patients prefer to occupy the same chair session after session. They return to the same spot and to the same physical relations with their fellow patients, although a patient occasionally changes location in order to be near another with whom he has become friendly or of whose support he may be in need. Because of this regularity, which has specific meaning, the therapist, as well, should have a definite place at the table. This uniformity of environmental setting is related to the patients' libido economy. It obviates the necessity to readjust to different persons at each session. Once accustomed to the person next to or in front of him, the patient continues in this environment, for it requires no effort to readjust. This mechanism is closely related to the repetition compulsion.

In psychotherapy we seek to conserve the psychic energies for the therapeutic activity rather than dissipate them in readaptations and readjustments to environment. It is for this reason that a psychoanalyst's interviewing room is not changed in its setting and arrangements. The patient is not required to reacclimatize to a new environment and to adapt to changes. Conservation of energies favors regression. The less the demands made by the environmental conditions the more is regression facilitated. The setting in the room in which groups gather, whether for activity or for interview, must, therefore, be constant.

However, as treatment proceeds and the patients attain greater emotional freedom and flexibility, the spatial rigidity is diminished or disappears. The emerging security makes it less necessary to defend themselves by uniformity in the situation. Patients have freer access to one another, and their capacity to adapt to the various personalities in the group is enhanced. Thus, the reality sense is heightened by their growing security and greater comfort in human relationships. At this stage, the seating arrangement becomes much less important. This growing flexibility and greater group mobility gives the therapist an opportunity to observe the reactions which in part determine the success of treatment and the readiness of some patients for termination.

To recognize when a patient is ready to terminate treatment is one of the skills a therapist needs to develop, a skill that is far from easy to acquire. Concepts of "recovery" vary greatly, since no criteria have as yet been evolved as to what it constitutes. Sometimes elimination of a disturbing symptom may constitute recovery. Most often, however, basic changes in the personality are necessary to prevent the recurrence of the symptom or the appearance of another to take its place. By and large, psychotherapy does not limit itself merely to eliminating symptoms: it aims at affecting more or less basic intrapsychic changes of an extended or permanent nature. To what extent psychotherapy, and even psychoanalysis, affects fundamental changes is difficult to establish. In our work with groups, we have given Rorschach Tests to patients regularly and periodically, at various stages in treatment. The tests indicate that structure changes in the personality have occurred.[12] Such tests can be used to determine the ending of treatment, but a practiced eye can discern whether improvement is permanent by observing the patient in a variety of situations and by the manner in which he deals with reality.

Different patients react differently to ending. Some imperceptibly lose interest on their own, and attendance drops off. In such instances, it is requisite that the therapist have an individual interview with the patient and terminate treatment planfully, rather than allow it to peter out. Other patients stop coming abruptly. Some announce that they are no longer interested; still others are aware that the difficulties for which they had come no longer trouble them. There are patients, however, to whom the group becomes a source of security and comfort which they do not wish to give up. They become inured to it and dependent upon it. This is analogous to the desire of some patients in individual treatment who come to depend upon the security and comfort of the transference. As in individual psychotherapy such patients in groups, also, have to be helped to affect separation, which may have to be done through individual interviews.

The approach of termination sometimes reactivates early symp-

[12] Miriam G. Siegel, "The Rorschach Test as an Aid in Selecting Clients for Group Therapy and Evaluating Progress," *Mental Hygiene,* July, 1944; also "Interview Group Therapy with a Neurotic Adolescent Girl Suffering from Chorea," in *Practice in Group Therapy,* ed. S. R. Slavson (New York, International Universities Press, 1947).

toms, behavior analogous to the infant's struggle against being weaned. The therapist must not be misled by it and should proceed with plans for termination despite this manifest resistance. Sometimes, a whole group may act out their anxiety induced by impending separation or termination. The following illustrates this:

At the last session before a group of ten-year-old boys and girls was to disband for the summer, they returned to play with the dollhouse, which they had not done for many months. They had developed beyond the dollhouse play stage, but regressed at this session. They also asked the therapist to get them some food so that "it would be homey," despite the fact that no food had been shared by this group for six or seven months.

Interpretation: This regression may have a number of meanings. (1) The children may have desired to test their own growth by reverting to their original play; (2) they may have wished to reexperience the earliest and strongest (pre-Oedipal) satisfactions from the group as a "keepsake," as it were, to take along with them for the summer, and thus retain that memory of the group and of the therapist; (3) it is more likely, however, that they were giving notice to the therapist that they had not improved and still needed her and the group experience. This regressive act served to convey their resistance to separation.

CHAPTER EIGHT

PLAY GROUP PSYCHOTHERAPY WITH PRE-SCHOOL CHILDREN

RECORD AND INTERPRETATION

THE RECORDS presented in this chapter and the next are of two groups of young children. The first consists of four boys, five to six years of age, the second of two boys and two girls between the ages of nine and ten. The reader will observe the directness with which these children act out their impulses, hostilities, and rivalries and speak of their feelings about themselves and others. One is especially impressed with the surface nature of their unconscious. Their death wishes, for example, are not hidden; they are there for all to see. The symbolic and direct acting out and the evident absence of restraint is also impressive. It is these elements, among others, that make therapy with young children in many respects quite different than with older persons. We find also ample evidence in these records of the fact that younger children substitute the therapist for parents rather than develop a (libidinal) transference, as is the case with older patients. Their ties to their parents are still primary and intense; other adults occupy only a subsidiary place in their emotional economy.

CASE HISTORIES

In the record of the younger group, we find Mike,[1] an only child, very bright, who came for treatment at the age of five and a half because of extreme stubbornness, whining, frequent illnesses, fears of being left alone, nightmares, complaints of being unhappy, continuous masturbation, and severe constipation. Masturbation be-

[1] See p. 80. Note: In some instances the case material in this volume does not seem to support fully the diagnoses at which we have arrived. This is due to the fact that the imposed brevity of the anamneses made it necessary to omit much of the supporting facts in the case histories.

came excessive when Mike was treated for multiple congenital stricture of the urethra at the age of three. Dilation of the urethra was performed regularly every six months. Mike had never played with children and slept in the parental bed at the time of referral.

Mike was unwanted. The father felt financially unready for the child, and the mother was extremely fearful of birth pains; delivery was by a Caesarian section. Toilet training was begun at six months and completed when Mike was eighteen months old.

The mother was a very disturbed, unstable and immature woman, cried a great deal, had a tendency toward hypochondriasis, was chronically sorry for herself, worrisome, entertained thoughts of and threatened to commit suicide, and had fears of going insane, occasioned partly by the fact that two of her sisters receive shock therapy for psychotic conditions. She was diagnosed as psychoneurotic, anxiety hysteria.

The father was a rigid, neurotic, compulsive man, unsympathetic toward his wife and her difficulties. He had gone to quack psychotherapists and accepted will power as a cure for all illnesses. He, therefore, had no patience with people with emotional problems. Actually, he had many fears and felt insecure and weak. He opposed treatment for both the mother and Mike.

Diagnosis of child: primary behavior disorder with neurotic traits (though a full-blown psychoneurosis can be suspected).

Another of the boys is Judah, who came for treatment at the age of five because he was hyperactive, aggressive, had severe temper tantrums, and was unable to play with children of his age. He was stubborn, defiant, destructive with furniture and toys, played with fire, masturbated excessively, picked his nose, chewed clothes, was irritable, screamed instead of asking for things, stuttered when excited, had sleeping difficulties, and moved his hips and legs in a jerky fashion. He was afraid of the dark and of being alone, of "boogy men," and strange people. When beaten by his parents, which usually took a severe form, he gave evidence of guilt. Among other difficulties were constipation and vomiting.

Hyperactivity was observed in early infancy. Defiant behavior and masturbation started at one and a half years. Fear of strangers was first noted at six months; other fears, as well as evidence of guilt feelings, at four years. Temper tantrums began to appear between the ages of two and three. Judah was unwanted, coming at a time of financial stress in the family. He was bottle-fed, except for a few days after birth, was weaned easily at two years, and slept in the parental bedroom until four years of age.

Judah lived with his mother, father, and maternal grandmother. There was one sibling, a younger girl, born after Judah began receiving treatment. The mother was attractive, petite, with the manners and appearance of a much younger woman. This had a psychological counterpart in that she rejected her role as wife and also, to some extent, as mother. She had a considerable drive toward placing men in inferior positions. She was, however, a woman with understanding and awareness of some of her weaknesses and their effect on others. She expressed a desire to improve the family situation.

The father appeared to be a friendly, good-natured man, who readily submitted to his wife's domination. He was employed at night and seemed interested in and fond of Judah, although he had little time to spend with him.

The maternal grandmother was a very narcissistic, rigid woman who cursed anyone who got in her way. She and her daughter, though living in the same home, maintained two separate households within their one apartment ostensibly because of differences in religious convictions. The older woman refused to care for Judah or help in any way. Judah openly expressed hatred for her.

Diagnosis of child: primary behavior disorder with neurotic traits with suspicion of psychoneurosis, anxiety hysteria type.

John came to the group at the thirty-eighth session, which created some difficulties for him. At the time, there were two boys and two girls in the group, and he became its fifth member. Later the girls were eliminated.

John was referred for treatment by the school because he was restless, had regressed in the preceding year, was indifferent and inattentive. Other difficulties included disobedience, temper tantrums, eye blinking, constant touching of nose and ears, nose picking and eating the nose excreta. He was inordinately afraid of doctors, of the dark, and of being separated from his mother. He presented feeding difficulties, was unable to fall asleep, was a restless sleeper, and complained of stomach pains that had no organic basis.

Disobedience and temper tantrums began at two years after placement in a nursery while the mother went to work. Since his first year, John had feeding problems, which were exaggerated during the fifth year. Eye-blinking appeared at about three, and fear of the dark, nail biting, and touching of nose and ears at about five years of age. There were school difficulties soon after he entered the nursery, including truanting. Stomach pains developed after the mother's second miscarriage soon after treatment was instituted with John. John was an only child.

The mother was a petite, attractive woman, very tense, rigid, and anxious. She had severe neurotic difficulties, with such symptoms as headaches, pains in arms and hands for which no physical cause had been found, frequent crying spells, many worries, difficulty in falling asleep, little appetite. She, too, was under treatment. The mother had been married the first time secretly, but separated the day after the wedding and later married her present spouse, who had been a friend of her first husband. She had had two miscarriages since John's birth.

The father was a short, dark, rather handsome man, who gave the impression of considerable ease and self-confidence, with underlying tension and fears. When John was a year-and-a-half old, the father suffered a nervous breakdown and was unable to work for eight months. The symptoms included unexplainable pains in various parts of the body, fear of meeting people, reaction to noises, anxiety while riding in subways, and refusal to go anywhere alone. He received brief psychotherapy. Recently he had made a fairly adequate adjustment in his work and at home. He was employed nights as well as some hours during the day.

Diagnosis of child: psychoneurosis with anxiety and conversion symptoms.

Noah, the younger of two children, whose sister is fourteen years older than he, was referred for treatment because of irritability, extreme hyperactivity, breaking things at home when angry, stubbornness, willfulness, being extremely annoying and demanding, and getting into difficulties with his mother, other members of the family and playmates. His speech was extremely immature, poorly formed, having a strange accent. The mother stated that when he was angry his speech was normal and distinct and only on ordinary occasions did he distort his speech.

He was blind in the right eye, which malady was said to be of tubercular origin—the father had been under treatment for tuberculosis.

Noah was an unwanted child and the mother continued to reject him severely. She was extremely punitive and threatening which she alternated with overprotectiveness, infantilization and pampering. The mother was described as being overanxious and complaining; she considered herself a martyr, stating that she gave her life up for her children. She was an extremely disturbed person with paranoid trends and was treated intensively both in a group and individually at the same time that Noah was in group treatment. This plan was adopted because it was felt that the boy could not be helped to any extent without some changes in the mother. The mother had suffered from rheumatism since childhood, had pyorrhea but had no money for dental care. She claimed that she had high blood pressure. Because doctors feared complications at the time Noah was born, no Caesarian operation was performed.

Initial interviews with the mother were described as being "highly colored by emotional tones."

The father who was under convalescent care through an agency dealing with tubercular patients was described as a devoted husband and father. About twenty years earlier he had been successful in business, but at the time of the boy's referral was ineffectual in all his relations.

In psychological tests Noah received an I.Q. of 80. The result, however, was questionable, since Noah was considered to be a very bright boy, as was also his sister. A Rorschach examination was administered. The results were found to be unreliable because of the boy's age, but the examiner felt that the child was considerably retarded.

Diagnosis of child: primary behavior disorder, pre-Oedipal type.

RECORD OF (66TH) GROUP SESSION [2]

The therapist came out of her office with Noah (a new patient) when John arrived. He seemed a little more subdued than usual and called out: "Come on; let's go upstairs." Both boys raced ahead to the "activity room," where the sessions are held. Noah went right up to the cupboard for his boat, but John first rummaged through the closet and soon began to wander around the room. (A)

He finally took some of the water-color paint out of the closet and announced he would use some of the "different kinds" (colors). He became a little excited, got hold of the pot and said he would make a mixture. It was going to be poison. The therapist said to John: "What do you mean by poison, John?" He answered, "It is what you think it is." The therapist said, "You mean something that is going to hurt someone?" John said, "Sure." The therapist asked if he wanted to hurt her. John looked startled and said, "No, it's just poison." He then poured paints of different colors into the pot. (B) He left his mixture temporarily and went to the cupboard, picked up an airplane that Noah had made and ridiculed it: "What kind of painting job is this, anyway?" Noah defended himself, saying it was camouflage. "It's all right," he said, "that's the way it's supposed to be." (C)

John then went back to his "poison" and the therapist said she thought John was angry with her because of Noah. John said, "That is right." He continued working on his mixture, when Judah arrived. John called to him to come and help with the "cooking." Judah (whose major interest is playing with fire and who is in rivalry for leadership with John when Mike, the undisputed leader, is absent), hesitated. At first he said no, then he said, "Oh, all right," and helped John in a sort of offhand lackadaisical manner. They put the pot on the electric plate, John plugged in the wire and they started to pour more water-color paint into the pot. (D)

Noah did not participate in this, working on his boat by himself, although at one or two points he called for help with putting two ramps onto the boat. John volunteered and went over to tell him

[2] It is suggested that the records in this and the succeeding chapters be read in full first, then reread with reference to the interpretations following each record.

how to do it. Judah and John kept adding paint to the mixture they were boiling. John said he was making "poison for her" (apparently referring to the therapist, which he had earlier denied). The therapist said it looked as though John was angry with her and wondered why. John looked annoyed and returned to his work with added vigor, adding more and more paint until the pot began to overflow and the stove sizzled. Judah cautioned him, saying, "Look, that is too much." John, however, kept inciting Judah to add more, saying, "Oh, it's all right. Let's see what it is like when it is filled." At this point Judah tried to put a piece of crayon on the grill "to see how it melted." John looked very frightened. He seemed alarmed and cried, "No, don't do that. That isn't a good idea; it will burn." (E)

Judah seemed to be calm but John was very excited. Judah began to complain about the smell in the room caused by the burning paint, and said, "We should stop this." The therapist had not interfered with this activity, but at this point she said, "Does everybody want to go out to eat today?" (Even though this was too early in the session, she thought it advisable to have John get out of this situation in this manner. He had been rapidly growing more and more excited.) Judah, in a very relieved tone, said, "Good." John joined in and said, "Yes, let's go; I have money." He pulled a quarter out of his pocket and showed it to the therapist. Very proudly Noah said the therapist was to let him have some money; he would give it back. His mother said it was all right. Judah, too, wanted money from the therapist. (F)

John had left his coat with his mother downstairs, and Noah had left his in the reception room on the floor below. The therapist said they would go down to get their coats. All went down to the floor below. John's mother gave him the coat and admonished him about his shoes, pointing out to him angrily that he had paint on them already, though he had been upstairs only a short while. John did not respond to her comment. He just took his coat and left the room with the others. Noah found his own coat very quickly and, as he was putting it on by himself, said anxiously, "Please wait for me; I'm going to hurry." He put his coat on rather quickly by comparison with his usual dawdling and delaying pattern. (G)

When the group came out of the elevator on the street floor, John suggested that they go downstairs by the "secret stairway." (This is a dark tunnel through the basement that is used as a fire emergency exit. The children used this tunnel many times; going through it is a more or less common experience for them.) All agreed and started down to the basement, with John leading. Noah took the therapist's hand; he seemed to be a little afraid. Noah had not been down in this passageway. (His anxiety may have been connected with his defect in vision, the vision of one eye being almost zero.) He did not act tense in places where there was a little light.

On the way down, John was full of bravado. "Come on," he said, "I'm leading the way. You don't have to be afraid. You take one step at a time. Here are two steps. One, two." He appeared very sure of himself and seemed to be also taking over the role of Mike (a very domineering member of the group who has been absent from the last several sessions). John even came up to Noah to show him how to walk down in the dark, but when the group got to the bottom steps, John said: "Let's all take hands here and we can go together." All did this. He suddenly hesitated as he came to the passageway itself, which led by way of three or four steps up to a door opening to the street. At this point, John became panicky, turned to the therapist and said, "You go first." Judah had been silent throughout all this. The therapist went forward and John now seemed overcome with fear. He screamed loudly several times: "Let's go back upstairs!"

Noah and Judah were apparently affected by John's fear and even though they were only a few steps from the exit, turned back. John said he was afraid. Noah reminded John of what he previously said and ridiculed him by saying: "No, go ahead John. There is nothing to be afraid of. It is just dark and you just put one foot ahead of the other." John now held back instead of leading the way as before, and clung to the therapist and Noah. Judah seemed to have no fear and went right along. John, on the other hand, beside himself screamed: "Let's get out as soon as possible! Hurry up, everybody!" All went back to the second floor and walked down the front stairway to the street. (H)

Once on the street, John and Judah ran ahead. Noah did not hold the therapist's hand as he usually did, but did remain near her. At the corner drugstore John was the first to order. He said he would order one thing first and would let the therapist know when he was ready for something else. He ordered a soda. Judah ordered exactly what John did. Noah decided on something different, a plate of ice cream. (In the past Noah had had sodas.) We have had difficulty with Noah's dawdling and slowness at a previous session, and the boys remonstrated with him then. Noah seemed to remember this, and as he started to eat, he said: "This time I want to know how much time I'm going to have." Judah and John ignored this.

John had a straw in his soda and Judah insisted that he too had to have a straw just like John's. He seemed quite anxious about this. The children sat on the swivel stools at the counter. The therapist did not eat with them, but stood behind them. She said that Judah would certainly have a straw, that his order had not come, and that is why he didn't have it as yet. Judah accepted this and said, "Okay, but hurry up." (I)

While waiting for his soda, Judah started to twirl his stool. John, too, tried to twirl his stool, but an adult sitting next to him told him not to do that. John asked Judah to change places with him. Judah refused and kept on twirling the seat. John became angry at this and tried to dislodge Judah, but not too violently. He then gave Judah a slight push. The latter told John that he was going to stay wherever he wished. At this point Judah's drink arrived, he stopped twirling and began to drink his ice cream soda. John was finished and got off his seat. Noah hadn't finished as yet and he started to count to himself: One, one and a half, two, two and a half." (Counting was introduced by Mike at a previous session when he tried to get Noah to hurry with his food.) The others ignored him. They did not hurry him, but just waited impassively. Finally Noah got up by himself.

Again Judah and John ran ahead when the group left the drugstore. When the therapist got to the corner the boys were not in sight. Judah called to the therapist from the steps of the near-by elevated station. He was laughing teasingly, but with no trace of hostility. He came running down the steps, hugged the therapist around the waist. John pulled at the therapist's skirt, and then the two of them started running again. Noah ran with them to the next corner where they waited for the therapist to take them across. (J)

INTERPRETATION

(A) John is shocked by the fact that Noah had been alone with the therapist (mother). This makes Noah the preferred child. John feels rejected and hostile, which feelings he represses, and, therefore, acts subdued. He calls out, "Come on; let's go upstairs," an expression of hostility to the therapist. Having been rejected he in turn rejects her.

When Noah and John race each other to the activity room, John attempts to show Noah that he is superior to him, stronger and more potent. He also wishes to be first, which usually represents the desire for primogeniture (the special value that is attached to being born first in primitive societies and the superior legal and social status in most European nations afforded the first born).

Noah goes directly to the closet to get his boat, satisfied now that he has received attention from the "mother." He was her only child during the time that he was in her interviewing room, and is, therefore, able to mobilize power and focus his libido on the job. The boat may have a symbolic meaning of the mother; by continuing work upon the boat, he continues his relation with the therapist (mother). His continuing directly on a project upon which he was engaged the previous week indicates that the group experience has not been entirely eradicated in the interval, namely, therapy continued through the intervening period.

John, on the other hand, is not able to concentrate because of his disturbance. He cannot focus his energies and wanders around the room, which may represent seeking love.

(B) Paint is an easy material to work with, i.e., one of low resistivity, requiring no special effort. It has also urethral-anal-sexual significance. He undoubtedly gets excited because, as we can guess, he is using red paint, which has sexual significance. (When the therapist was asked about it, she confirmed that the paint he was using was red.) John's answer that poison "is what you think it is," may be a stray statement or it may be a recognition of a very important psychological principle. He verbalizes in a disguised form his fear of his impulses toward his mother. The therapist rather unwisely translates this in terms of herself: she substitutes herself for his mother. Interpretation of this nature must not be given too soon. Poorly timed interpretation either disturbs a patient (John is startled) or causes him to reject it as implausible. He could not at this point accept even the fact that he is angry at the therapist.

Our surmise that John is overexcited because of the sexual connotation of his activity is supported by the fact that he is psychoneurotic. It also finds support in the succession of his symptom development. Note that the following symptoms have set in at the age of five (at the height of the Oedipal conflict): fear of the dark, nail-biting, touching of nose and ears.

(C) John by now is angry with the therapist (mother), but as is usual in groups (families), displaces his anger on Noah (sibling) and ridicules his work.

(D) John now returns to his making of "poison" and the therapist interprets his anger and the cause for it, which is correct. He can accept this. It has to be explained why he now confirms his anger, but denied it before. This is evidently because he had brought his hostilities into the open when he criticized Noah's airplane, and, since he was not punished, he is no longer afraid of admitting to being angry, which demonstrates the importance of timing in interpretation.

When Judah arrives, John invites him to help with the "cooking." By this stratagem, he punishes the worker as he prevents her from having Judah. It also constitutes a rejection of Noah, and support of himself in his hostile activity. After a brief period of vacillation, Judah decides to work with John, but extends the activity beyond just mixing paints to include his own interest, namely, using the electric grill (fire).

(E) Noah is isolated because he is a new member and also because to John he seems to be the preferred child, but when Noah asks for help he admits his inadequacy, and John helps him, thus asserting his power as a strong person in relation to the therapist (mother). Again the Oedipal conflict is acted out.

Having received support from Judah, John is now able to reveal his real intention, namely, to poison the therapist, who continues making the mistake of interpreting John's anger. John is now annoyed, his anger rises, and as a retaliatory act, pours in more paint so that it overflows and sizzles. Judah is frightened, but John wants to continue punishing the therapist; he, also, establishes by this his superiority over Judah, with whom he is in rivalry for supremacy. But when Judah tries to put a piece of crayon on the grill itself, John becomes frightened that *it* will *burn*. This undoubtedly is a result of his castration fears.

(F) The therapist had done well suggesting this relief from the mounting tension for both Judah and John. John's castration fear is abated and to confirm it, he produces money from his pocket to show it to the therapist. The fact that he shows it off with pride is of particular significance. It represents potency. Noah, too, not to be left out, asserts himself, but he does it by monopolizing the therapist: she is to give him money (she is to give him power); his mother said it was all right (as the mother gives him power). Here he replaces the mother by the therapist (substitution).

(G) It is rather unfortunate that the children had to return for their coats and thus expose John to his mother's outburst. The coats and the other belongings of the children should have been taken up before.[3] What is significant is that John does not respond. This is a good demonstration of cathexis displacement; now that he has the support of the therapist and is anticipating pleasure that she will give him, the mother's remarks are less significant than usual. Noah becomes aware of his dawdling and is afraid of the consequences; he gives up his infantile behavior of the past for social approval (social hunger).

(H) John is full of bravado, an expression of his wish for (penis) potency. He leads the way. However, when they go down to the bottom steps he becomes apprehensive and suggests that all hold hands. John's fear mounts as they reach the narrow, straight, dark tunnel and this, too, can be interpreted as a castration fear. He asks the therapist to go first and the therapist does so, but instead of his fear becoming allayed, he grows panicky. He is suddenly overcome with a feeling of impotence, and when he asks the therapist to go ahead, and she does it, she confirms his weakness. This throws him into a panic. Had the therapist reassured and supported him by saying he can go ahead and that she is right behind him, his anxiety may not have set in.

[3] The routine was later changed. The children were brought by the mothers and "social work aids," who fetched some of them directly to the activity room. The mothers waited in the waiting room downstairs instead of calling for the children after the sessions.

The fear of the tunnel may also represent fear of actualizing his sexual impulses in relation to the therapist (as a mother substitute). This is quite likely because of the intensity of John's Oedipal conflict.

(I) Again, John and Judah race to see who arrives at the destination first. Noah seems at this session more independent than he had been before (he does not hold the therapist's hand). There may be two reasons for this: one, that the therapist had supported him at the session; the second, that John, the dominating person, revealed himself as being weak. Noah, however, is still not a part of the group and it is possible that he is not ready for group therapy, a fact that should be evaluated. Judah continues to act out rivalry with John when he chooses the same food, and insists on having a straw, too. Noah again isolates himself by choosing a different type of food, even though the other boys ordered the sodas that he used to take. Noah's maturing through group pressure is once more revealed when he becomes aware of his dawdling.

The therapist should eat with the children at a table, family fashion, act out her mother role, and create a family atmosphere. This is the practice in the group therapy room and should be continued outside.

(J) John and Judah are again in rivalry in the drugstore with John succeeding in reestablishing his feelings of power. (He is served first; he has a straw; he finishes first.) The value of the group as a means of correcting character defects is again demonstrated when Noah attempts to control his own tendency to dawdle. This is a result of Mike's check-up at previous sessions, which helped Noah to recognize his dawdling. According to the case history, his mother could do nothing with him in this respect.

The rivalry between Judah and John asserts itself again when they run ahead. Some of the earlier negative feeling toward the therapist had been dissipated. Because she has acted out the role of a good mother, a provider and protector, the children now have positive feelings toward her. They accept her protection when they wait for her at the corner. Noah now joins the boys at running. This is considerable growth for him.

DISCUSSION

Several points in the conduct and process in this group need to be highlighted to demonstrate its particular characteristics. In addition to dynamics set forth at the beginning of this chapter, noteworthy is the functioning of the therapist. In pure activity groups, the therapist does not react verbally to any of the children's activities. Here, she helps John to bring to consciousness his resentment of her for giving special attention to Noah. He becomes aware of his rivalry with Noah and Judah. We have here demonstrated the fact of substitution in the therapeutic relation when John wants to poison the therapist as a mother substitute. Activity catharsis is clearly seen in the behavior of all the children, especially Judah who acts out his sexual aggression by using fire, overboiling the paint mixture (making it sizzle), and burning the chalk. John, too, acts out his hostile intents, and when he is not punished becomes more accepting of the new and different mother (therapist).

The importance of tact and timing of interpretation is dramatically shown. John is unable to admit that he wants to poison the therapist, but can accept the idea that he is angry with her for being good to Noah and not to him. Later when he is ready, he can also face his destructive feelings toward her. It must be noted that despite his hostility toward the therapist, the negative transference is only temporary. The basic transference is positive and is soon reestablished.[4]

[4] For another record and interpretation of a session of the same group, see S. R. Slavson, "Play Group Therapy for Young Children," *The Nervous Child,* July, 1948.

CHAPTER NINE

ACTIVITY-INTERVIEW PSYCHO-THERAPY WITH CHILDREN IN LATENCY

RECORD AND INTERPRETATION

CASE HISTORIES

THE FOLLOWING record deals with a mixed group of boys and girls, nine to ten years old. Among them is Alice, about nine and a half years old. She presented a problem in adjustment with children, had no friends, stole, lied, was brazen at home and school, quarrelsome, and always insisted on having the last word in quarrels. She dramatized herself, was sloppy, careless, indifferent and annoying, a "great talker," demanded attention, was spiteful and reckless in school to the degree of destroying blossoms in the Nature Room.

Her conversation usually centered about herself and her voice trembled when she talked about her problems. She was a sulky loser. One of her favored occupations was throwing lighted matches out of the window, an activity that began at a time when her mother was hospitalized. She was a nail-biter, talked in her sleep, had nightmares, used to chew her hair, but later chewed her handkerchiefs. Her tendency to dramatize gave her the appellation of "little Sarah Bernhardt." Alice was in constant conflict with her brother, six years older. There was well-founded suspicion of sex play between the two.

The mother came from a disturbed and unpleasant home environment. She was a sickly woman with a cardiac condition, which necessitated her taking things easy. The father, a friendly man, was devoted to his family, but seemed to have played into his wife's patterns.

Diagnosis of child: primary behavior disorder, Oedipal type.

The other girl in this group is Sylvia, I.Q. 112, who had a brother seven years older, and was referred for treatment because she whined, did poorly at school, and her behavior was extremely attention-getting. She did not get along with other children, was resistive to, and unhappy about, going to school. She sometimes appeared unable to hear when addressed, was disobedient to her mother, refused to go to bed, lied, was generally unreliable and in strong rivalry with her brother.

Her father and mother were separated. Sylvia seemed confused about this and spoke of her parents' life as "a mystery" to her. She preferred to play with boys, and during treatment displayed considerable preoccupation with sex. She often lapsed into baby talk to an extent that it was difficult to understand her.

The family consisted of the mother and the two children, who lived in a crowded section and in unwholesome conditions. There had been considerable conflict between the father and mother before the separation. The father was a weak, inadequate man, very dependent upon his own mother. In fact, he and his own family lived with her for thirteen years until she died. As a child, Sylvia witnessed physical combat between the parents. In recent years the mother had acquired a man friend and Sylvia witnessed their fondling each other; frequently Sylvia left her bed at night to go into the room where the couple were.

Diagnosis of child: behavior disorder, Oedipal type.

Richard, I.Q., 106, was referred because he disturbed the class routine, ran around the classroom, talked loudly and out of turn, insulted teachers, lied, was histrionic, and stole. His hyperactivity was so great that a diagnosis of chorea was made, but this was not confirmed later in treatment.

At home he refused to go to bed, was overinquisitive, sucked his thumb constantly and vigorously so that the saliva ran down his chin, on his clothes, and on objects around him. He bit his nails, picked his nose, was spiteful, and so violent that at camp he was nicknamed "the killer." He urinated frequently, was exhibitionistic, talked and mumbled in his sleep. He was in strong rivalry with an older brother, with whom Richard was compared unfavorably. He liked to climb high places and tore his clothes.

Richard was unwanted because his mother wanted a daughter. When he was an infant the mother tied him with a rope to the bed to control his hyperactivity, and to prevent his thumb sucking, placed celluloid cuffs over his hands. When the boy was five years old, the mother was forced to go to work because of the father's illness. Richard was placed in an orphan asylum for a period of one and a half years. There he changed completely from a hyperactive to a subdued and inactive child.

His maliciousness had a long history. At four years of age he pulled girls' hair and took toys away from children. Richard was unable to concentrate on anything, his interest being of very short duration. He was aggressive, dominant, bossy, and forceful. His parents were incompatible and in constant conflict with one another, and he was continually threatened with placement.

Diagnosis: behavior disorder, conduct and habit type, with neurotic traits.

According to his mother, James suffered from many "imaginary ailments." He identified with sick people, was very anxious and worrisome, afraid of dying, and when he heard of someone's death, grew panicky about dying and demanded that a doctor be summoned. He suffered from psychogenic cramps, suspected his mother of poisoning his food and refused to eat it. He grimaced, twisted his mouth, blinked his eyes, made peculiar sounds with his throat, cracked his knuckles. He had difficulty falling asleep. He felt guilty about his behavior, but explained that he could not help acting as he did.

According to the mother, James had masturbated violently and excessively up to four years of age, but had stopped abruptly. The boy, however, stated that he had masturbated at the time of referral and during treatment, until his penis "got red." He daydreamed a great deal, disliked teachers, hated his maternal grandmother who lived with the family, and refused to stay at home with her. He complained of lack of attention from his father. Up to the age of six, James slept in the parental bedroom, but at the time of referral slept in a room only with his father. When, for a period, he slept alone in the living room, he had frightening nightmares that woke him up, and he then would crawl into his mother's bed. When alone at night he saw strange objects moving around the room and then wanted to get into bed with his father. James stayed alone at home a great deal, read comics excessively, and did not play with children.

The mother was a cold, rationalizing, unemotional person, verbose, impersonal. She had been very strict and rigid with James and at the same time quite anxious about him. She denied herself to the boy as well as to her husband as a defense against having her personality invaded. She said, "I keep myself away from James because he is dying to touch me." She was sexually frigid and found sexual intercourse intolerable.

The father, though a man in his forties, appeared like an aged person. He was stooped, thin, haggard looking, and anxiety ridden. Always dependent upon his own father; he had been in business with him until the latter's death, when he went to work for another relative. The father was described as being strongly attached also to his mother, who lived with him. For a period, he had anxieties about having cancer. The father called James names such as "dope," "imbecile," "brat," "stinker," "louse." These epithets were particularly concentrated around the boy's studies and homework.

The paternal grandmother had chronic asthma, and James witnessed her severe attacks. She was an extremely worrisome person, hypochondriacal, anticipated illness, and continually exhorted James to be careful so as not to hurt himself or get killed. It is suspected that the boy wished his grandmother to die so that he could have her room to himself. He also dominated his parents.

At school James attempted to outdo the other children and dominate situations. He was described as extremely talkative, dawdled, was inattentive, and when he got into difficulties, wanted his mother to fight his battles for him.

Before James was born, three children had died. He himself was not planned and was unwelcome. His was a difficult birth; he presented feeding difficulties from the very outset, was allergic to mattresses and human milk, and as a baby suffered from rashes. He had colic, always lived on a restricted diet, was partially blind in one eye from birth, necessitating glasses from the age of four, and he had a tendency to squinting. His food allergies were particularly severe between the ages of six and eight when he had severe cramps and the sight of food sickened him. At seven years of age he developed a tic consisting of an up and down movement of his head.

Diagnosis of child: psychoneurosis with hypochondriacal trends, possible schezophrenia.

RECORD OF GROUP SESSION (FOURTH)[1]

The children had to wait for the therapist, who returned late from a meeting. She had notified them by postcard, asking them to come a little later, but they all came on time. While waiting, they engaged in rough play in the waiting room. (A)

The therapist telephoned to the receptionist to tell the children to come to her room, which is one floor above the reception room. The children came tearing down the hall. (B)

Because time was rather short, the group did not go into the activity room, where the sessions were held, but gathered around the table in the therapist's room. There was some milk chocolate which Alice distributed to the children. (C) Immediately after they had calmed down, Alice, as the spokesman for the group, said she had a secret. The others said they all had a secret from the therapist, but they felt she should know it.

Richard playfully ran out of the room, and within his hearing the therapist asked whether Richard was in on the secret. Yes, he said, he knew about it. The therapist said: "How do you feel about Richard's not being in the room?" and Richard poked his head in the door and said to Alice, "Yes, tell it," and hovered near the door, listening. Alice said, "He is ashamed." James seemed embarrassed and ducked, but Alice proceeded to tell how Richard had picked up a nickel from the counter in the store, how he had stolen some chewing gum and candy on a number of occasions, and that this time he tried again and was nearly caught.

Richard now came into the room and seated himself quietly. The therapist asked him whether he had heard everything that was said. Yes, he heard it. Had he taken other things, too? Yes, he once stole

1 See note 2, p. 129.

a ring from the five and ten cent store. He said: "I just can't stop myself when I see something I want." (D)

Alice said she has that same trouble. If she wants something, she can't stop herself. The therapist asked her what she takes. Generally pennies. James now said that he, too, has at times stolen little things, but, "I generally think, should I or should I not take?" The therapist asked, "Well, what happens?" He said at times he takes and again he doesn't. Richard, in self-defense, said the most he ever took was five cents. Alice reminded him of the ring he stole in the five and ten, and continued to say that her mother now knows that she used to steal pennies. She has given up stealing entirely.

Sylvia, who had been very quiet, now commented that she, too, used to steal but has stopped. She hasn't stolen for a long time. Then looking thoughtfully at the children, she said cryptically: "Crime does not pay." (E)

The therapist wondered if they ever thought why it is that they take things that do not belong to them. Sylvia said quickly, "For revenge." The therapist said maybe they could talk about this and they could figure out what happened. Alice was the first to speak. She said when she is denied things, she gets angry, but because she is afraid of being punished, she doesn't show her anger. Instead when she got a chance, she took money from her mother's pocketbook. This she doesn't do any more; she has given it up. Richard said he tells lies. James remarked that sometimes he lies but not as much as he used to. Why do they lie? They said they knew, and almost in unison added, "To protect ourselves from a beating." (F)

Then James asked whether we could not continue with a story that he and Richard made up when they met here alone before Richard was ill. As all of the children wanted to hear the story and asked the therapist to read it from her notes, she opened the notebook and began reading. She read haltingly because she had only an outline and her writing was not too clear. Interestingly, James recalled from memory, word for word, the story and began telling it, in a much more coherent way, but Sylvia said, "Let's read it." It had to do with pregnancy. First James spoke very fast and imitated Danny Kaye; then Richard took up the story: "There were many babies, all eyes, pregnant, looking at him. It was a nightmare;

walked in his sleep." James said: "Then at breakfast he couldn't eat. The food was too cold, so he went down to play. But he doesn't feel well. He could play all sports but now he doesn't feel well, so he takes a course in punchball. Before he wasn't well, he was the best ball player, but not being well now, as he threw the ball it fell over the fence and there stood a little house." James was delighted to get commendation because he had remembered the story so well. The therapist asked Richard if he remembered it. Richard said he can't remember about the baby's pregnancy because it was a nightmare. (G)

The therapist followed this up and asked whether a boy can be pregnant. Richard said no, because it is a difference of sex. At this point, Richard and James ran out and brought back some water. They had taken a drink and spilled some of the water on the floor. When they came into the room, Alice said: "You both got mothers, boys. Why are you ashamed?" Richard said, "She [Alice] knows." The therapist asked Richard does he know? Richard then drew a picture and when the therapist asked for an interpretation, he said: "First comes graduation, then comes marriage, then comes James with a baby carriage."

At this point, Sylvia rose from her chair and recited several little limericks somewhat on the "smutty" side, and Alice laughingly said that she asked a question which went unanswered. "I still want to know in marriage, what does a man do to a woman?" Richard said: "He kisses her, he undresses her." Alice said: "Uhuh, I guess we are getting closer to facts." Richard giggled and said he would have to have a drink. James excused himself politely and said he wanted a drink, too. (Up to this point there was no twitching of his face, but now twitching has returned. He also seemed to be trying to keep his eyes open wider.) The boys were gone but a moment. (H)

When Richard returned, he seemed quieter. (He had been acting as though he were overstimulated.) When he returned, he said to the therapist he wished she would draw a picture. The therapist asked what kind of picture he wanted. He said, "A boy and a girl." The therapist asked, "Why can't we all draw pictures?" The children at once gathered around a table and all began drawing. Richard and James said they were going to keep their pictures in their wallets. While the therapist was drawing they all gathered around her and directed her work. The outcome was a pregnant woman and a man, both with genitals and other sexual details. As the therapist drew them, she gave them the proper names. Each of the children asked for a copy, and the therapist made one for each. Richard then said he knew the difference between a man and a woman. The woman, he said, has a lot of hair. He saw his mother as she was pulling off her nightgown over her head (illustrating the movement) and then he saw a lot of hair. The children were serious and did not giggle, but listened attentively. The therapist said, "Don't men have hair, too?" "Yes," said Richard, "but not so much as a woman."

Sylvia again recited some limericks in which the word f— appeared. The children spelled out the word. The therapist told them it is also known as intercourse. (James and Sylvia displayed more anxiety than the other two children.) Since they ran over their time, the therapist told the children the session was ended and that the group would meet again next week. (I)

INTERPRETATION

(A) We don't know whether the children came early because they were rigid about schedules or because they were anxious to come to the session. It is also possible that they came early to raise havoc, which they did, as retaliation for being displaced in the therapist's affection. It is undesirable for patients to foregather anywhere but in the therapy room and in the presence of the therapist. Being unsupervised in the waiting room, the children gave vent to aggression and as a result came to the session in a set mood, namely, aggressive.

(B) It would have been better if the therapist had gone down for the children and brought them back with her; they must have been in a state of anxiety while waiting. They may have thought the therapist would not get there at all, and running hilariously through the hall was a reaction to this anxiety. It may also have been an expression of hostility, since they had been told several times that they should not make noise in the hallways. The rivalry factor may also have been present: each desires to arrive first, to be the first born. In an activity group such behavior is accepted; the therapist does not react to it. In an activity-interview group, such as this one is, the therapist might have commented by saying something like: "My, you are noisy. I guess you don't like being kept waiting." Later the actual motivation for rowdy behavior can be discussed.

(C) The giving of food presents a problem here. To the children it may be a peace offering from the therapist—she was late and wants their forgiveness for it. The effect on the children should be understood: the foodgiving activates guilt; the children have been rowdy and destructive, yet instead of punishing them the therapist is good to them. This makes them contrite and prevents acting out of hostility toward the therapist for neglecting them. One of two effects may result: therapy may be blocked, though expression of hostility is a major need in psychotherapy; or, as we shall see presently, the direction of the emotional flow and the content of articulation may be changed. There is, of course, the practical problem that children at this age need a snack after school, and some means should be provided for it. Perhaps the best solution would be for the parents to give the children money for this purpose on the days of the therapy sessions. When the parents are poor, the clinic can supply the money, as it does in the case of carfare.

There is, of course, the problem that children as young and as disturbed as these may dawdle in the stores and come late to the interviews. The sessions should, therefore, be scheduled at a time of day that would allow them reasonable time to travel from school and get their refreshments. If they do come late, this should be treated as a form of resistance and discussed with the group.

The above does not mean that occasional feeding of children is entirely ruled out. Refreshments may be indicated as a part of therapy in group, as it sometimes is in individual treatment.

(D) The children are repaying the therapist for being good to them. They gave up their secret to her, but at the same time, they displace on Richard their hostility toward her. He had stolen on a number of occasions before, but it is this particular time that they choose to expose him. Also, as already indicated, the situation blocked recitation of individual problems; instead they are all preoccupied with Richard's stealing. There is unanimity, and when there is unanimity there is hostility toward the therapist.

Richard is the scapegoat of the group's aggression. (It is interesting to note in this connection that although Richard had been in individual treatment for over a year with the same therapist, rather unsuccessfully, before he was transferred to group treatment, he never mentioned his stealing. Nor was it known that the other children stole as well, although they, too, had been in individual treatment.)

The therapist makes the mistake of asking Richard if he stole other things. The wrong emphasis was placed on the act and she elicits a confession from the boy. While confession reduces anxiety, it does not lead to the intrapsychic activity that is necessary in therapy.

Note that James, who is intensely psychoneurotic, is the most embarrassed one in the group.

(E) We see here four children freely confessing to prohibitive acts. It is a mass confessional, but what are they actually saying? First of all, they are in effect saying to the therapist: "We know that you understand us, that you are not going to punish us. You are all-loving and we know you will forgive us and cleanse us." They are looking for forgiveness from the therapist, which she cannot give them. The therapist cannot condone, nor can she punish. She must retain her nonjudgmental role. The main motivation for the confessionals is, of course, allaying of guilt and the fear of punishment. The secondary motivation is to reduce the stigma they attached to Richard. They feel guilty of their disloyalty, and put themselves in the same category with him. Thus the superego is enriched through identification.

(F) Sylvia's reason for stealing is quite correct. When the therapist gives them the opportunity to probe into the causes of their conduct, the children respond with insight. Sylvia demonstrates the capacity young children have for recognizing unconscious motivations, a capacity which is further manifested in this passage. While there are also other reasons for stealing, revenge is one of them. To Sylvia, it is a retaliatory act for frustration and rejection. In suggesting that they talk about this the therapist plays out her role well: she neither condones nor condemns the stealing, nor does she interpret it; instead, she treats it as a natural manifestation that needs to be understood. To this, Alice reacts by elaborating, displaying good understanding. She sees the connection between frustration, aggression, and substitute gratification: she is afraid to express her anger against her parents so she finds another way of getting even. She also recognizes that she has improved. She does not steal anymore, that is, she can now better deal with frustrations and with her impulses.

Richard sees the connection between stealing and lying as hostile acts. James lies as well as steals. Both boys say they use more than one weapon to express their aggressions, and James recognizes that he has improved (which is true). This confession is particularly valuable to him since he has a full-blown psychoneurosis. His superego is now less tyrannical and his ego is strong enough to permit recognizing his transgression, in which the other children help him.

This passage illustrates well the relation of the basic dynamics of psychotherapy: transference, catharsis, insight, and reality testing. The children test themselves against one another and especially against the therapist. Will she punish them? Will something happen to them as a result of their crimes? It must also be kept in mind that hostility to the therapist is also present here. They are telling her of their transgressions against her world. They trampled her adult codes underfoot, as it were. (This is analogous to the expression of hostility to the therapist in activity groups when children break or destroy materials and tools and damage the room.) Are they repaying her for neglecting them and keeping them waiting, and, instead of displacing hostility on Richard, do they now direct it where it rightfully belongs?

(G) James grows too anxious and seeks to escape into a fiction story. The others are anxious enough to fall in with his plan. The story is very clear in James's mind; he remembers it word for word. His anxiety rises, and he escapes into comedy by imitating Danny Kaye. His anxiety is evidently associated with birth and babies, but he emphasizes "all eyes." They see him. Thus the center of his fears are sex, birth and dead siblings who accuse him (all eyes).

James tells us that he had siblings of whom he is afraid and has nightmares. Indeed, he is so upset that he walks in his sleep and cannot eat. He kicks his siblings around (punchball), but falls over the fence where there is a house. We have here a complete birth-sibling rivalry-death-family phantasy. The punchball is a sibling whom he has destroyed or rejected. (Three children preceding James died at birth and his mother often talked about it. James was the only living child.) We have, therefore, a child who is inordinately preoccupied with death and birth, and at the same time guilty of having something to do with causing the death of his siblings. This is a rather sick boy, who should receive individual as well as group treatment. It was well to build up James's ego at this point by telling him how well he remembered the story.

(H) Note that Richard says, "The baby's pregnancy." The therapist rightly follows this up by asking whether boys can be pregnant. Evidently the boys, especially James, are confused on this issue; they are not clear whether they can have babies. In the story they do not specify that a woman was pregnant; the story is just about pregnancy, generalized. The therapist's question was aimed to clarify this for the children. Richard, who is much less disturbed than James, supplies the answer.

Both boys run out of the room for a drink, which is a convenient way of escaping anxiety. They spill water on the floor, which can be viewed as an hostile act against the therapist to punish her for causing them anxiety. This could have been interpreted with profit either at the moment, or a bit later. Interpretation of transference is, as we have seen, an important aspect of this type of group psychotherapy.

Alice perceives their embarrassment, which is in relation to their Oedipal conflict, and brings forth the matter of mothers, and when Richard says that she understands their problem ("she knows"), the therapist tries to bring their phantasies to the surface by asking him if he knows. To this, he responds by escaping into drawing. But here the therapist makes the mistake of asking him what he is drawing. This is the third question directed to him by the therapist and it seems as though she is pursuing him. She is pressing him too much. Richard fends her off by bringing in James as the center of his drawing, which is a transparent fiction.

Note that Richard did not include a wife in this setting and the impression one gets is that James gave birth to the baby. Marriage is a ritual for having a baby. His lack of awareness or refusal to acknowledge sexual intercourse is characteristic of the period of latency, but in this instance it is part of the boy's problem. When

Alice asked, "What does a man do to a woman?" his answer was, "He kisses her, he undresses her." The bars having been let down, Sylvia recited "smutty" limericks, and Alice, who is very disturbed and preoccupied with sex (sex play with a brother) entered into a conversation with Richard. His reaction is again escape under the pretense of getting a drink.

James is also frightened. "He excuses himself politely" and leaves the room. His tension is so great that twitching of the face returns and staring of the eyes sets in. His efforts to widen his eyes is probably a result of his struggle against a desire to withdraw from the situation. As he became tense and frightened, he automatically tended to shut out the noxious pressure (the group and its discussion) by shutting his eyes. He either began to sink into a pseudo-stupor or felt sleepy ("subdued"), but forced himself to "stay awake" by widening his eyes. The effect of this discussion upon James illustrates how a group interview can prove too distressing to a given patient.

In Alice we see a young girl whose sexual curiosities and whose intimacy with the subject are way beyond her years. The suspicion that she indulges in sex play with her older brother would seem on this evidence to be justified and we should look to a strong unresolved Oedipal conflict in this girl, for the brother is probably a substitute for the father. It would also be well to investigate if she was sleeping or had slept in the parental bedroom beyond a permissible age.

(I) Since Richard is not as neurotic as James, he calms down more easily after he leaves the room. When he asks the therapist to draw him a picture, he asks her to enlighten him on the relation of a man and a woman (father and mother). It is a disguised way of asking for the same information that Alice had requested more directly. There is also another implication here: if the therapist, who is a woman, tells him the truth, she will become accessible as a sexual object. Since she is not hiding anything from him, then she does not resist him. The therapist, therefore, becomes what he wishes his mother would be, namely, sexually accessible (substitution).

The therapist asks him what kind of a picture he would like, and he promptly says "A boy *and* a girl." This was uppermost in his mind and confirms our hypothesis as to his intent in asking for a picture. His phantasy, however, is preoccupied with the relation of his father and mother. The therapist then suggests that they all draw pictures, which they do, but soon gather around her, ask her various questions about human anatomy.

Although the children got their way, the therapist missed the point of Richard's question. She did not perceive that his asking her to make a drawing had a direct connection with what the children had been discussing (associative thinking and free association). She rather took it at its face value and suggested that they all draw. Instead, she should have asked him how he wants the boy drawn, in what position, where the girl should be drawn and what her position should be. The phantasies he had built up would thus have been brought to the surface. As it is, the children got what they wanted, but less directly. They suggested the therapist draw in the details, which they themselves were afraid to do.

There is little doubt that, despite the considerable anxiety they were exposed to, this experience had given the children great relief. Unfortunately we do not have all the details as to who was the more active in this situation and who suggested drawing in the most prohibited organs, but we would expect James to be the least assertive and the most anxious. His therapy may have been of a spectator type. It is regrettable that we do not have information on the pictures that each child drew for himself. These would be very revealing. The therapist did well in giving the proper names for the various parts of the body. Her objectivity and calm during the entire proceedings must have given the children great security, released them of a great deal of tension, and cleared channels for further catharsis.

Sylvia's reciting of smutty limericks and the others' spelling out the four letter word may be a manifestation of the release they achieved through all this. It may also be a challenge to the therapist, an expression of hostility. They were aware of the unacceptability of such language in the presence of an adult and they either tested or defied her. It must be noted that the children were not interested in intercourse. Their curiosities were limited to the genitals. Since these children are in latency, the word for intercourse means nothing to them. It was just a prohibited word.

DISCUSSION

The important point must be noted that the children had been in individual treatment from six to twelve months by the same therapist and none ever talked about stealing, but discussed it freely at the fourth group session. Universalization, identification, and mutual support played an important part in facilitating this catharsis. But of even greater importance is that it demonstrates how cathexis displacement operates. In individual treatment, the therapist was the object of cathexis, while in the group this cathexis was diminished and resistance was correspondingly decreased.

The record demonstrates many of the general principles and dynamics suggested and elaborated throughout the preceding pages. This would make further comment repetitive. One feature ought to be noted, however, and this is the free acting-out pattern of the children as compared with the sessions of older patients. They use stories and drawings to communicate their phantasies; when they feel uncomfortable they leave the room, and when hostile they disturb the occupants of the building and spill water on the floor. The value of the less-conflicted patients to the more anxious is well demonstrated by Alice, who spurs the others on to boldness in exploring areas of which the others were afraid.

CHAPTER TEN

ANALYTIC GROUP PSYCHOTHERAPY WITH GIRLS IN PUBERTY

RECORD AND INTERPRETATION

CASE HISTORIES

ANNE came for treatment at twelve and a half years because she was moody, obstinate, cried easily, had difficulty in making friends, and was particularly unhappy when boys did not pay attention to her. The mother described Anne as an ungrateful, sloppy, insolent girl, who constantly sought attention. She lied, fidgeted, bit her nails, and was a restless sleeper and a finicky eater who never ate meat. Her dreams, of which she remembered many, revealed frustration and fear. One of the recurrent dreams was that she fell in front of a moving train and just escaped being injured or killed. Anne was aware of feelings of inferiority. She said she was too fat and unattractive and had a poor complexion. She was a brilliant student and was accelerated two years at school.

Anne was the eldest of three children. A sister, three and a half years younger, had died a year before Anne came for treatment. There was also a brother, two and a half years old. She had been in very strong rivalry with the younger sister, whom she pinched, beat and terrorized by telling horror stories. When the sister died of encephalitis, the mother went into a marked depression. She blamed Anne for the child's death, claiming that it was brought on by Anne's striking the younger child on the head. Anne could not bring herself to cry when the sister died.

Anne was an unwanted child and presented feeding difficulties from the very beginning. She felt that both parents had rejected her (which was quite true). She particularly disliked her father, with whom she was in intense conflict and who beat her frequently. He was a cold, undemonstrative person and a strict disciplinarian, while her mother was a neurotic woman who had suffered severe depression since the younger daughter's death. There was constant friction between Anne and her mother regarding conduct, household duties, cleanliness and details of family life. Up to the time of her sister's birth, when Anne was three and a half years old, she slept in the parental bedroom. In the belief that Anne was old enough to care for herself, the mother had completely neglected her and devoted her entire attention to the new baby.

Anne was very antagonistic toward her parents; she felt that they treated her cruelly and unjustly, and she hated her maternal grandmother to such an extent that she left the house when the latter came to visit. She, however, liked her paternal grandmother. Menstruation began at eleven and a half, and had occurred regularly. Anne planned to run away from home.

Diagnosis: primary behavior disorder, Oedipal type, with conduct disorders and neurotic symptoms.

Yolanda, twelve years old, a tall, obese girl, was brought for treatment because she associated with older, undesirable companions, both boys and girls. She stayed out late nights, threatened to leave home, lied, made demands for money and clothes, and when denied stayed in bed, cried, and refused to talk to her mother. She was described as being difficult, uncooperative, and disobedient at home, and fought violently with her mother. At school she had marked difficulty in concentrating on her studies and in understanding the subject matter. She was retarded in reading.

Yolanda suffered from many fears, such as staying at home alone and hearing murder stories on the radio. She could not fall asleep because she kept thinking of these stories. She also had crying spells, felt unhappy, had ticlike movements of her tongue, picked her lips, and continually touched the region of the navel with a rubbing movement. She was a nail-biter, untidy about her person and neglectful of her belongings.

Yolanda was the youngest of four children. Three of the older siblings were boys, one of whom died. The marital relations of the parents had always been strained. The parents frequently quarreled and actually beat each other in the presence of the children.

The mother beat Yolanda frequently and severely. Both brothers had been behavior problems. The father deserted the family on a number of occasions but always returned; he threatened to leave again unless a better and more harmonious life could be affected. Yolanda was fonder of the mother, who was an inconsistent, overanxious, sado-masochistic woman, who would at times overprotect the girl, then suddenly become domineering, rigid, and imperious. She demanded that Yolanda become brilliant, self-reliant, independent—in spite of her own infantilization of her daughter. The latter was unable to express her aggressions and handled her feelings by withdrawing and turning them inward. She clung to people in an overpossessive, dependent way, only to find herself rejected and excluded.

Diagnosis: mixed psychoneurosis, infantile character and conduct disorder.

Betty, thirteen and a half years old, was the third of five girls. The father had died when Betty was three years old, but the mother lived with her daughters. She had remarried shortly before treatment began with Betty.

The mother was a narcissistic, withdrawn person with paranoid features, irresponsible, unable to cope with her problems, completely indifferent to the family, neglectful of home and children to a degree that there was seldom food in the house. The girls had had to shift for themselves since childhood. The mother was very extravagant with money and ambitious for her children with regard to their education. At the same time she was envious and in a state of rivalry with them. She complained incessantly of ill health, and at the slightest excuse stayed away from home, where in any case she spent very little time. Two of Betty's sisters had also been under treatment.

Betty was an attractive girl who had had many serious and chronic illnesses. She had an attack of spinal meningitis at the age of three years, suffered from rheumatism, arthritis, and a defective heart, and had attended a hospital cardiac clinic for about nine years. Being an invalid from the time she was a little girl, she received instruction at home from teachers of the Board of Education. Betty was an isolate, had no friends, was in severe conflict with her siblings, entertaining particularly vicious hatred with homicidal phantasies toward one of her older sisters, as well as her mother. She was stubborn, very dependent on her mother, demanding that the latter stay close to her. Betty described herself as "my mother's shadow." She was given to temper tantrums, was sarcastic, and when she lost her temper, would bite and scratch. She was rigid, felt "dumb" and inadequate. At the time she was accepted for exclusive group treatment, Betty was still at home, tutored by a visiting teacher. (Soon after she was able to leave the house, attend school, and make some friends.)

Diagnosis: psychoneurosis.

Ella was twelve when she was referred for treatment by the school authorities because of suspected sexual activity with girls, specifically a younger colored friend. It must be noted that these accusations had not been confirmed. Because her father was dead and her mother employed, Ella was without supervision for most of the day. As a result she had been staying out late nights without permission and was becoming increasingly difficult to manage at home. The mother complained of her disrespectful language and the girl herself complained about having no friends.

Ella was one of two children. The brother, two years older than herself, like her father suffered from a heart ailment; he had also suffered from chorea. After the father's death, when Ella was eight years old, the brother attempted to take over the former's role and to discipline and manage Ella, who rebelled against him. Later this relationship between brother and sister became very warm, and there was suspicion of sexual play between the two. The brother was particularly protective of the girl and insisted that she look her best physically (see p. 166).

Ella was described as a strikingly beautiful girl with red hair and so well developed that she could easily be mistaken for a girl of seventeen. Despite her surface sophistication, she was immature and dependent. She was preoccupied with her appearance, was extremely careful with her English, and was trying to give the impression of being "refined." When, at the age of ten, menstruation began, Ella was unprepared and was somewhat frightened by the experience. She was described as a "bad milk drinker" and over-fastidious about food. At the time of referral her only friend was a girl several years older, who was reported as being sexually promiscuous. Ella talked considerably about a recent transfer to Junior High School and seemed to focus her interest on the sexual activities purported to have been carried on between the boys and girls. Her interest was disguised by protestations of horror at these occurrences.

The girl was antagonistic to her mother and despised her because of her very small size and foreign accent. Ella emphasized that she could not bear her mother's old-fashioned customs. The father, on the other hand, was a superior person in the girl's eyes. He spoke English perfectly and was socially very active. At the time of referral she identified herself with her father's family and saw herself as gay and active and looking like her father's brothers.

Diagnosis: primary behavior disorder, conduct type, with trends toward sexual delinquency.

RECORD OF SESSION (TWELFTH) [1]

Present: Ella, Yolanda, Betty, Anne.

The girls all came on time. As usual, Anne proceeded to hold the attention of the group. This time she asked permission to read a poem. Ella showed some irritation and told Anne that she had read her poems so many times at camp last summer that she knew them by heart. Anne did not seem to mind this rebuff and repeated her request. Betty and Yolanda now said they would like to hear it and Anne read her poem.

Disillusionment

Often I look up at the stars
I marvel at their loveliness
And strive to reach but one
But always it eludes my outstretched hand
And slips away into the inky sky.

Though I may climb to dizzy heights
The stars which seemed within my reach
Climb higher still, and slide
Out of my eager grasp.

[1] See note 2, p. 129.

When finally I have closed my hand
About the object of my desire
The sun's rays blind me
And I let it fall.

The therapist asked Anne what the poem meant to her. Anne said that whenever she attained her desire, there was always something else, something higher that dazzled her and she drops whatever she has. (A) Betty said she is not at all like that. She always likes what she has, but it is never enough for her. (B)

Ella always makes sure that she gets what she's after, and if she doesn't get it, she is very disappointed, "sensitive, I would say." Yolanda says that she tries and tries but rarely accomplishes what she is after and so she gives up. Ella said she is entirely different. She never gives up. The therapist asked her to give an example. Ella said that recently she missed two weeks of school. "By hook and by crook, I got my back lessons done," she added. The therapist asked her how she accomplished it. Ella said, "By being quiet and well behaved in class." Another example she gave was when she wanted to go to the circus. She had never seen a circus before and begged her mother to let her go, but her mother refused to give her money for it. Raising her head in a challenging way, Ella said: "So I went out, got a job sitting with a baby and made enough money by myself and went to the circus." (C)

Betty, who was doodling, said that is the only way she gets an allowance; no matter how sick she may be, she always manages to sit with some child and earn some money. (D) Yolanda said she tries very hard to be independent and carefully saves her money. She once finally accumulated a few dollars but her father needed the money, so she gave it to him. She has now given up all hope of getting what she wants—a new dress. (E)

Anne said that this was not so easy; it's hard to give up something. She finds it very difficult to part with anything that belongs to her. "I am a little bit like Yolanda. I'm charitable on the spur of the moment but then when I get to thinking of all the things I could have done with the money if I hadn't given it away, I feel unhappy. I know I am impulsive." The therapist asked whether her impulsiveness gets the better of her. No, she has learned to think twice, but she believes she is troubled with indecision, particularly when she goes shopping with her mother.

Ella wondered whether Anne's position is different from that of any other girl, and said: "It is a universal mother-daughter problem." Anne said it was the constant difference of opinion between herself and her mother that is at the bottom of it. She likes tailored clothes; her mother likes to see her dress in feminine things. (F)

This stimulated a discussion regarding the relation of age to the type of clothes one wears. Anne said that parents have a feeling that they never can learn from children. Betty disagreed with this; her mother lets her pick whatever she likes. (G) Ella said she prefers to turn to friends to help her. (H) Yolanda worked as a salesgirl last winter and her feeling is that in general, people are not considerate of salespeople. Now that she has herself experienced how badly people behave toward their sales help, she is very thoughtful of them. (I)

Anne again spoke of the difficulty she had had with her mother because of a dress that was to have been purchased for her. Whenever Anne selected a dress she liked, her mother preferred another one. Anne said vehemently, "I could have choked her with that dress." When the therapist asked her about this feeling, Anne at once expressed ambivalence. She said that she knows down deeply she really wants to please her mother, and proceeded to tell a story of a man she knew, whose wife drove him nearly crazy by nagging him and continually comparing him with another man, with whom she had once been in love. (J)

The question of flirtation came up. The girls were unanimous about being very self-conscious. Ella told Betty that she thinks Betty has a "deep inferiority complex." The latter turned directly to the therapist and asked why she is so self-conscious. The therapist turned the question on her, and she laughed, saying *she* was asking the questions. The therapist said that there were many reasons. (K)

Ella then said that she had read a book about "sex aberration and fetishism." Anne remarked that when she read "Idylls of the King," she got the feeling that in those days any woman was placed on a pedestal and worshiped by men, and men did everything for woman's glory. Ella said: "Why talk about 'Idylls of the King' and the women there; let's talk about masturbation. I read about that in a book." Betty looked directly at Ella and asked whether it had anything to do with sex. Anne also recalled reading about masturbation. Betty interrupted to change the subject, suggesting a discussion about interior decorating. Ella looked sharply at Betty and said that she "rudely interrupted." (L)

Anne then told about an argument she had with some boys about the supremacy of the male over the female. Of course, a fellow said that the male was superior, but "I just couldn't let him get away with it." Her mother gave her a stack of books on sex to read: "My mother is naive. She can't tell me herself and so she thought I could read about it." Ella recalled that she began asking her mother about sex; but when her mother put her off, telling her she would find out in due time, when she was older, Ella thought to herself, "It may be too late." (M)

Yolanda said that her friend Rachael's mother and father are both doctors. They had a sixteen-year-old patient who knew nothing at all about sex, so the patient and her boy-friend "experimented" and the girl became pregnant. Ella turned her conversation to her brother. Her brother punches her in the abdomen and she quarrels with him a great deal; but they make up easily. She said she has intimate talks with her brother. (N) Betty expressed her envy over Ella's having a brother. She wished she had a brother. (O)

Anne said that each time she goes out with a fellow, she notes that he becomes "wolfish," and she was wondering if maybe it's something in her that brings out the "wolf." She thinks that most boys are open to flattery. Anne cannot be flattered. She doesn't believe things that people say to her. (P) Betty spoke of an older man she knows who criticized his wife as he compared her with Betty. He spoke of Betty's "beautiful long fingernails" and his wife's that were in poor condition. He also spoke of Betty's neatness, and such things. (Q)

Ella said that Betty might have played up to the man. She herself does not do that; she is too blunt, and she is beginning to realize it gets her into trouble. Her teacher once said to her that she must not show her feelings. She knows she is very frank. Anne spoke of having had a crush on a fellow. She frankly asked him whether he liked her and tried to date him up, but he put her off. Betty said, "If he had taken you out, it would have been only to please you." She, Betty, could not possibly be frank with a fellow. Ella said that she, too, is that way. (R)

The session had to end abruptly as another group arrived, but the girls did not want to leave, saying, "We love the meetings." (S)

INTERPRETATION

(A) Anne's poem reflects her feelings of inferiority, inadequacy, and frustration. Her striving for "higher things" is a compensation for her failure, especially in her relations to her parents, and for physical unattractiveness and failure with boys. By setting her aims so high, inadequacies in ordinary matters become less important, failure less disturbing, and the threat to the ego is diminished. Anne's entire pattern is one of ego-defense. Ella, who has strong masculine drives and penis envy, responds to Anne in a characteristic manner. Anne's feminine interests irritate Ella. Of great value to Anne is the ego support she receives from the other two girls when they display interest in her poem.

(B) Betty, having been circumscribed and limited in her social experiences and affectional life, is unable to identify with Anne's strivings. She rather would like to have more love, more affection. In this statement she reveals her "affect hunger." It also makes her stand out as different from Anne, which gives her some satisfaction, but we can suspect that Anne's creative effort and her drive for "higher things" creates anxiety in Betty.

(C) Here Ella reveals her basic masculine drives, which is her nuclear problem. She cannot submit to anyone. She must always be the potent, successful person. This becomes plausible from our knowledge that she is close to her brother, which she reveals later in the discussion (p. 160), and probably indulges in sex play with him. She expresses here her desire to possess the potency of her brother, namely, a penis like his. To possess a penis means to master. It may seem that by being quiet in class, quite unlike her, Ella submitted to the teacher. Actually, this was not submission, but a technique leading to mastery, and a means for attaining what she wanted. This is confirmed by the manner in which she raises her head in a challenging way when she describes how she earned money to get what she desired.

Yolanda, on the other hand, reveals basic feelings of inadequacy. Her intelligence is low, and she is generally an undeveloped and infantile person. She is resigned to failure and accepts her subordinate position without demur. The fact that Yolanda can bring her feelings to the surface without losing status is very helpful; this fact becomes quite evident in later sessions and in her general improvement.

By asking Ella how she made up the two weeks lost at school, the therapist changed the course of the girl's free association. It would have been better to ask *why* she did it, and thus help her delve into her motivations. The therapist changed the focus from the intrapsychic process to the *modus operandi.*

Betty is made more aware of her inadequacies through the comparative strength of the others. She reacts to anxiety by doodling and claiming that she, too, has earned money as a baby sitter. This is doubtful, since she is a very sickly girl and could not go out of the house evenings; but she now has a motive for not appearing helpless or less adequate than the others. As treatment proceeded we found that Betty was physically more robust than she had appeared, and she became active and independent.

This incident again demonstrates the importance of proper grouping. The discussion emphasized Betty's inferiorities, which may have had an undesirable effect had she not had the strength to deal with her feelings at the group sessions.

(E) Here Yolanda reveals her rivalry with her mother and her desire to replace her. She had given up to her father that which she cherished most; she also demonstrated to him that she is better to him than his wife. (This is confirmed in a later interview, when she actually verbalized that her mother is not worthy of her father, and implied that she could have made him a much better wife than her mother.) The fact that she sacrificed a dress may have special meaning, namely, that she was willing to undress for him, and may have special significance at her age when the Oedipal conflict is reactivated.

(F) Throughout this discussion, as in many other statements, Anne reveals ambivalence in everything she does. She is good, then regrets it. She realizes that she is impulsive, but denies it when questioned by the therapist. However, she recognizes that she is "troubled with indecision"—a very important step toward emotional maturity, namely, the elimination of ambivalence.

Her preference for tailored clothes may be a defense against being a woman, that is, a rejection of anything that resembles her mother, a form of adolescent rebellion, or masculine identification.

One can expect two therapeutic results from such interchange. By asking Anne whether her impulses get the best of her, the therapist gave the girl an opportunity to examine her mechanisms and gain insight into her own mental processes. Another important therapeutic result from what Ella says about the "universal mother-daughter" problem is the diminishing of Anne's guilt through universalization.

(G) It seems that whatever the subject of conversation, Anne's conflict with her mother is uppermost in her mind. In saying that parents think they cannot learn from children, she says: "I am as good as my mother and I can be as useful to my father as my mother is. But my mother blocks me. I am a child and I must submit to her. I don't want to submit to her. I want to submit to my father." At this stage Anne is in negative transference toward the therapist who represents the mother figure.

(H) Ella, who rejects her mother, turns to friends for help. In this statement we must suspect that Ella is also telling the therapist that she too is a bad mother and that she rejects the therapist as she does her real mother. The therapist overlooked an opportunity to deal with the transference at this point. A question like, "You don't trust me either," or, "Are you telling me that you don't like me, too?" would be in place. The negative feelings that Ella has toward the mother and therapist should be brought out and dealt with.

(I) Yolanda, who feels inferior to the other girls, identifies with a subordinate group, salesgirls, whose friend she is now.

(J) Again Anne brings forth her conflict with her mother: she continues in her groove. When she says that she wanted to strangle her mother, Anne gets nearer to her wish and, as the therapist focuses attention on this, Anne is frightened by the revelation and denies it. The therapist's question had set up anxiety; and, Anne, as a placation to her superego, tells of a man who almost went insane because his wife nagged him the way her mother nags her. The fact that she brings in insanity at this point is significant, but its meaning is unclear. Could it be that she perceives the relation between insanity and her incest drives?

(K) Anne's story of the nagging wife who had been in love with another man brought the idea of flirtation to the fore, namely, a relationship without sexual intercourse, which is what girls of this age desire. This is in turn associated with self-consciousness.

The therapist failed by evading the question. She should have explained the nature of self-consciousness, that it is a transitional stage in the development of young people which disappears as they grow older. Explanations of this order are helpful at such times. It would also have been helpful to Betty had the therapist explained that since she spent so much time at home, she could be expected to be self-conscious more than most, but that now that she gets out more her self-consciousness will diminish. This would have given the situation a realistic base and Betty would have been reassured. When she turned to the therapist with her question Betty was seeking reassurance which she did not receive.

Sometimes it is possible to deal with such matters more deeply and to indicate that self-consciousness is a conflict between sexual desire and the fear of it. For girls of this age, the present explanation is more suitable. Older adolescents may be given the latter explanation. However, the significance of the conversation does not escape even these girls, as we shall see in what immediately follows.

(L) Ella perceives the meaning of the subject discussed and speaks about sex. Sexual aberrations may have some connection with the brother about whom she speaks later in the session. Because the therapist has evaded the question, Ella, who is preoccupied with sex, punishes her by blurting out the most prohibited of subjects: perversions. This defiance was evident in her manner.

Anne, made anxious by Ella's remark, diverts the discussion to women being placed on a pedestal and worshiped by men, a common adolescent wish. But Ella, whom we suspect of being no stranger to sexual abnormalities, and who is not psychoneurotic, is not afraid to bring the question forward. She says bluntly: "Let's talk about masturbation."

Betty being the least mature and the most restricted does not know, or pretends not to know, the meaning of the term. Encouraged by Ella, Anne, who sought to prevent this conversation, now confesses that she recalls reading about it, indicating that Anne's anxiety has been diminished through Ella's "boldness."

Betty, who is less informed on sexual matters than the others, does not understand the conversation and naively suggests the subject be changed to interior decorating, which is a major interest with her. (She is planning to make it her profession when she grows up.)

In this conversation the girls reveal their hostility toward the therapist. With the possible exception of Betty, they are all in negative transference. Ella, being the least conflicted, serves as a catalytic agent, but this discussion also illustrates the difficulties patients experience when in a given situation their psychologic syndromes are not homogeneous (see p. 239). Anne is shocked by Ella's frankness and Betty remains confused and puzzled.

(M) Again Anne relates a conflict. Now the conflict is between maleness and femaleness, which is rather significant in terms of the homoerotic undercurrent in the group at the moment. Anne's anxiety reasserts itself, and on this score she brings the element of maleness into the conversation. There is also implied an attack on the therapist for not having boys in the group. This resentment was openly expressed by the group of girls in the institution (p. 214), but it is in the background here as well. Denial of boys by the therapist is one of the sources of negative transference in groups for adolescents and girls in puberty.

As Anne recalls the male-female conflict, the image of the mother appears and she talks of her mother's inadequacy. The mother cannot even explain to her "the facts of life." Mother is not only a poor wife to the father, but a poor mother as well. She is useless in both roles. When she says, "My mother is naive," she really means, "My mother is inadequate." The mother is too "naive" to understand Anne's desires to possess the father. When Ella says that, when she herself learns about these facts, "it may be too late," and is probably referring to her relation with her brother.

Again the girls reveal their negative transference to the therapist when they talk about the inadequacy of their mothers. The therapist, however, fails to interpret it or to help the girls explore further their attitudes toward sex, boys, and themselves. At some stages it is in order to supply direct information that patients are unmistakably seeking. Educational therapy at this point would have helped Anne, especially.

(N) Yolanda at once senses the meaning of Ella's statement ("it may be too late") and tells the story of the girl who became pregnant, and Ella associates this with her relation to her brother, giving further credence to the suspicion of sex play or more serious sex activity between the two.

It may be helpful to note the following in relation to Ella and her brother. Her brother, had suffered from chorea, had been "cured" but was now a cardiac. We do not know whether his illnesses are psychogenic or somatogenic. His ambition is to be the most perfect specimen of masculinity in the United States, and he indulges in a variety of exercises to accomplish this. The boy is well built and very attractive and insists that his sister, too, must look beautiful. He demands that she make up to look outstandingly pretty but forbids her staying out after ten o'clock in the evening.

The meaning of all this is quite evident. He wants his sister to himself; therefore, he does not wish her to be out late and be exposed to the possibility of anyone else having her. He wants her to be pretty so that he can be attracted to, and proud of, her, and is himself doing all he can to be desirable so that she would have no interest in other boys. In the light of this, Ella's saying, "it may be too late," has special meaning. She is vaguely aware of the danger. The brother's punching her abdomen is both a sexual attack and a prohibition against becoming pregnant.

(O) Betty probably means: "I wish I had what your brother has. Then I would be stronger, healthier, and more adequate than I am."

(P) Anne is an unattractive girl and is not sought after by boys. In speaking of boys becoming wolfish, she actually expresses a desire to be attractive and sought after. She covers it over by saying that she wondered whether it was something in her. The statement that she cannot be flattered and is difficult to get is pure phantasy. It is a stratagem to build up her self-esteem.

(Q) When Betty speaks of an older man who compared his wife unfavorably with her, it is quite possible that she has in mind her stepfather, who, we know, is very fond of and very good to her. By this statement she expresses her wish, or probably her conviction, that her stepfather is so nice to her because he really desires her and not her mother. Considering Betty's immaturity, restricted life, and feelings of inferiority, this reference to herself in such a complimentary way is very significant. It indicates a growing self-image of a healthier nature.

(R) Ella reveals her lack of interest in boys; she is blunt with them, that is, she doesn't want them; she really wants her brother and therefore resists the advances of other boys or is afraid of a repetition of her relations with her brother. Anne can now reveal her basic inadequacy in relation to boys, which she has heretofore tried to cover up. This is a truer picture of herself than the earlier one. Just as Betty is able to accept a more positive image of herself, Anne is now able to accept a more realistic view of herself.

Her ego is strengthened by being accepted in the group, which gives her courage to see herself as she is. Such self-acceptance is one of the major aims of psychotherapy.[2] An adolescent girl who was particularly unattractive, physically, had been committed to an institution for sexual delinquency. After being helped to discover a genuine artistic talent and to appreciate her intellect, she once said: "I was thinking about myself. I know I am not good-looking, but not all men want good-looking women. Some like them smart." [3]

(S) It is unfortunate that other arrangements had not been made that would not require the group to be displaced by another. The schedule was rearranged. The girls' expression of their love for the group is unquestionably a disguise for the negative feelings toward the therapist which characterized this whole session.

DISCUSSION

The group interview of these girls, at the age of puberty, differs in several respects from that of the girls in later adolescence (Chapter XI).[4] In the first place the sexual content is not so boldly expressed; the girls are still in a state of latency or just emerging from it. There is no reference to intercourse, nor has there been any reference to it in the entire course of treatment in this group, while

[2] S. R. Slavson, *An Introduction to Group Therapy* (New York, Commonwealth Fund, 1943), pp. 197–201.

[3] Slavson, "An Elementaristic Approach to the Understanding and Treatment of Delinquency," *The Nervous Child*, October, 1947.

[4] See pp. 182–189.

this subject appears frequently in the interviews of the older girls. The younger girls are also less homoerotic. There is little interest expressed in each other's appearance, clothes, figures, and such matters. The girls also do not dance with one another as the older girls do.

There is considerable diversity in the levels of development and maturity in individual members of the group, especially in matters of sex and social maturation. Ella is by far more sophisticated than is Anne or Yolanda, and Betty lags far behind the others.

The central subject of the discussions is independence rather than a manifest sexual drive. They seek freedom from the domination of their mothers, even though behind it is the Oedipal involvement. The period of individuation is still in operation here, as against social reintegration in the case of older girls. The topics of conversation and the special target of their hostility are their mothers and not the fathers. They are closer to the Oedipal conflict.

Anne's conflict with her mother has a realistic foundation. Her mother is a rejecting and cruel person, but Anne's repetition of the topic has meaning in terms of the transference to the therapist, which requires clearing up.

CHAPTER ELEVEN

ANALYTIC GROUP PSYCHOTHERAPY WITH ADOLESCENT GIRLS

RECORD AND INTERPRETATION

CASE HISTORIES[1]

SANDRA was a very attractive girl. Her blonde hair was bleached and touched up to appear "glamorous." She used cosmetics excessively and actually appeared older than her age. She affected a carefree air but grew serious when discussing music and art, in which she had superior talent. She was excessively interested in herself and spoke about her abilities a great deal of the time. She had many phantasies, especially after retiring at night, and frequently spoke of harmonious family life in her home as a reality, which was far from being the case.

Sandra came for treatment through the police department, who apprehended her after a run-away escapade with another girl, Helen. In this Sandra was aided and abetted by her mother, who was in serious conflict with her husband and whom she disliked intensely. Sandra stayed away from home overnight on a number of occasions and picked up sailors on the street. There was constant wrangling in the family about money, the father being a miserly person, giving the family insufficient funds to meet expenses, and grudgingly at that. Sandra truanted from school a great deal until she was transferred to an art school, in which she was interested.

The father was a punitive, rejecting, strict person. He indulged the second of his three daughters, Sandra being the youngest. There was very strong sibling rivalry between these two girls, for which Sandra was blamed by the parents, who considered her a "trouble-maker." The mother, who infantilized the girl and had never given her any responsibilities in the home, complained of Sandra's stub-

[1] The ages of the girls in this group at the time of referral were 15.6 to 17 years.

bornness and described the girl as restless and as having a very short span of concentration. The father, on the other hand, was distrustful of her and called her abusive names, such as "tramp." Sandra described herself as lazy and "dizzy" and admitted that she got herself into trouble. The father was so restrictive that even on hot summer nights he insisted that Sandra go to bed at nine o'clock in the evening.

The girl was upset by the friction and strife between her parents. The mother was considered inferior to the father, both by him and the daughters. It seemed that the father was unable to meet the mother's sexual demands, and she had sexual relations with other men. (At one of the group sessions Sandra said she wished she could have been somebody's favorite child; she always wanted a father whom she could love; she wanted to be affectionate with her father. She remembered that even when she was a little girl, she could not bring herself to put her hand in his and call him "Daddy." She wished she could call him "Daddy." What does she call him? She giggled self-consciously and said, "Pa.")

Diagnosis: behavior disorder, pre-Oedipal group, conduct type.

Rose, a refugee from Nazi Germany, had undergone a series of traumatic experiences as a very young child, on the flight with her family from Europe. She was raped on at least two occasions during this flight. When she came for treatment, Rose cried frequently for no apparent reason, and was suffering from frightening dreams, nightmares, and "general nervousness." She frequently became irritated and depressed, the reason for which she could not fathom. She was suspicious of people, unfriendly, seclusive, and distrustful of men particularly. Rose bit her nails when excited and had bodily tremors, which dated back to eight years of age, when she also began to scream at her mother and brother.

Rose's father suffered from depression, largely because of the sharp decline in his social and economic status. From his status as a wealthy businessman in Germany, he had been reduced to that of a menial worker here. Rose was very sensitive about and reacted intensely to her father's moods. The father treated her as an infant and was unable to accept her strivings for independence as an adolescent. Rose was an only child for six years, and recalls how her father played with her when she was about four, something he had not done since. Although she had wanted a brother, she resented his coming and vomited at the time of his birth.

Rose was a well developed, attractive girl, who seemed eager for friends but unable to establish relationships. A study of this case revealed that the girl's early Oedipal drives had not been adequately resolved and that her sexual preoccupations were very intense. These she shared with only one girl, her closest friend, who was also under treatment. Menstruation set in at ten years, and had always been accompanied by pains. She knew about menstruation, but did not confide this knowledge to her mother. The girl considered herself a martyr and she saw herself as a mother substitute to her brother from the time she was eight years old. She bathed and fed him, which, it seemed, her parents expected her to do, and took over much of the household duties from the time she was ten.

Diagnosis: psychoneurosis with obsessional elements.

Bertha was a tall, slender girl of sixteen, I.Q. 126. Because of her thin face and prominent nose, she was sometimes referred to by her teachers as "Pinocchio." She had brown hair, often worn in extreme fashion, but seldom neatly combed. She had very attractive large blue eyes. Her clothes were always messy and she was generally neglectful of appearance. Under individual treatment she began to take better care of herself and to use lipstick, wearing a cupid's bow.

Bertha was not self-conscious, related well to people, and spoke with candor and ease, but in a monotone. She seemed to lack affect and talked of all matters impassively, as though she were discussing the weather. She had a strong sense of justice and reacted with anger to anything she considered unjust, whether it was directed against her or not.

Bertha truanted from school and her mother complained that she was "loud-mouthed, stole money from an older sister, and had a quick temper." She kept late hours, lied, had undesirable friends, fought with her seventeen-year-old brother, invoked God when in difficulty, acted in a precocious manner, was always late, even for meals, and was distrustful toward her parents (it was suspected that she knew about her father's extramarital relations).

The parents had been at loggerheads since the beginning of their married life; even when the mother was pregnant with Bertha, the father carried on affairs with other women. The father was attached to and influenced by Bertha to such an extent that whenever the mother wished to get anything from him she asked Bertha to intercede for her. Bertha and the mother, on the other hand, had violent quarrels, and the girl tended to ignore her mother, an unhappy, insecure woman who had borne seven unpremeditated children. She was disappointed in her marriage and insulted and humiliated by her husband, children, and her daughter-in-law.

In Bertha's many altercations with her brother the mother sided with him, to Bertha's great resentment. She complained that her mother cursed, insulted, and humiliated her even in the presence of her friends. The fights between the daughter and mother were so violent that they threw things at one another, on one occasion breaking a large mirror.

Bertha was brought up on a farm and had come to live in a large city only a year before she was referred for treatment. Before Bertha was born, three children were killed in accidents, and both father and mother felt guilty about it. A maternal aunt was actively attempting to set Bertha against her father.

Diagnosis: behavior disorder, conduct and habit type, neurotic symptoms.

Reva was extremely infantile and felt inferior. Although good looking, she considered herself unattractive, was unable to meet responsibilities such as getting to school on time or keeping appointments, was withdrawn, and felt that no one liked her because she was too quiet. She had no friends, stayed home from school a great deal of the time, and constantly fussed with her face, imagining she had pimples. She was described as nervous, screamed when angry and bit her nails. She used to be afraid of the dark, of strangers and of dogs. Reva was always jealous of her younger brother, who by now was much taller than she and more mature. She frequently fought with him. When Reva began attending school, she cried a great deal and vomited.

Reva saw herself as babyish and having little self-confidence. She did not feel "as good as other people," and said that she was unable to look directly at them. Generally, her attitude toward herself was that she was a failure. Exacerbation of psychoneurotic symptoms had occurred six months before her treatment when a dog that she was taking care of fell from a roof and was killed.

Reva was the oldest of three children, the others being boys. Both father and mother and the next younger brother were all diagnosed as psychoneurotic. The youngest, who was around nine years of age, was also retarded and such a serious behavior problem that he had to be institutionalized. The mother overprotected all the children, while the father, an irritable man, got into temper tantrums and beat them severely.

The central problem as revealed by this girl was her very strong envy of her brother and attachment to her father. It was felt that she was in the midst of the Oedipal conflict and was functioning on the level of a very young child. Reva had not taken on any of the adolescent mannerisms or behavior common to youngsters of her age. She dressed and fixed her hair neatly, but in a childish manner. She was generally insecure and shy, either twisting a handkerchief or pressing it tightly in the palm of her hand when speaking to someone. When she came for treatment she spoke in a confidential tone, complained of headaches and that her eyes got red when she studied or read. In individual treatment Reva was very resistive and proved to be inaccessible. She constantly broke appointments, partly because she was indifferent to the time factor, but largely because she was unable to establish a personal relation.

Diagnosis: psychoneurosis with infantile character development.

Lydia was a tall, slender girl, with a stiff, upright carriage, and an attractive and refined appearance. She wore her hair in a bizarre fashion, with a high pompadour, her lips heavily rouged, harlequin glasses, and stared for long periods without blinking. One of Lydia's characteristics was her lack of affect. Even when she spoke of the death of her favorite grandmother or her hatred for her mother's boy friend there was no change in her expression. She rarely smiled.

Lydia was one of two children; her sister, three and a half years older than she, was married.

In a psychometric test Lydia received a rating of 135. She had an excellent school record, which suddenly deteriorated. The specific complaint was that formerly a quiet and well-behaved girl, she had begun to go around with young people older than herself, kept late hours, and did not disclose her whereabouts. She suddenly changed from a good, studious, rather submissive and obedient girl into an aggressive, quarrelsome individual. She was also enuretic.

The mother and father had been separated since Lydia was about nine years old. The father visited the home after remarriage and made sexual advances to his former wife. Lydia was strongly affected by the separation of her parents. She felt she had been let down by them, especially by her father. The mother, a very strict woman, never seemed satisfied with Lydia's achievements and even when she brought high marks from school, the mother thought that they should still be higher. Lydia was greatly disappointed at this.

She once attempted to run away from home with a girl friend; the latter stole a watch and a ring from Lydia's sister for the purpose, but instead sold the watch and bought clothes for herself.

Diagnosis: latent schizophrenia.

Paula, with a minimal I.Q. of 94, presented a confused picture in her psychosocial development. When she came for treatment, she walked and acted like a boy, spoke in a low-pitched, coarse voice, used profane language as early as the age of twelve. At the same time she dressed prettily and her hair was arranged in numerous curls that hung all around her head. She said she liked to have curls so that boys could pull them.

Paula was a short, stocky, well-developed girl with dark eyes and a small pale face framed by the numerous dark curls. Menstruation began at ten and a half. Paula had an overpowering hostility toward her mother and all women. Women angered her very easily. She adored her father, and was described as "man-mad." She built all sorts of romantic stories about herself in which innocent male friends of the family played unsavory roles. At school, she did poorly, giggled, talked a great deal, and was retarded in some subjects. One of her ambitions from early childhood was to be a policewoman.

As a child Paula tried to push her mother out of bed so that she could get in with her father and even at the time she was in treatment, would call her father in to wash her hair while in the nude. She openly resented her father's attention to the mother. Paula's chief problem was seen as a fairly serious confusion in her sexual identifications. She could not accept the female role and phantasied herself as a boy, largely because her father was the love-giving person in the family, the mother being harrassed, disturbed and authoritarian. The father, on the other hand, had been an irresponsible, youthful person; he was rather fond of Paula, though he had serious conflicts with the two boys older than our patient. There were also two younger girls in the family, one of whom was a baby.

Intensive individual psychotherapy was required for this girl. Transference to a female worker was the chief aim; however, it was found that to enhance her identifications with women, it was necessary for her to have a group experience. She was, therefore, referred at the age of twelve to an activity therapy group in which she remained for four years. This experience was of inestimable value to the girl, both in terms of observable results and her own intense enthusiasm and the feelings of satisfaction that she derived from it. At one point it was found that there were only two women in the world whom she trusted. They were her caseworker and the activity group therapist.

When Paula reached the age of sixteen, she was placed in an interview group. After a year and one half of this, it was decided to terminate treatment altogether and give her an opportunity to test herself against the world, with an option to return if she so desired.[2]

Diagnosis: behavior disorder, Oedipal type, with severely narcissistic character.

At thirteen and a half, Georgia was referred for psychiatric treatment because of general social maladjustment, lack of friends, excessive dependence upon her mother, resistance to going to school, shyness, and bizarre choreoform tics which included facial grimaces, movement of the tongue and lips, head jerk, and involuntary shuffling of the feet. The tics were first observed when she was seven years old and diagnosed as Sydenham's Chorea. The girl received hospital treatment for more than six years. The physicians at the

[2] See abstract from record on p. 64.

hospital finally suspected psychogenic causes and referred the patient for psychotherapy. After a period of individual treatment, she was referred to group therapy at about fifteen and a half years of age. On referral, Georgia was still subject to tics, spent much time daydreaming, staring into space until her eyes "blurred." As a small child she dreamed of dragons and snakes and had nightmares of dragons crawling on her and lifting her high into the air. When she came for group treatment, her dreams were about boys and dates. She considered herself worthless, had no friends, and was exceedingly hostile toward her mother and older sister.

The parents were seriously maladjusted, the mother being a power-driven, aggressive woman, who managed the household and the children with an iron hand and beat Georgia mercilessly to stop the tics, the cause for which the mother could not understand. Georgia was the butt of her mother's criticisms and fault-finding; she was constantly compared unfavorably with other children and her older sister. In addition Georgia was very tall and the children called her "daddy long-legs."

The father was a narcissistic, infantile, provocative person, given to temper tantrums, and resorted to yelling and screaming. He neglected the family but liked Georgia, though even with her he was usually inconsistent. She was strongly attached to him.

Diagnosis: mixed psychoneurosis with hysterical features, depression, conversion and withdrawal symptoms.[3]

RECORD OF SESSION (THIRTY-THIRD)

Present: Rose, Sandra, Paula, Reva, Georgia, Lydia, Bertha [4]

Paula, Rose, Sandra, Reva and Bertha came on time. Paula did not look well. She had a wan expression on her face and appeared to have lost weight. Sandra told the girls that she had left high school. The girls expressed their disapproval; they thought Sandra should continue with her schooling, but she said she had given the matter a great deal of thought. In fact, she had not fallen asleep until three in the morning before she made her decision as to whether continu-

[3] For a detailed anamnesis, full treatment history and outcome on this case, see *The Practice of Group Therapy*, ed. S. R. Slavson (New York, International Universities Press, 1947), 197–218. In that report Gloria is named Lilly Sloane, both names being fictitious.

[4] See note 2, p. 129.

ing school could or could not help her. She had decided on her future work and school would only hinder rather than help. She wants to be a song writer and, to do this, she needs to have not only time to practice, write the music, orchestrate and arrange it, but she needs to spend time with the lyricist and to contact publishing agencies to sell her songs. She practices the piano a great deal and finds that school interferes. She simply must give up something and it is much easier for her to give up school. (A)

Georgia came in at this point and, not being aware of the content of the conversation, interrupted. She apologized for being absent from the last session. She was very ill, having become ill in the office and her boss was extremely kind to her. She was greatly affected by his sympathy. Since she had a discussion with him on politics, just prior to the elections, he had "treated her royally." In fact, the boss's wife, too, has become a friend of hers. Georgia was wearing a corsage and this was commented on by the girls, to which Georgia responded with much animation. She said that she had had a date with Leon the night before and gave some details about the entertainment. With this she showed the therapist her report card. She was disconcerted not to have received one of the highest marks in shorthand. (B)

The entertainment that Leon had planned for her was not a great success. He had given her three choices of places to go. She had to work all day from nine to five-thirty and was so tired when she got home that all she could do was go to a movie. She displayed her corsage and let all the girls smell the roses. (C)

The therapist said at this point that it was difficult for her to take down all the conversation and wondered about the possibility of having a stenographer at the meetings to take notes. Georgia at once volunteered, saying that it would be very helpful in learning stenography. The girls thought it a splendid idea. The therapist gave Georgia a notebook and two sharp pencils.[5]

By this time Lydia had also arrived. All the girls complimented Reva, who seemed to grow more attractive with each session. She now wore her hair very becomingly and dressed attractively. At this session she wore a very pretty dress and the girls spoke of it. Reva acknowledged their compliments modestly and added that even her

[5] This plan was abandoned after this session by the girls themselves.

mother said that she has a "pretty form" in it. Lydia began to talk about food fads, when Sandra interrupted to tell a dream she had had since the last session. (D)

Sandra dreamed that she was at the piano giving her best efforts to practicing when a small ape, or it may have been a small polar bear, came and stood near her and interfered with her practicing. She was a little afraid of the animal, but actually didn't mind it too much. Finally when it persisted in trying to interrupt her, she ran to her mother's room, but the ape followed her and she begged her mother to take it away. The ape, however, stuck to her. Sandra then ran out of the house, but the ape clung to her. She struck it, and the ape sank its teeth into Sandra's arm. Sandra kept trying to free herself and the struggle continued for sometime. Laughingly, she said: "It's just like in dreams," for suddenly there was Helen instead of the ape. Helen said: "Don't go in again and practice. If you do, I'll turn into an ape again." Sandra paid no attention and turned to go back home. As she reached the threshold, Helen changed into an ape again. (At this point Sandra stood up, stooped over, and let her long arms dangle forward and said that was just the way the ape's arms were hanging down.) She then awakened.

Sandra herself interpreted the dream. "Just as I have said before, I think Helen holds me down," and the ape is supposed to be a human animal but of low mentality. (Helen had induced Sandra in the past to go on blind dates, pick up sailors, run away from home and participate in other delinquencies. Sandra had often told the girls that Helen was not bright.) Bertha said that Helen clings to Sandra, though Sandra wants to shake herself free of her. Sandra said that she can still recall how scared she was. Lydia said, "Sandra, I believe you're cutting your nose off to spite your face by going with Helen. Helen seems to do you more harm than good." The therapist then asked Sandra whether, instead of the ape being Helen, it might not have been her father. (E)

Sandra giggled briefly and said that when she was little, her father used to frighten her by making faces and threatening her. She said, "I hate him, and I pity him." Bertha said Sandra was involved with her father too much and that he clings to her, too. Her own father, Bertha said, often gets mad at her and then he looks like a beast ready to pounce on his prey. Paula laughed out loud and said, it's queer that Bertha should have said this. Her father sort of frightens her, too. He has a habit of yelling. She thinks that he yells because he is in pain. (F)

Bertha had taken care of her sister's baby the preceding Friday night and arranged to sleep away from home. She told her father about it, also that she would be sleeping with her sister's neighbors. The mother visited her sister and Bertha told the mother that she planned to sleep there again the following night. No one from home telephoned to inquire about her, and her sister commented that it looked as though her parents did not care much about her. When Bertha got home Sunday night, her father was very angry and asked her: "Who the hell said you could sleep over?" He insinuated that she slept "with a fellow." Bertha was almost in tears. Reva asked Bertha why her father didn't trust her. She doesn't know why. She was "giddy in the past," but she had been "acting much better lately." She was so angry at her father that she told him that he was far from being an ideal parent to her; she talked to him at great length. But before she finished, he began to hit her and for once her mother took her part and threatened to leave home if he beat Bertha. Bertha said that her father is jealous of her mother and he used to accuse her of having affairs with other men. It finally got to a state where each accused the other of extramarital relations. Last night, when her father was so angry and beat her, Bertha cast it up to him and reminded him of the kind of environment they were creating for her. She asked him whether he felt that it was the proper thing to do for a growing child. Her father made no reply to this. (G)

Rose said that her father has his peculiarities, too. He "stirs up his anger and then there is murder." Lydia believes there is insanity in her father's family. Her paternal grandmother committed suicide. Two of her paternal aunts became mentally unbalanced. Laughingly she added, "My father is wacky." She described how, when they lived in the suburbs in a beautiful, attractively furnished house, the family were once seated around the dining room table, chatting. Her father suddenly threw a candelabra at his mother. He threw his lighted cigar at her and then broke the dishes and windows. In fact, he wrecked the house. Lydia described in detail the lovely carved oak furniture, the gold-lace curtains, the candelabras.

The cause of his anger was an argument between her mother and the grandmother. Lydia said that her sister had the same kind of temper. Sandra said that while in her family things do not reach such extremes, her father, when he gets angry, throws the silverware at her. Georgia recalled distinctly that when she was a little girl, her father used to be like that, too. He would wreck things, kick at the door, and was generally pretty destructive. (H)

Bertha said that listening to all of this and thinking about it, has made her realize that she never loved her father, but like Sandra, she pities him. The reason for this conclusion is that she senses weakness in him. Today her father humbly apologized to her and sort of offered to buy her off by telling her that she could buy whatever clothes she wishes.

Sandra said that at this point she couldn't sympathize with her father very much, she felt angry at him. Why angry? Because when she returned home after her runaway, he suspected her of having had sexual intercourse. Rose asked Sandra what else could she have expected. Sandra very angrily asked, "What do you mean?" Rose said that her father apparently was aware of her habit of picking up sailors, but she could understand why Sandra ran away. Sandra said: "Well, why not? I did it to make up for the love I don't get at home." Lydia asked if Sandra felt like an outcast in the family, and added, "Sandra, I guess it is hard to break a vicious circle." Sandra said that her father should have realized that people run away from home because they are unhappy, not because they want to be bums. (I)

At this point Sandra said timidly that she had been rewriting her biography, and the girls asked her to read it to them. All sat in rapt silence as Sandra read it. Rose and Lydia seemed most impressed by Sandra's talent. The others, as well, gave Sandra a great deal of praise. Reva (not to be outdone, it seemed) raised her voice and said that she, too, was writing. Her's is not a biography but a short story. The girls asked her to read it, which she did. The same attention given Sandra was given also Reva. When Reva read her story, the girls were so affected by it, that Georgia said it brought tears to her eyes and she had noticed that several other girls looked tearful too. Reva read with much feeling and at the end, Paula offered to type as much of Sandra's biography as was ready, and said she would continue typing it until it was completed. Sandra handed the sheets over to Paula. At this point, Bertha offered to type Reva's story.

The girls commented that though Reva's story was very nice and very interesting, she had made a few grammatical errors. Bertha asked whether Reva would mind if she corrected them while she typed. Reva said she would be very glad; she was aware of having made some errors. Lest Sandra feel underpraised, the girls again gave her a great deal of credit for her biography. They said they recognized that in her description of the delinquent girl, she was talking about herself. (Sandra displayed no affect when this was pointed out to her.) (J)

Rose returned to the discussion of fathers. She said she was still thinking about her relationship with her father. She repeated an incident she had narrated many months ago in individual treatment. When she was a little girl and misbehaved her father used to threaten to make her poor, to throw her out of the house so that she would become a beggar. With a note of sarcasm in her voice, Sandra said that her father used to threaten to cut off one of her braids, so that she would look grotesque.

The therapist said that it seemed that all the girls fear their fathers and asked what it is they are so afraid of. Paula interrupted to say it is not only the fathers. Her boy friend Jim told her that her mother is "sinister." Paula did not know the meaning of the word. The girls looked it up in a dictionary on the therapist's desk. Paula said with a sad expression on her countenance, "I've been jipped." She added, "You see, it isn't only the fathers; it's the mothers, too."

When Paula's father saw her on Jim's lap, he told her to get "the hell off his lap." Paula argued with her father and questioned why he should feel like that about it; they weren't doing anything. Her father ought to be glad that she sits on Jim's lap in his presence rather than when his back is turned, but her father called her vile names just the same.

Bertha said she could never pet or fondle a boy friend or sit on his lap in the presence of her father. In fact, she can't even let a fellow hold her hand. Lydia said that in the presence of all, the family and friends, she sat on Max's lap and went *into* Joe. Paula didn't let her finish and said, "Lydia, I think you want what Joe has." Lydia said she doesn't want anything that Joe has. Paula asked her how long had she been going with Joe. Lydia said from February to June.

Paula then said, "Lydia, I think you want Joe's penis." Lydia raised her head challengingly and said, "Not if it were offered to me on a silver platter." She tried to explain what she had meant to say, but Paula sort of laughed her down and said: "Anyway, Lydia, you made a nice slip ('into')." Lydia denied that it had any special meaning and said that she kicked Joe out of the house only last night. Lydia went on to say that she had moods when at school. She was not interested in boys; boys did not affect her as much as they seemed to affect the other girls. Sandra and Rose both said they had moods and "can imagine things and cry over them."

Reva had tried several times to say something and finally got her chance just before the end of the session. She has met several times the sailors (of whom she had spoken to the group before), and spent some time talking with them. (This was during World War II.) They were very nice, respectable boys and Reva enjoys talking to them, but her father acted strangely about it. He yelled at her so that he scared her, he was so angry. He told her that she must never see them again. Reva tried to explain that she had made no dates; she never knows when she will meet them. She can't help it if they happen to be on the street when she is, but her father was adamant and said she must not see them again. She will, of course, do as she is told, but if the boys meet her, she will talk with them. However, she soon will not have to worry about it because their furlough is up and they will be leaving. As to whether she will write to them, she thinks she may. She sees no harm in it whatsoever. "I'm not marrying them," she said. (K)

Because the hour was late, the therapist terminated the session rather abruptly.

INTERPRETATION

(A) Sandra is still in conflict and feels guilty about quitting school; she brings her problem to the group as she would to a good mother. I have already reported that a therapy group can be a substitute for a mother in some patients' unconscious. Actually Sandra is hoping for but does not receive approval. The discussion illustrates clearly sibling transference. Leaving school is a regressive act, the meaning of which becomes clearer when later she interprets her running away as seeking love. Sandra's ego is weak and she tends to run away from difficulties.

(B) Georgia comes in all excited and acts hastily. The excitement stems from guilt because she had gone out with a boy the night before; she was disloyal to the girls in her (homosexual) relation to them and to the therapist (mother), Leon symbolically represents her father and she has to placate the therapist (mother). She begins by explaining (apologizing for) her being absent so that the therapist will not be angry with her. She directly tells how her boss and his wife were good to her, suggesting that the therapist, too, should be good to her and not punish her. She proceeds to further placate the therapist by displaying her school report card (an act of submission), expresses her dissatisfaction with herself for not being better than she is, thereby fending off any possible criticism (punishment), and holding out a sort of promise that she will be a good girl.

The therapist did not perceive Georgia's intention, namely, her need to be forgiven and does not respond. The therapist should have in some way reassured the girl by saying something like, "I hope you had a nice time." The therapist could also have interpreted the transference by asking, "Do you find it necessary to apologize for going out with Leon?" But this may be rather risky at this point. Georgia's "animation" when the girls call attention to her corsage is really a manifestation of anxiety which she seeks to allay by offering them all a smell of the flowers.

(C) Not having received the forgiveness of the therapist, Georgia seeks here to placate her and the girls by saying that she really did not have a good time (therefore deserves no punishment). Her sin gave her no pleasure.

(D) Georgia's spending an evening with her boy friend activates sexual phantasies in the girls. The object becomes Reva, the most feminine, demure, and "sexy" (the girls' own characterization of her). Interest in her appearance, dress, hair, unmistakenly stems from homosexual trends. Sex seems to disturb Lydia, which is transmuted into oral preoccupation and food. As a result of the attention she had been receiving from the girls in the group, Reva, who had been an untidy, infantile, unpunctual, and irresponsible girl, sloppily dressed, has greatly improved in all these areas and now derives ego satisfaction. She is now even able to accept praise without being disturbed. Reva's mother comes to mind (since her nuclear problem is Oedipal involvement with her father and her intense desire to displace her mother) . She says in effect, "I am worthy of my father, even my mother admits it." The sexual content of the conversation activates Sandra to associate it with a dream, which can be expected to have sexual connotation.

When the therapist introduced so peremptorily the question of a stenographer, she changed the course of the girls' free association. This is an illustration of some of the principles described in Chapter III. When administrative matters must be brought in, it should be done at the end of the session, not in the beginning or during the group interview.

(E) In this dream, and because of the sequence in which it is told, Sandra brings forth her homosexual involvement with Helen. The fact that the two girls go out, pick up sailors, and run away from home together, is evidence of the homosexual attachment between them. The symbolism of the monkey or bear, is quite evident (pubic hair),[6] and the dream expresses her struggle against Helen's seductiveness which prevents her from being "good." When Sandra speaks of wanting to go back to play the piano, she means she wishes to be "good," but Helen arouses forbidden impulses and these are evil as the monkey (sex) is evil, and she is afraid. The therapist had rightly recognized that Helen was a displacement for Sandra's father and has given an interpretation which is entirely correct, if we are to judge by the sequence of the interview. Note also that in the dream Sandra runs to her mother for protection (against her sexual impulses), but her mother is not there.

(F) Sandra's giggle confirms the correctness of the therapist's surmise which is still further confirmed by her childhood memories of her father. In her unconscious, the monkey, the "bad" impulses, the father's "monkey faces" that so impressed themselves on Sandra are all related. Her father arouses in her evil impulses that are symbolized in the monkey "or bear." Bertha interprets Sandra's problem correctly. Sandra and her father cling to each other too much. Bertha too visualizes her father as a beast (one who can attack sexually) and Paula expresses her death wish towards her father when

[6] See discussion of pubic hair on p. 45.

she says that when he yells she thinks he does so because he is in pain (for pain is a preliminary to death).

The noteworthy element of this passage is the way members of the group interpret each other's unconscious. We see how correct are their insights and how they help one another in releasing and understanding impulses and phantasies. Catharsis, identification, universalization are all present in this. The flow of the interview demonstrates further the importance of grouping patients on the basis of a common syndrome, in this case incestuous strivings toward their fathers. This similarity favors mutual understanding, support, catharsis, and insight.

(G) Bertha vaguely perceives the sexual involvement between her and her father. The fact that he suspects her as well as her mother of illicit relations places her in the same category with her mother and his other women. The father's beating Bertha, as it appears in the context, can be interpreted as a form of sexual aggression. The objectivity with which she now deals with her father reflects considerable emotional growth in the girl. It also demonstrates the principle of cathexis displacement.

(H) Lydia, whose schizophrenic process has been held in check through individual and group therapy for almost ten years, gets very close to her problem. She is preoccupied with insanity, and is also able to perceive the relation between incest and insanity. At a previous session, the twenty-ninth, Lydia recalled that as a very small child, somehow her face was covered over by a blanket and she began to choke in her sleep. She clearly recalls the terrible fear she had experienced. She related also other terrifying experiences. She said once that she was born with a tumor on her head, "which was removed by X-rays." She then laughed and added, "maybe some of it is still there." The therapist asked her what she meant. Smilingly, Lydia said, "Maybe I still act kind of crazy." The therapist asked, "Do you think you do?" Lydia laughed without answering. Much later in treatment it was Lydia who revealed that once she cut a cat across the abdomen,[7] and that for some years she had regularly stolen from stores. Reva made no comment during the entire conversation about fathers. Her involvement with her father is too great at this point for her to be able to talk about him so directly.

[7] See p. 110.

(I) Bertha's statement about her father indicates considerable improvement. She now sees her father realistically, having been helped to do so through psychotherapy. She no longer idealizes him and her ambivalence is decreasing. She is clearer about him (cathexis displacement). She sees him as a weak person (which he actually is). Sandra too is beginning to be more objective about her father. She no longer feels guilty about her hatred of him, which is justifiable in terms of the real situation. Stimulated by the views of the others, Sandra reveals excellent insight into her motive for picking up sailors and for running away from home. Lydia who is a very perceptive person, characteristic of schizophrenics, makes the significant remark about breaking the vicious circle. In later sessions the girls discuss this thought and their role in it.

(J) When Sandra speaks at this point of her biography, she is actually continuing the story of her relation to her father. Her biography dealt largely with the intense suffering that leads to delinquent behavior and the struggle a girl goes through in her attempts to avoid it. Since all of the girls, and especially Sandra, were on the threshold of establishing the association between delinquent acts and relationships with fathers—all of this session was really devoted to it—the therapist should have attempted to bring this relation out into the open. Such interpretation might have been appropriate and desirable at this point. Sandra gave the lead in her previous statement that her behavior stems from her cravings for love.

The close attention of the girls as Sandra reads about the psychological basis for delinquency and the struggle with her environment and her own impulses indicates the girls' identification with her. This is valuable to Sandra and to the other girls. Sandra's ego is built up by the recognition and the impulses and feelings of all are clarified by the story. This is therapy through identification. Sandra's narrative was so written as to describe and interpret each girl's feelings much as a therapist would do.

Reva (who came to the group as a demure, shy and withdrawn "yes girl," as she had been characterized by the others) has now become assertive and is able to enter into open rivalry with Sandra, for Sandra places her in the subsidiary position she is forced to take toward her mother in relation to her father. This demonstrates again the variety of transferences that emerge in a group when a fellow patient may become the recipient of one's feelings toward parents. The identification with the story as revealed by the girls' tears takes the form in Paula of actual participation in typing it.

(K) In this interchange the girls' real castration anxieties appear. To Reva, being turned out of the house and becoming a beggar is to take away the security which she received from the father, while Sandra's fear of losing one of her braids has quite evident meaning. This is confirmed later when Lydia and Paula speak plainly about wanting "what Joe has." Castration anxieties are clearly shown by the girls, as demonstrated by the following incidents. During the sixth interview, Lydia said that she is especially concerned about her subway travel, because there are many men on the subways who get close to her. At this, she drew out of her purse a hat pin which she said she always carries for protection. The others laughed, and each of the girls took the pin and handled it. With the exception of Sandra, all the girls said they carry long pins with them. The adolescent girls' preoccupation with castration is demonstrated in another group. Betty asked Ella [8] whether she was wearing a real man's shirt. (Ella also wore men's ties.) Ella rather proudly stuck out her chest and said: "Yes, and it buttons down the front." Anne said, "She even has a fly on her skirt." At that, Ella seemed quite disturbed and vehemently denied it. There had been pencils and paper on the table and the girls took them up and remained silent for a period. . . .

An even more direct expression of adolescent girls' preoccupation with castration is revealed in the following story, written by Yolanda. The story takes place in the year 2040.

"After the war which the Allies won, there was a battle of the sexes. The women won and now their positions are reversed. The men have the babies, do the housework and do everything connected with the home, while the women work and earn a living. Now the scene opens in an office. A woman presses a buzzer, in comes a man to take dictation. Mr. Jones sits on the boss's lap to take the dictation. Says Mrs. Smith to Mr. Jones, 'What are you doing tonight, honey?' She's just about to kiss him when in walks her husband with a gun: (Haaa, haaa, these women, you can't trust them!) He bangs Mr. Jones on the head. Jones falls. He is worried: 'I've

[8] See p. 153.

killed him; now who'll take care of the children?' The wife says: 'I'll protect you.' They go to the policewoman, who puts them through a third degree." Here Yolanda demonstrated how the policewoman sticks pins into Mr. Jones.

At another session, Betty said with much feeling: "They [women] are paid less for the jobs they do as good as a man and even better." She went on to say that when she reaches the top of the ladder she will fix men. They are impolite, stupid. "Even my father [stepfather] is stupid for living with my mother," and she gave a number of illustrations of the neglected home and her mother's inadequacy and neglectfulness. Betty feels sorry for her stepfather for marrying her mother. He is a nice man, good and kind, but has a "rotten life" with her mother.

Returning to the dialogue in the record, we find revealed the close association between fathers and boy friends and the ready substitution the girls make one for the other. The incest drives toward the father are now displaced. Bertha conveys this when she confesses to being too guilty to pet or fondle her boy friend in the presence of her father. She is vaguely aware of her father's interest in her and her interest in him, and to come in physical contact with another man in his presence is an affront to and a sexual rejection of him. She is afraid of hurting him and suffer his wrath that would follow. Lydia, on the other hand, is characteristically narcissistic and has a less sharpened awareness of the effect on others. She does not inhibit her actions. She unintentionally reveals her penis striving which Paula at once recognizes. When faced with it, she vehemently denies it. Lydia also reveals her autistic character when she avers that boys do not affect her as they do the other girls. Reva's description of her father's reaction to her seeing the sailor boys in the neighborhood reveals his attitudes toward his daughter. Interestingly enough, she ends up by saying, "I am not marrying them," which is to say that "my father need not be afraid that I will marry them; I will marry him." In the light of this girl's basic problem, namely to replace her mother, this statement is significant.

Paula's sexual confusion and intense striving to have a penis makes her readily aware of a similar striving in Lydia, and she at once recognizes and interprets Lydia's unconscious. She also understands the significance of the word-error "went *into* Joe." Both statements strike a responsive note in Paula. By sitting on Jim's lap, Paula acts out her basic infantile unawareness of the significance of sex and her general infantile character. But there is in it also an element of seductiveness toward her father. The girl is strongly fixated on her father, who was the more kindly of the parents, and by sitting on Jim's lap in his presence she seeks to make him jealous, in which she succeeds.

The therapist attempted to stimulate the girls to further exploration of their incestuous strivings by asking why they are afraid of their fathers. Paula blocks this line of discussion, since her attachment to the father makes it necessary for her to see him in a better light, and she throws the onus on mothers as well.

DISCUSSION

This record is fairly typical of a group interview of adolescent girls when the conflict between Oedipal drives and the normal sexual interests are at their greatest. We see the girls' dependence upon, and death wishes toward, their parents. This is quite clear in Paula, though less evident in the others. We must note the easy catharsis, free association, and associative thinkings, and the low levels of resistance. The girls are singularly free of "shame," and their revelations of "bad" impulses meet with no disapproval. Identification is very clearly demonstrated here in all the problems discussed; emotions are acted out, as well as talked through.

The girls act as therapists to each other, giving clear and sometimes profound interpretations of unconscious motivations. This type of interview leaves very little for the therapist to do, since the therapeutic flow occurs without her participation. The therapist is passive, but at appropriate times she brings out a point to help the patients toward insight and further catharsis.

Expression of the girls' hostility toward the parents was made possible in this session by cathexis displacement facilitated by the acceptance, security, and affection and closeness that the girls feel toward each other and toward the therapist.

Spotnitz,[9] who has analyzed the basic trends of the interviews of

[9] Hyman Spotnitz, "Observations of Emotional Currents in Interview Group Therapy with Adolescent Girls," *Journal of Nervous and Mental Diseases,* November, 1947. From a paper presented at the Fourth Annual Conference of the American Group Therapy Association.

this group of adolescent girls, has found that they were motivated, in part at least, by two forces. "Those forces which tended to bring the group together, and those forces which tended to disrupt the group and break it up," and that these forces were the same. They were emotional drives associated with "the reproductive constellation" which was counteracted and disturbed by the girls' feelings of inadequacy as potential mothers. Spotnitz characterizes the latter as "the inadequacy constellation." He has found that "after about two years of [group] therapy, in the main, there had been a definite movement from a curiosity about children and how they are made, to a greater interest in producing them and in properly taking care of them." This change occurred because the girls found "that many of their fancied inadequacies were not inadequacies but based primarily on social disapproval, and as they learned to tolerate the group disapproval and came to understand themselves, many inadequacies turned out to be assets and others tended to disappear."

I believe this analysis applies very well to this group of girls.

CHAPTER TWELVE

ANALYTIC GROUP PSYCHOTHERAPY WITH ADULTS

RECORD AND INTERPRETATION

IN THE interest of space economy the present chapter is intended to serve two purposes. One is to demonstrate the process of analytic group psychotherapy with adults, the other is to show how it is applied specifically in the treatment of mothers.

It has long been recognized that mothers are the greatest single factor in the emotional maladjustment of children. Unless the interpersonal relations in the home are corrected, efforts at treatment of some children are frequently frustrated. The younger the child, the more essential it is to include parents in the treatment plan.

Because of this, hospital out-patient clinics, social service agencies, child guidance clinics, and private practitioners treat parents, especially mothers, of their young patients. The usual aim is to change the mothers' attitudes toward their offspring, though it is frequently necessary to affect basic changes in their personalities through psychotherapy.[1] Experience indicates that it is not possible nor advisable to limit the treatment aims once the process had been started. Whatever the original aim may be, the group therapeutic

1 Fannie Amster, "Collective Psychotherapy of Mothers of Emotionally Disturbed Children," *American Journal of Orthopsychiatry,* January, 1944; Helen E. Durkin, Henrietta Glatzer, and Jeannette S. Hirsch, "Therapy of Mothers in Groups," *ibid.;* Etta Kolodney, "Treatment of Mothers in Groups as a Supplement to Child Psychotherapy," *Mental Hygiene,* July, 1944; Lawson G. Lowrey, "Group Therapy for Mothers at the Brooklyn Child Guidance Center," *News Letter of the American Association of Psychiatric Social Workers,* Winter, 1943, and "Group Treatment for Mothers," *American Journal of Orthopsychiatry,* October, 1944; S. R. Slavson, "Group Therapy," in *Progress in Neurology and Psychiatry,* ed. Ernst Spiegel (New York, Grune and Stratton, 1946), and "Current Practices in Group Therapy," *Mental Hygiene,* July, 1944.

process is such that it inevitably leads the members to explore their backgrounds, difficulties, marital and social maladjustments.

Some of the nonclinical criteria for selecting mothers for groups are: (1) Women with social cravings and a desire to be with others, but who cannot participate in the ordinary neighborhood or social clubs because of personality difficulties. (2) Women who are solely preoccupied with their children and families and who need to redirect interest, and find some self-fulfillment outside the family circle. Reduction of emotional drives toward their children frees the children to grow more normally. Treatment groups are a step for such women in the transition to wider social participation, (3) Conversely, mothers involved in too many interests outside the home and needing to face their home situation more responsibly are helped by the discussions of common problems with other mothers. (4) Women who are intellectually limited and emotionally blocked can gain in ego strength through group participation and universalization. (5) Mothers who, because of competitiveness and power-drives find it difficult to enter into a close relation with an individual therapist, can be referred to groups either as preliminary to individual therapy, as sole therapy, or as an educational experience to change their attitudes toward their children. (6) Mothers who suffer from more or less severe pathology can also be included in these groups as long as they can relate to people. They can benefit through correcting their attitudes toward their children through identification and the other dynamics already described. (7) Mothers can be included in groups as any other patients in accordance with the established clinical criteria (Ch. XIV).

The following record of the eighth session of a group of women clearly demonstrates some of the process in the treatment of mothers as well as group treatment of neurotic adults. For ease in following the interview, we have chosen the record of a session at which only three women were present—Mrs. Allen, Mrs. Farmer and Mrs. Koenig.[2]

RECORD OF A SESSION (EIGHTH)

Since Mrs. Koenig was a newcomer, the therapist introduced her to the other two women.

[2] See note 2, p. 129.

Mrs. Allen brought candy and placed it on the table. She commented, laughingly, that she talked to Mrs. Farmer at the last session and it looked as though the group was built around her, Mrs. Allen. She is being helped here, although Albert (who was treated in a group as well) was getting "very bold." Mrs. Farmer said that this is just a stage children go through; she never resents her son Nathan's behavior. She accepts it. Mrs. Allen had threatened Albert that her husband would punish him. Mrs. Koenig thought this very bad. Both Mrs. Allen and Mrs. Farmer agreed that one should not put the father in a bad light with children, but Mrs. Allen added that both her children cling to her. Rickie won't let his father even come near him, which makes her husband miserable. Mrs. Farmer thought that if the father ignored the boy, he would come around. At this point Mrs. Farmer said that it is different in her family. Nathan prefers his father: they have so much in common. (A)

Mrs. Koenig had been quiet throughout this discussion and the therapist asked her how things were going. She said her little girl clings to her very much, but she tells the child she doesn't want that; she would rather she showed her love in deeds. She went on to narrate how closely she had kept the child tied to her. Mrs. Allen and Mrs. Farmer thought this was bad and said it was Mrs. Koenig's own fault. Mrs. Farmer went on to say that Mrs. Koenig is not the only one in this, a neighbor of hers does the same thing to her child, though in their case it is the father who curtails the child's freedom. It is better in Mrs. Koenig's case because she is at least aware of the problem and is trying to remedy it. Both women asked Mrs. Koenig to tell them some more about her difficulties. Mrs. Koenig told of her fear to let the child travel alone to see her caseworker at the clinic. They felt that she should let her do this. Mrs. Koenig, however, held her own, protesting that she does let Jean travel to other places, but the neighborhood of the clinic is bad. (This is a form of resistance for the neighborhood is populated and quite safe.)

All three then went on to discuss Mrs. Koenig's handling of Jean, the latter's fear of children, and how Mrs. Koenig tried to get the girl to join a club unsuccessfully. Mrs. Allen said: "Well, look, other children can be cruel, so that Jean may be afraid of making advances. Why don't you take the initiative and ask friends to come to your house?" Mrs. Farmer agreed with Mrs. Allen even though

Mrs. Koenig said she was afraid to do this lest she give Jean the feeling that she is again taking the initiative for her. Mrs. Farmer asked if Jean had any school friends, or any hobby. Mrs. Koenig said that the child is mechanically inclined and likes to fix watches, like her father. Then, too, there is the problem of the older sister. The older sister always pushes Jean away from her own friends, and the younger girl is very jealous of the older one's social success.

Both Mrs. Farmer and Mrs. Allen described their older children as jealous, too, but Mrs. Allen added that this was something different. Mrs. Koenig's girl is seventeen and in her prime. She is going out with boys and everything, and of course the younger child would be jealous. A five-year difference between children is too much. Mrs. Allen herself badly wanted to have her children closer in age. Mrs. Farmer said not she; she did want a second child, but didn't want him any sooner. After all, her husband and his brother are only two years apart, and they are not friendly with each other. Mrs. Allen went on to say with emphasis that it is all in the way children are brought up. In her father's family they are all close in age, but her uncles and aunts have no love for each other. This is true also of her mother's family. Her own brothers, on the other hand, are very close, but she is the one who has to be the rallying point for her husband's family. Mrs. Farmer said that in her own family they too are close, but her husband's family are not, and there she also is the center. (B)

Mrs. Allen said her husband is very anxious to have his family close to one another. She went on to describe the family difficulties. Her maternal grandfather died when her mother was thirteen. She was the oldest child and took care of her sister, because the mother went out to work. Then an uncle cheated the family out of their money. The three boys were boarded out and never had a real home. There are differences of personality in her own family. When Mrs. Allen's mother and brother get angry, they just stop talking; Mrs. Allen and her younger brother fight it out. Despite this, they are all close to each other. In her husband's family he was the dominant person. Mrs. Koenig said it sounds like a typically European setup, but, she said later, perhaps there were differences in all countries.

Mrs. Allen returned to her narrative, describing how she quarreled with her mother-in-law, because the latter thought her "lawyer-son" was such a great prize for any girl. She was considered a good catch, herself, because she came from a well-to-do family. Her husband's older brother ran off at the age of fifteen and was gone for nineteen years so that when he came back anything he did was acceptable. She spoke of her mother-in-law, finding it hard to understand how the family could have sent her alone, a girl of twelve, from Europe to this country. (C)

Mrs. Koenig said she left home at nineteen. She now took over the discussion and related that her husband had slept with his mother till he was twelve years old. She herself slept with her father until she was thirteen. Mrs. Allen said her husband always loved his mother, but his father was the underdog. Now she will not tolerate his being mistreated. She takes her father-in-law's part. (D)

The therapist here interjected the statement that this conversation was reminiscent of last week, when Mrs. Farmer and Mrs. Allen said that such a reaction can actually hide resentment. Mrs. Farmer said that if she had a mother, she would just take whatever came from her. Of course, she probably felt that way because her mother was dead. When her mother was alive, she answered her back, but she respected her. Mrs. Farmer said flatly, "Parents cannot be wrong." The therapist questioned this. Mrs. Farmer went on to say, "Well, yes; my father was wrong in regard to my stepmother." Mrs. Allen said that at times she disagreed with her father and even told him that some of the things he did were terrible, but they were always able to talk things over and come to an understanding.

Mrs. Farmer said feelingly that she resents so many things in her father, but she cannot face him with them. The therapist wondered why, and she said, "Well, he wouldn't listen." The therapist encouraged her to think more about why she could not talk to him freely. Mrs. Farmer said, "Well, actually I am afraid I might lose whatever relationship there is left between us." Mrs. Allen said that was true. She cannot really talk to her mother either; her mother starts to yell, and she, Mrs. Allen, begins to cry. (E)

Mrs. Farmer went on to speak of her father very feelingly. Several times she was on the verge of tears. She wants to tell her father that he is mistreated by the stepmother and stepdaughter, but she just cannot bring herself to do it. She and her siblings never did such things as they do to her father; it hurts her terribly. She can't even have five minutes alone with him anymore. "He takes it all; he is just a jerk." Mrs. Allen suggested, "Maybe he is happy this way." Mrs. Farmer replied: "How can he be? He forfeits his own children. He can't want that. Now his own children don't even go to see him. They are the ones who are treated like stepchildren. He doesn't even call me." Mrs. Allen said, "Probably his wife talks him into it." Mrs. Farmer: "Can't he see what is going on?" Mrs. Allen again said, "Probably not; he may be hurt by your not going to see him." Mrs. Farmer said his wife certainly has power over him. She herself had been very close to her stepmother and did everything for her. Six months ago there was a break—and this after nine and a half years of friendship. Mrs. Allen said she should swallow this for her father's sake. Mrs. Farmer said dejectedly she had tried but she just can't do it anymore. What should she do about Mother's Day, and Father's Day? Should she buy her stepmother a present, as she had done every year in the past, though this year she would rather give her poison? If she doesn't give her mother-in-law a present, how will it be when she gives her father a Father's Day present? Mrs. Allen again repeated she should still do these things for her father's sake.

The therapist commented that what makes it so difficult is that Mrs. Farmer is so greatly hurt by her father's indifference. Mrs. Farmer said she would like to have at least a little love from her father. He didn't even telephone to inquire when the baby was sick, although everyone else in the family did. Mrs. Allen said Mrs. Farmer should call up her father; she should talk up for herself. Mrs. Farmer said she is afraid she would burst out crying. Mrs. Allen said that is all right; it is still better to talk these things out. "You should insist on a chance to talk to him. Maybe he doesn't realize what is going on, and thinks that you just changed toward him." She also called Mrs. Farmer's attention to the fact that after all she is out of the home, and they cannot be as close to each other as they used to be when she lived at home. Mrs. Farmer said maybe when she goes up on Saturday, she may find him alone, and then she will talk to him. Mrs. Allen said even if he is not alone she should talk with him, and went on to tell Mrs. Farmer what to say.

"After all it is not all the stepmother's fault," she said. Mrs. Farmer should be humble if necessary. The latter responded she would rather cut her throat than be humble. Mrs. Allen: "You will be more at peace with yourself. You will know where you are at." To this Mrs. Farmer replied: "I can't be humble. That would give them the upper hand. Now at least I have my independence. Maybe I could talk to my father alone, but never in front of her [stepmother] and give her satisfaction." Mrs. Allen said: "You will be the one to get the satisfaction. You are torturing yourself this way." Mrs. Farmer said she preferred it. Suddenly she said that in this very difficult situation her husband is no help to her. He is fighting against her father, too. (F)

Mrs. Koenig said apparently Mrs. Allen and Mrs. Farmer are different types. Some people feel that if their pride is gone, they have nothing left. Mrs. Allen said well, Mrs. Farmer wants her father's love; to this Mrs. Farmer responded emphatically that she will not "beg for it." Her father must give it freely, as a father should, to his children. Mrs. Allen interjected that one ought to try. Could Mrs. Farmer ever forgive herself if anything should happen to her father, say if he died at this point with this misunderstanding between them? Mrs. Farmer said that is not the point. She prays for him every minute of the day, but things are so very different. It is the stepmother's fault. The father would not now offer them even a glass of water, while in the past his refrigerator was always open to his children. Mrs. Koenig went on encouraging Mrs. Farmer to go further, and try to understand the father's point of view. He can't just leave his wife, she said. Mrs. Farmer quickly said: "I don't want him to, but he should have been different ten years ago and stood up for his rights and the rights of his children." Mrs. Allen: "You can't lead his life for him." Mrs. Farmer said she doesn't want to do that. In fact they always took the stepmother's part in arguments against the father. Now, when she tries to stand up for her father, her husband attacks her father, too. Mrs. Allen suggested that when her husband attacks her family she should knock his family in return. Mrs. Farmer said: "That's no good. After all you can't knock his mother. She is dead." At this Mrs. Allen went on to say that she had seen the movie, "Stairway to Heaven," and the idea in the picture upset her. (G)

Mrs. Farmer went on to say that death is not nice, no matter how it seems in the pictures, and Mrs. Koenig added that it is hard on the living who are left. Mrs. Farmer elaborated on her fear of death. Mrs. Allen rather fears pain. Mrs. Farmer knew the pain of labor, but it was still preferable to death. She thinks of herself as living forever. She hesitated for a moment, then said she is terribly frightened of being buried, in the cold earth, and especially of being buried alive. Mrs. Koenig wondered why she should have such ideas, and smilingly suggested that she might have a telephone put in her grave, a situation she once read about in a story. Mrs. Farmer said this had been an obsession with her since the age of twelve when she lost her mother. She saw her mother's corpse in the coffin. Her mother was thirty-seven years old and Mrs. Farmer feared ever since that she herself would die at the same age. Mrs. Allen's only concern is about her appearance. She doesn't want to be seen not looking her best, and told her husband that when she dies she must be dressed and made up perfectly, with lots of flowers and a beautiful funeral. (H)

The group had overstayed its time and the therapist commented on this. She said that the question of death had come up before and it should be brought up soon again, because of the difficulty they all had in talking about death with their children. Mrs. Allen said that she has a problem with her son Albert. She wants to go out to the cemetery with her father, but would rather not take Albert along. Her mother, her brother, and her husband all know that she may be left alone for a few minutes to talk to her father. They all leave before she does. It is not that Albert would be upset because of her father, but she feels that he would become sad at the cemetery.

Mrs. Farmer spoke with resentment of the fact that her husband and his family were going out to her mother-in-law's grave on Mother's Day, although her husband would not take her when she wanted to go to her mother's grave. She had asked her brother-in-law if they would drop her off at her mother's cemetery on the way, and was very much hurt when he refused. Because of this she will not go with them to her mother-in-law's grave. (I)

The therapist later saw Mrs. Farmer for a few minutes outside the waiting room and commented that she had seemed very upset during the session and wondered how she felt. Mrs. Farmer said yes, this whole question hurts her terribly. She feels that she has to work out something with her father and is sure she will be able to do it. (J)

INTERPRETATION

(A) Mrs. Allen reveals at the very outset her narcissistic character (which dominated her relations with her husband and, before him, with her father) when she says that the group seems to be built around her. She perceives herself as its center. This is negative transference toward the therapist, that is, she is displacing the therapist in the group as she had displaced her mother in her family. Being afraid of the therapist's retaliation, she placates the latter by saying that she is being helped, but finds fault with the clinic (which the therapist represents) when she complains that her son (who is attending an activity group at the clinic) is becoming bold. Actually the boy, who has been a very frightened and insecure child before, is becoming more outgoing and normally less fearful. Mrs. Allen does not like the fact that he is becoming assertive; he now begins to challenge her self-centered, narcissistic power-drives. Mrs. Farmer consoles her that this is only a stage of a child's growth—it is not a personal matter with her or specific to her problem. Mrs. Koenig helps Mrs. Allen understand that it is bad for a boy to be afraid of his father and place the father in a bad light.

Continuing in her narcissistic power-drives, Mrs. Allen announces that she still is the boss of her household; both children cling to her, and Rickie, the younger one, does not let his father come near him. This makes her important also in the group. Again Mrs. Allen attacks the therapist. The fact that Rickie avoids his father pleases Mrs. Allen; it puts her above her husband. This may have a number of implications, for which we have no evidence at this point, but opens up possibilities for speculation, one of them is that her basic drives are masculine, probably as a result of identification either with her father or brothers. She is generally a castrating person.

Mrs. Farmer helps Mrs. Allen in two ways; one is when she says she gives Nathan freedom and suggests that Mr. Allen ignore the boy until the latter comes to his father. But at the same time she expresses envy of her husband, because her son prefers him. The "two men" in her family seem to have much in common. This too can have a variety of meanings, the most obvious of which is that they both possess something she does not (a penis), and this disturbs her.

The value of the peroration lies in the fact that mothers help one another in dealing with their children; they share common problems; they make each other feel more at home with their difficulties. We can observe here universalization, dilution of transference, reduction of guilt and lessening of anxiety.

(B) Mrs. Koenig was brought into the discussion by the therapist because she seemed to be outside of the group, being a newcomer (new sibling). The therapist at this point felt that it would be more advisable to include her in the discussions and keep her interested in the proceedings, so that she would not feel unwanted. It is interesting to note the freedom with which Mrs. Koenig is able to reveal her own inadequacy in relation to her daughter, such as her overprotectiveness. The readiness with which she makes the admission must be viewed as a form of resistance. Being the new member (sibling) she is attacked by the others. Sibling rivalry comes to the fore here, and is mitigated when Mrs. Farmer relates the story of the neighbor. Mrs. Koenig conveys her resistance to treatment again when she says that she lets Jean travel by herself to other places, but not to the clinic. (The clinic is only half a block from the elevated station.)

Mrs. Allen in her characteristic dominating manner takes the prerogative of telling Mrs. Koenig what to do—she must ask children to come to her house. As the two women continue to explore Mrs. Koenig's family situation her chief problem comes through; her daughter is like the father. They both like mechanical things and to fix watches. The sibling rivalry between Jean and her older sister comes out at this point and all find that their children are jealous of each other.

This discussion brings to their consciousness, by free association, their rivalry with their own brothers and sisters and with their husbands. They associate directly the situations present in their families with their childhood. They see their children's behavior in the light of their own relations to the members of their respective families. Because of the activation of these early feelings, Mrs. Allen and Mrs. Farmer get into rivalry, for having become friends in the group (siblings) they act out rivalry when both claim they are in the center of their husband's families.

(C) Mrs. Allen again reveals her rivalry with her husband and her drive to superiority in relation to him. Even though he is a lawyer, she came from a well-to-do family. Besides, his older brother ran away from home, and her mother came alone as an immigrant at the age of twelve. Her own mother was a strong personality: she took care of her siblings. Mrs. Allen does not approve of the fact that her husband is important in his family and is loyal to it. This jealousy is further revealed when she admits to being in conflict with her mother-in-law. She cannot share.

(D) Because the question of relationships between children and parents was opened up, Mrs. Koenig can bring forward her problem; her husband's sexual attachment to his mother and her own to her father. The latent meaning of this statement is sensed by Mrs. Allen when she associates this with her husband's love for his mother (which she unconsciously perceives as having incestuous connotation), and becomes angry at her mother-in-law for being unkind to her own husband. The latter is now treated like Mrs. Allen's father. She takes up the cudgels for her father-in-law as she did (or would) for her own father against her own mother. In other words she prefers her husband's father (that is, her own father) to her husband. Mrs. Allen's father fixation is transferred upon her father-in-law; because he is an older man, she prefers him to her husband. In this Mrs. Allen continues her involvement with her father, who, as we know from the case history, preferred her and who had made a great deal of fuss over her.

(E) The therapist points out the relation of this conversation with the one of the preceding session in which Mrs. Farmer and Mrs. Allen also talked about fathers. When the therapist speaks of resentment, Mrs. Farmer becomes guilty about her repressed hostile feelings toward her mother and says she would submit to her mother if she were alive. She allays her guilt: though she quarreled with her mother, she respected her. This is a rather important statement for Mrs. Farmer. She fully reveals her Oedipal conflict with her mother with the accompanying feelings: she challenged her mother but respected (feared) her. This ambivalence is characteristic of her. She seeks to further allay her guilt feelings when she firmly says that parents cannot be wrong. The therapist rightly questions this and Mrs. Farmer reverses herself by saying that her father had been wrong when he took a second wife. By this she implies that he would have done better had he taken her as a wife. This surmise is confirmed in her statement when she says that she is afraid, as a small child is afraid, lest she lose him altogether. Quite evidently her love for her father is of a regressive, infantile character. Important to note is the ready transition to her father made by Mrs. Farmer as she talks about mothers. The Oedipal conflict is evidently uppermost in her mind.

Mrs. Allen, too, sees herself in the same light as Mrs. Farmer, but when she disagrees with her father, she is able to talk it over with him. Her relation to her mother is different. With her she begins to cry. In other words, the relationship between herself and the father is warmer and more secure than that with the mother, whom she resents strongly and, therefore, deals with in a regressive manner.

(F) Mrs. Farmer feels about her stepmother as she felt about her own mother. She could make a better wife to her father than either. Her newly acquired siblings are displacing her in her father's graces as her own siblings had displaced her in her own family. Throughout, she expresses resentment of her father who abandoned her for another woman. She feels strongly about this, is very emotional and weeps. She feels abandoned and unloved and would like to eliminate her rival, her stepmother, by giving her poison. She reveals herself as an infantile person, very dependent on her father and very much in need of his love. Being infantile she is unable to deal with the situation in a controlled, mature manner, and work out an enduring relationship with her stepmother. Neither can she humble herself, for to do this would mean to accept secondary place in her father's esteem. She wants to come to her father a strong, worthy individual and not humble and broken down. Now the association of her father and the husband comes to the surface. Just as she expected her father to extricate her from her difficulties, she now expects her husband to do the same thing. Here is revealed the direct displacement of Oedipal conflicts from the father on the husband, a rather common occurrence among neurotics.

(G) Mrs. Farmer reveals even further the depth of her infantile dependence. She wants her father's love to be given her without any effort on her part to earn it. It must be given freely. She also wants to be fed: his icebox should still be open to her. By pursuing Mrs. Farmer and urging her to make amends and establish a relationship with her father, Mrs. Allen is displaying considerable identification. The urgency of her arguments would seem to indicate that in doing this she is attempting to resolve some conflict within herself. She is working through, one may guess, a difficulty similar to the one by which Mrs. Farmer is oppressed. Mrs. Allen speaks her mind when she associates Mrs. Farmer's need for her father with his death (which is presently tied up with her mother's death and her own). If one has an incestuous relation with one's parents, one dies and the husband who serves as escape from incest is expected to take the place of the father. But instead of supporting his wife and recognizing her struggle, he attacks her father, thereby causing her to withdraw from him and return to her father. Her anxieties are increased because of the husband's lack of understanding which drives her even closer to her parent. This is confirmed by the fact that she cannot fight her husband as she cannot fight her father. She is afraid to lose them. So that when Mrs. Allen suggests that she attack her husband in retaliation, she quickly says, "That's no good." She rejects the idea, ostensibly because her husband's mother is dead. Mrs. Allen, significantly changes the subject.

(H) Death, incest, and childbirth are all now fused in Mrs. Farmer's mind. She is afraid to die because at the age of twelve she had seen her mother dead at thirty-seven, which probably was a fulfillment of Mrs. Farmer's unconscious death wishes toward her mother. Hence, death holds special terror for her. It is accompanied with fears of punishment (being buried alive). The phantasy of being buried alive may have another meaning. She cannot think of ever being dead, for then she cannot have her father. She, therefore, will be alive after death so that she can still have her father. Mrs. Allen, in her characteristic narcissistic way cannot identify with this. She wants to look pretty even when she is dead. Because when you are pretty and attractive, you are desirable (particularly desirable to father). Mrs. Allen is secure with her father and she does not have the same qualms and doubts as does Mrs. Farmer.

(I) The therapist makes the mistake of changing the flow of the interview by bringing the difficulty that the mothers had revealed in discussing death with their children. At this point the center of preoccupation was not death itself, but incestuous drives. The center of preoccupation was infantile dependence and regressive sexuality as manifested in the unresolved Oedipal strivings, which were projected on the husbands and other members of the family. The therapist had shifted the center.

Despite the interruption, Mrs. Allen returns to speak of her father, and Mrs. Farmer again expresses her resentment against her husband and his loyalty towards his dead mother. Mrs. Farmer expresses her jealousy of her dead mother-in-law in relation to her husband; the same kind of jealousy she had had toward her mother in relation to her father. This unconscious association of her relation with her mother, father, and stepmother, which she transferred to her husband and son, Albert, will have to be clarified for her in treatment.

(J) The therapist did well to recognize Mrs. Farmer's disturbance. This understanding and sympathy, as that of a good mother, helped Mrs. Farmer to abandon for the moment her demanding, helpless attitude when she said that she must work out something with her father. It is clear from this session that the center of treatment both for Mrs. Farmer and Mrs. Allen at this point is their involvement with their fathers. This must be cleared up to some extent, at least, before the two can function adequately as wives and mothers.

DISCUSSION

The content of the interview of this group is similar in some respect to that of the group of adolescent girls (see Chapter XI). The Oedipal conflict and its irradiations is the central preoccupation in both. This similarity is not confined to the two records reproduced in this book, for they were taken from a mass of records at random. It is rather characteristic of nearly all the group interviews, though very definite differences also become apparent as one studies them in greater detail.

The similarity arises from the fact that women who come for psychotherapy seem to have been fixed psychologically at the stage when the Oedipal conflict is reactivated and they have not affected libidinal separation from their fathers necessary to function in the subsequent roles of wives and mothers. This situation in itself stems from the unresolved Oedipal conflict. Thus the fixation can be considered as being on an infantile or adolescent level. Mrs. Farmer's attitudes and dependence leave little doubt as to this conclusion. It is revealed by her helplessness and open craving for her father's love. It is equally apparent in Mrs. Allen's primary narcissism, which stems from her infantile wish to be desired by her father and to monopolize him.

We have seen that the cathexis in girls in puberty (Chapter X) was focused on mothers and that of the adolescent girls and the adult women on fathers. All are at the stage when the Oedipal conflict is being reactivated, but in the latter two—the adolescent girls and the adults—the sexual content is more obvious and more pronounced than in the pubertal girls. This is even more apparent and more at the center of the problem in the adolescent girls. Theirs is a clear driving force—consummation of their sexual urges and, as later interviews reveal, also of their procreative desires and phantasies. These drives had been accomplished by the mothers, even though not too satisfactorily. At least parts of the phantasy elements had been eliminated and some stark realities are faced. In later interviews the mothers confess to unsatisfactory sexual adjustment, a fact that seems to stand out in nearly all the women we have had under treatment in this and other groups.

The psychological constellation is still further complicated by the presence of children. This is an additional cathexis focus not present in the treatment of adolescent girls. We have here, therefore, a network of psychologic forces that reinforce one another. The women have a much stronger feeling of being trapped than do the girls. The latter may still look forward to jobs and marriage as means of escape; to the women these avenues are closed or can only serve as minor and secondary escapes and satisfactions. The realities of the two are quite different, varying in the admixture of actuality and phantasy. The sexual phantasies of the two of necessity must be different and the feeling of hopefulness is effected correspondingly.

The mothers have at their disposal sublimation outlets through sexual activity, for what it is. The adolescents weave webs of phantasy, guesswork and conjecture, around these urges. The adults also have coitus, as unsatisfactory as it may seem, and periodically at least have a means for releasing neuro-vaso-muscular tensions and establish, even if temporarily, balance in endocrine activity. But their frustration and hopelessness are much more vivid and intense. The day-to-day functioning in the pressing and inescapable duties as mothers and wives against their own unresolved cravings for parental love, and living in a sexual relation where the sexual cathexis is weak or lacking, is a great psychological load to bear.

The group interviews of adolescents, as can be expected, reveal vastly more direct concern with sex than do the interviews of adult women (and men as well). This is quite evident and understandable. The mothers, too, talked frequently about their sexual activity, but they were never as persistent, and seldom as direct, as were the adolescent girls. The women have other foci of cathexis—husbands, in-laws, children, material problems—that force themselves upon them. They are more multifocal than are the girls.

It is clear that treatment has to be adjusted to these variations in the two types of patients, even though they are identical in terms of basic and fundamental content. In the interview cited we see that the mothers' first interest are the children and their relations to them. They start nearly all interviews by a recitation of what had happened since the preceding group session and how they dealt with their offspring. Since the central difficulties are not their children but rather their own unconscious drives and conflicts, it is inevitable that they should, through catharsis and free association, turn the discussions to more fundamental dynamics within themselves. Thus despite the therapist's desire to confine her therapeutic effort to the limited field of the women-as-mothers, the patients themselves make this position untenable.

Leaving for the present the general discussion and turning to a few of the specific details in the record under analysis, we find a rather interesting phenomenon in the relation of Mrs. Allen and Mrs. Farmer. We see how the women support and in a sense reinforce one another. Both are deeply involved with their fathers and both suffer from unresolved Oedipal conflicts. But what is striking about this situation is the extreme difference in the way the two women were affected by it. Mrs. Farmer is a crushed person, masochistic, helpless, and dependent. Mrs. Allen, on the other hand, is more poised, confident, independent, and narcissistic. The former's maladjustment is a problem deeply rooted within her own personality; the latter came to the clinic not because she suffered, but because her children presented adjustment difficulties. The syndrome is the same in both—Oedipal conflict—but the resultant personalities are diverse. One of the reasons for this is the fact that one succeeded in gaining the attention of her father, the other failed.

Mrs. Allen became her father's favorite child; that is, she succeeded in displacing her mother and siblings in his affections, whereas Mrs. Farmer failed utterly in this. It is this difference—success vs. failure in attaining the infantile aims—that constitutes the difference in the nuclear problems of the two patients. One weeps for love like a baby, the other has retained the infantile narcissistic quality. While treatment in each case is directed toward the same traumatic focus, it must of necessity follow different routes. What these are cannot be explored here without going too far afield. The point must be emphasized, however, that the group therapist must be aware of and constantly keep in mind the nuclear problems of each patient.

Because Mrs. Allen is stronger as a person, she therefore supports Mrs. Farmer. That is, she is the latter's supportive ego. Mrs. Farmer leans heavily on her (these two women were seeing one another outside the group sessions), but this relation was made possible by the fact that both have the same difficulty and, therefore, talk to each other's unconscious. Mrs. Allen can identify with her friend, because fundamentally they are alike, even though their manifest difficulties are different. This closeness between the two leaves Mrs. Koenig out of the group. She is on the periphery for this reason, but also because she is a newcomer. She is in the "out-group" while Mrs. Allen and Mrs. Farmer are of the "in-group." This situation is corrected by the presence of other patients at later sessions, and, thanks to her fairly constructive attitude, Mrs. Koenig makes her way into the group.

The discerning reader will have observed the numerous openings the therapist had during the group interview to interpret the patients' attitudes and unconscious. She advisedly refrained from so doing. In the first place she was still observing the patients for diagnostic material. Secondly, the patients and the various transference relations did not favor further exploration and interpretation.

CHAPTER THIRTEEN

ANALYTIC GROUP PSYCHOTHERAPY IN AN INSTITUTION

RECORD AND INTERPRETATION

WE ARE concerned in this chapter with the use of group therapy in correctional schools, commonly referred to as "reform schools." The striking characteristic of the residents (or inmates) of these institutions is the surface nature of their aggressions and their open hostility toward staff members, including the clinical staff. The residents here do not differentiate between the maintenance, clinical, and administrative staffs, all of whom, of necessity, have to exercise some authority. Resentment is general, diffuse, and universal. This is unavoidable, for removal from one's family and social group inevitably spells rejection and deprivation—rejection by one's family and deprivation of the pleasures and comparatively secure relations in the normal setting of life.

Ambivalence is more widespread and intense in a free setting than it is in an authoritarian and restraining institution. Although the staff, and especially the clinical workers and psychiatrists, are friendly, helpful, and protective, they still are impediments to the enjoyment of infantile indulgences. One of the benefits of institutional life is the lessening of ambivalence through helping the residents accept the situation and adjust to it as part of reality. Another is the opportunity offered them to use this flexible and conditioned environment for their own satisfaction and to the maximum advantage for all. These are treatment opportunities that can be effective only when the total climate helps strengthening the ego, favors the establishment of identifications, and builds feelings of self-esteem.

It is not the intention here to describe management of institutions.[1] Rather, our concern is the pertinence of the use of the group for therapeutic ends in this setting. This involves at least three types of groups of major importance. These are the groups that emerge spontaneously, are planned for effective community living, and are specially structured for therapy. Our interest here is in the third category.

This chapter will be devoted to a discussion of one interview, the first, of a group of adolescent girls. For the sake of brevity no case histories will be given, since we are interested in the *process.* Among those participating in this session are three girls of sixteen—Marian, Rhoda, and Myrna—and one of fifteen—Clara.

The girls had been prepared by their workers for the group and their programs were arranged so that they could come to the session.

RECORD OF GROUP SESSION (FIRST) [2]

Marian came first. She came on time, to the minute, and told the therapist that she had already been looking for her, but that the therapist was not in the office. Marian was friendly and eager, she looked freshly scrubbed, with her hair tied up in pigtails. She sat down rather self-consciously on one of the chairs placed in a semicircle around the therapist's desk.[3] Because she seemed self-conscious, Marian was encouraged to talk. She said she knew the other girls in the group and that they would be coming along. The discussion veered to the time of the "meeting" and her program, which the therapist compared with those of the other girls. The therapist asked Marian what she had been doing this day, since it was a holiday. She had some cottage duties in the afternoon and helped one of the staff's family in the morning. She took over the children. She loved it. She was particularly enthusiastic about taking care of the baby. She loved babies, and added that she was a little sorry that

[1] For a more extensive description of this see this author's "An Elementaristic Approach to the Understanding and Treatment of Delinquency," *Nervous Child,* October, 1947; his "Milieu and Group Therapy in Institutional Treatment," *Year Book of the American Probation Association, 1948;* and, with Harry Schulman, "Reeducative Activity for Delinquent Youth," *Jewish Social Service Quarterly,* June, 1936.

[2] See note 2, p. 129.

[3] The arrangement of the room is unsuitable for interview therapy, and this had been changed at later sessions. The group met in a room where they all could gather around a round table, which is best for this purpose.

she had no younger brothers or sisters. She had an older brother and sisters older than she. (A)

Rhoda came into the office explosively. She bounced in angrily and had a sullen expression on her face. She seated herself on a chair next to Marian. The therapist said that they were waiting for the other girls to come and had meanwhile been discussing the program of each girl, so that a convenient time for all could be arranged. Rhoda volunteered information about her own program as well as those of the other girls. She also announced that Mary would not come to the meeting, but did not say why, though Mary said earlier in class that she was not coming and gave some reason for it. Rhoda said that she was not sure that she herself wanted to come. She did not know what this was all about. She had just come from her social worker and she was very mad. She freely expressed hostility toward Miss Brown, saying that while she would not exchange her for any other social worker, Miss Brown certainly made her mad. She knows that Miss Brown says the sort of things she does for Rhoda's good, but she doesn't like it, nevertheless. Then she went on a rampage against the school. She does not know what other people think, but she certainly does not want to get herself in any more trouble and have her parole put off. Marian disagreed with her quite definitely. She liked the school and felt it had done much for her. (B)

At this point, Clara came into the room and sat down in a chair somewhat removed from the group. She had a disdainful smile which remained with her for a long time. She sat quietly through most of the following discussion. The girls disagreed about what the school did for people. Rhoda said perhaps it does some good to other girls, but does nothing for her. When Marian shook her head in disagreement, the therapist asked what Marian thought about it. Marian said she knew what the school had done for her—she had learned respect and how to do better on a job. Rhoda shook her head violently. She said that perhaps it is important to respect people, but not all people deserve respect.

The therapist asked whether Marian thought that not respecting people created problems. The girl answered that this had been her problem, and she is glad that she can now respect her elders.

Rhoda thought that there were a lot of people in the school whom she does not respect and who do not deserve respect. What kind of people should one respect? Well, there were people around the school, even—and here she grimaced—including the staff, who lose their tempers too easily. Not that she doesn't like some of the staff, but there are some that she cannot stand. Of course, she knows people do lose their tempers; she loses hers, too. She loses her temper when she is irritated, as now. She wants to go home and the school does not let her go home. Of course, she knows that she can't expect to ask for something and have people say "Yes" all the time. This is not like home, when you ask to go to the movies and somebody says "No." At home you go into a temper, but here you can't go into a temper just because somebody says, "You can't go home." (C) What does Rhoda do when she loses her temper? Oh, she feels like throwing things. Marian knows it well because she has thrown things at Marian. Marian, with a little startled look on her face, agreed with Rhoda. But Marian, too, has an impulse to throw things when she is angry. This she said somewhat regretfully. She used to throw things when she was home, but she must admit that she does not like throwing things around. The therapist asked, "I wonder what happens when a person loses his temper?" Marian said, "People don't like you, and you give people a wrong impression of you." (D)

Clara had been sitting quietly with the same smile on her face. She said nothing but frequently nodded her head. At this point the therapist encouraged her to come closer, asking her what she thought. Clara moved closer to the group and, instead of answering the question, said she wanted to know something first. When Miss Brown had told her about the group, she had asked Miss Brown if she would have to talk about personal things. Miss Brown said that she would have to ask the group therapist at the meeting. She continued to say that it was hard enough to tell Miss Brown personal things; she did not think she could talk about them in front of other people. (E)

The aim and *modus vivendi* of the group had not as yet been presented to the girls. At this point the therapist suggested that perhaps they could talk about what the group really was, since she felt that they had some question about it and seemed all to be concerned with talking about personal things in the presence of others.

The therapist explained briefly what the group was for. It was a way of helping girls with their problems, and just as the things which they talked about with their caseworkers were confidential, so were the things they discussed here. While they might talk about personal matters here, these were not to be discussed outside the group meetings. Rhoda said that she does not know whether she will talk about personal things. It's hard to talk about such things to people; but she can talk about general subjects. However, it does not bother her so much, and perhaps she will come to the group. She is very angry, however, because she did not think she is such a problem child that she needs to be in a group as well as see a social worker individually.

Marian agreed that it is hard to talk about personal matters with other people present. Clara and Rhoda in particular thought that when confidential matters are discussed, they "get spread around." Did this mean that the girls would gossip if they learned things about each other? They said that is exactly so; girls always gossip. Why would they spread gossip about each other? Well, girls are jealous. All agreed that girls are always jealous of each other. When asked why, Rhoda pointed out that sometimes one may have a boy friend that another girl wants, and to get even the other girl will spread gossip. Clara was definite and quite emotional as she agreed that girls are all very "catty and love to talk about one another." (F)

At this point, Marian, who merely nodded her head occasionally in agreement during most of the conversation, asked a question which she said often bothered her about boys. Sometimes very nice boys choose girl friends who are "really nothing very special." They could have any girl they wished, but choose one who doesn't look very nice or isn't very smart; yet they seem to like them. Rhoda explained that it is not only a girl's looks that is important, but her personality. "Beauty is only skin-deep," she said. "Sometimes, girls don't look as well as they might." She knows that she is not pretty, but she takes care of herself and is very clean and neat. "I can't stand girls who are sloppy and who don't take care of themselves!" she exclaimed with feeling. It is very easy to be clean if one is not just lazy. Marian joined her in this discussion, saying that girls who are sloppy and do not take care of themselves are just lazy, because there is no other reason for it. The therapist said she wondered whether this was just laziness and nothing else. All felt that a girl can always do something about herself to make herself look better. Rhoda pointed out how much make-up can do for one.

Clara, who is a very untidy-looking girl, did not participate in this discussion, and looked a little uncomfortable. Marian said, perhaps it wasn't just laziness; maybe a girl had other things on her mind. The therapist asked what she meant. Rhoda said sometimes a girl doesn't care; and when she does not care about other things, she does not care what she looks like either. For example, when she herself feels the way she does now she doesn't want to do anything. She just wants to go off by herself and sit in a corner. Marian murmured agreement and Clara nodded her head. (G)

Marian wondered about girls who always sit by themselves instead of participating with other girls. Rhoda thought that they were self-conscious and could not mix. The therapist said maybe these girls would also like to be with the others in the group who are having fun. Rhoda said now she has fun and always mixes with girls except when she is feeling angry, and then she sits by herself. She used to be self-conscious, would sit alone, and never had a good time at parties. At first she couldn't dance, and then even after she learned to dance she imagined people were watching just to poke fun at her if she made a mistake. Marian nodded her head in agreement. She is self-conscious and sits on the side at parties. She knows how to dance, but somehow does not feel comfortable and wondered how Rhoda was able to change and become the way she is now. Rhoda giggled and said she just made up her mind that she was going to have a good time and forgot all about her self-consciousness. Clara did not participate very much in this discussion. Nodding her head, she said something that was rather hard to understand. It sounded like a jumble of words. When questioned, she said it was hard for her to explain. The therapist encouraged her, saying that she understood what Clara meant. (H)

The question of parties with boys and girls came up. Now all the girls belligerently attacked the school's new policy of separating the boys and girls. Marian was very conciliatory, saying that she was sure that the school knew what it was doing, after all it did things only to help the children. Clara and Rhoda denied this vigorously.

They were very derogatory about the new rules that prevented boys and girls being together at recess periods and about the deprivation in the past week. They did not believe in punishing the group just because of what a few children did. Clara said the trouble with staff is that they have "low minds and always think that something is going to happen between a boy and a girl just because they talk to each other or sometimes a boy kisses his girl friend." Marian still took the school's side. The therapist remarked that there seemed to be a difference of opinion and that each no doubt had her reasons for the way she thought.

Clara asserted that the school did no good for anybody. Rhoda thought that it might help some people, but not all. Marian again repeated that it is a good place, and helps "kids." Rhoda asked her point-blank what it could teach a girl, to which Marian replied that she learned many things, such as how to work, how to keep herself neat, and so on. Clara denied this vehemently, saying that if one was on a work-detail all the time, one didn't learn anything. She was very bitter as she spoke. Rhoda, too, was against doing the same chore every day, pointing out how boring it was. Clara said they learned nothing, even in class; it was baby stuff. Marian said one learned in class if one wanted to, and maybe those people who had to do low-grade work were just not so intelligent.

The therapist kept completely quiet during this heated argument. Rhoda said she was now sorry she had asked to come to the school, describing how she begged the judge to send her here. Now she regrets that day. Others react differently. For example, her brother likes it here, but after all, not everybody responds in the same way. Marian, too, likes it here. Clara cannot understand how anyone could like the school. The therapist asked why they disliked the school. Again they emphasized the attitude toward the relations between boys and girls. Rhoda said that rules are made to be broken. Did she mean all rules? No, the ones about the boys and girls. She said it is natural to want to talk to your boy friend despite the rules, and most of the children do not obey such rules. Rhoda was the most outspoken in this part of the discussion. She described how at field day the boys were supposed to stay on one side of the field and the girls on the other. "But how was it possible for the school to expect this could be carried out?" she asked. The boys and girls did congregate anyway. Rhoda, in particular, was very angry as she said, "After all, it's your boy friend." (I)

Rhoda said quite definitely that she had spoken with her boy friend the day before even if it was against the rules. The therapist asked if Marian had too, since she was nodding her head in agreement. Marian said, regretfully, that she had no boy friend, but she thinks it is natural to want to speak to him, if you have one. Clara talked belligerently about how suspicious and distrustful the school had been. Marian said that she does not blame the staff; after all, they only carry out the orders of the higher-ups. What did they mean by this? All three girls, but particularly Rhoda and Clara, brought out great hostility against the Director. Even Marian blamed Mr. Golder for all of their dissatisfaction with the school. Rhoda described how intensely she dislikes him. She called him "false," and imitated his "constant grin." (J)

This brought on a discussion of a visit of the boys from one of the cottages to a girl's cottage late one evening. Marian brought this up in connection with the staff's reasons for feeling that the boys and girls might get into trouble. All were very critical of this incident. Clara, in particular, was outspoken in blaming the girls for what had happened. It was not at all the boys' fault if the girls had invited them to come up. At first Rhoda said that she blames both. The girls had no business to invite the boys, but the boys had no business going there. Marian said that the boys should have known better and should not have gone. She feels that a boy is just as much at fault because if he knows that he will get into trouble and maybe spoil his parole by doing such a thing, he shouldn't do it. He should know better. Rhoda then said that she thinks it is really the girls' fault. She can put herself in the boy's place; if he knew he could get something out of a girl, why he would be a fool not to go. Therefore, it is all up to the girl. She can understand how a boy feels. If he is in the city, and if he has to have a girl or, as they say up here, "if he gets hard up," he can go to one of those places where they pay girls. But here that is impossible, and, therefore, if a girl encourages a boy, well, then she is in for trouble. Rhoda insisted that it is up to a girl to encourage or discourage a boy, and Clara elaborated on this further, pointing out that if a girl lets a boy put his hand on her, then she can expect him to go further if she doesn't stop him at that point.

The therapist suggested that a girl may find it hard to know how far to let a boy go. Clara and Rhoda agreed, and said that sometimes a girl wants to fool around, too. At this point, Rhoda said that since the therapist had said that they could talk about anything they wanted, this was a very good subject—boys and girls. The therapist said that was all right, it is a pretty important subject, and something that all were interested in. All three remained quiet for a moment and then Rhoda said, after all, it is natural for girls to be interested in boys. However, she does not know where to begin. She has to think about it first.

It was nearly at the end of the session when Myrna came in. She announced that she was late because she had been unable to leave the art group. Mrs. Rubins, the teacher, insisted that Myrna finish her painting. With this, she handed a note in confirmation. In a semihumorous manner, but in a somewhat defiant tone of voice, she repeated that she could not leave her art group until she was finished.

The therapist said that the time was drawing to a close and perhaps the group should discuss the time for the next meeting. The girls suggested different times. Rhoda stated that she is very busy; she has meetings Monday and Friday nights, rehearsal with the glee club on Tuesdays, and so on. She seemed quite amenable, however, to the various suggestions made by Marian, who, in fact, offered most of the suggestions. Rhoda agreed that she would find some time to come. Clara raised objections to one day, saying that she had to do her ironing that day. Rhoda said that Clara could do her ironing another day. The girls all agreed that the meetings should be held after school hours. Marian thought perhaps she and Rhoda could miss one meeting a week of their other club. Rhoda said that important things might take place, and they must not be absent. The day suggested by the others did not suit Myrna because it was clean-up day at her cottage. Marian and Rhoda, who lived in the same cottage, overruled her saying that they could do clean-up some other day. Marian said that one "has had to give up something in order to come to the group." Myrna announced quite defiantly that she would not give up her art group to come for anything. The therapist said in support of Myrna that it is true; sometimes we had to choose between things. It depends on the girl and what she really wants. Rhoda said that she really has not decided yet whether she will want to continue to come, but she will see later. By that time the rehearsals for the operetta will be over, and she will have an additional free night in the week. Finally a date was set for the next session. (K)

INTERPRETATION

(A) By her punctuality, behavior, manner of speaking and dress, Marian reveals herself as a submissive, conforming person. She reveals striving for love when she speaks of her affection for babies and her wish to have a younger brother or sister. It is also possible that "reproductive constellation" comes to the fore here. One would suspect that she has difficulties with her older siblings.

(B) Rhoda's bouncing in angrily and explosively is characteristic of her behavior generally. She presents a problem in behavior disorder, while Marian is obviously psychoneurotic. It is interesting to observe the difference in the initial reactions of the two girls especially in terms of the clinical diagnoses. Rhoda reacts with aggression toward adults in her environment (caseworker, group therapist), which is characteristic of a behavior disorder. But apparently treatment had made inroads on her for she is now ambivalent about her caseworker. She is beginning to relate to an adult. She is also ambivalent about the group. Though she says she does not want to come, still she did come; she will also try in the future. She is ambivalent also about the school: she does not want to express freely her feelings about it because other people may feel differently.

We have here a girl whose life pattern is a series of inner conflict and vacillation. She has no clarity of feelings in regard to anything. She wavers, but is driven by anger, resentment, hostility, and aggression. One gets the impression that underneath it all she is really weak and lonely, with a defensive façade of overdetermined positiveness. Marian, on the other hand, is submissive and placating. She has a good word for the school, for to attack the school would mean also to attack the therapist. When Rhoda says that she dislikes her caseworker she is also saying that she dislikes her group therapist. This creates anxiety in Marian and she comes to the defense of the school to allay it.

(C) Clara enters the room full of resistance. She places her chair apart from the others, wears a disdainful smile, and for a long time remains aloof. But underneath this mask there is apparent intense fear and shyness.

The therapist must keep in mind that just as Marian has to be helped to release the repressed hostility which she is covering up, and Rhoda to come to see the projection of her feelings upon others, Clara needs to be reassured and her self-esteem built up.

Rhoda is still aggressive. She evidently has an oral character, and the value of the school to this girl lay in the fact that she is discovering that irascibility and infantile omnipotence are of no avail. Rhoda discovers the inexorable pressures of reality and is beginning to submit to them.

(D) The therapist quite correctly explores Rhoda's statement and asks appropriate questions that help the girls examine their behavior. Rhoda does not seem to convey any regret about it, but Marian, being psychoneurotic, feels guilty and contrite. The value of this discussion is that she is able to admit having aggressive impulses. The therapist correctly explores the feelings behind Marian's temper outbursts, but the girl evades understanding her hostilities. Instead her explanation is on an objective base; people do not like you and you produce a wrong impression, she says. However, a beginning has been made in individual treatment with both these girls. Particularly is this valuable for Marian because her defenses are being loosened.

(E) The therapist recognizes in Clara a readiness to articulate her feelings at this point, for nodding is a form of passive participation. Clara is no longer a passive spectator; she is now a participating spectator. The therapist plays out the role of the accepting mother, and Clara responds to it. Our suspicion that the girl's remoteness and disdainful smile were a fence against fear is thus confirmed. Because of the reassurance she has received she says she would like to talk about personal matters, but is afraid.

(F) The therapist takes the opportunity to interpret the function of the group at this point, since Clara raised the question, and, undoubtedly, it was unclear to the others. The reaction to the therapist's statement on Rhoda's part is rather interesting. She again says she doesn't know if she will talk, but a few minutes later states that perhaps she will come to the group. Her ambivalence continues. She cannot be definite about anything. In addition, she recognizes a stigma in attending the group—another form of resistance.

It seems all the girls recognize the difficulty in speaking about personal matters in each other's presence. Because the transferences have not as yet been established in the group the resistances are strong. Some identifications of a mild nature, particularly between Clara and Rhoda, are evidenced, however. Both are behavior disorders and therefore have similar reactions. When Clara and Rhoda accuse the girls of gossiping, they are projecting their own tendency to gossip. The denial of access to their boy friends seems to be the source of their resentment toward the school. It is noteworthy that even in this brief interlude the girls were able to reach the center of their difficulty, find points of identification, and reveal what really troubles them. They are in conflict; they want boy friends and also feel guilty when they have them.

(G) Apparently Marian's problem is that of being rejected by boys, though she cannot speak about it. She, therefore, disguises it in the form of a question, in which she apparently expresses a hope that though she is not very attractive, she would be acceptable to boys. Rhoda is less sensitive and speaks of the fact that she does not consider herself pretty, but, "beauty is skin-deep" and she makes herself desirable to boys anyway. In expressing her violent feelings against girls who do not keep themselves neat and clean, she is expressing her homosexual interest in girls. When they interpret the fact that neglect of one's person may be a reflection of general emotional disturbance, the girls display good insight. The therapist helps them do this by asking an appropriate question well timed, for they were on the threshold of this understanding. Rhoda at once identifies with this and applies it to herself. The other girls express their assent; they all understand it.

(H)Marian again relates her problem to her adjustment to boys, and perhaps also to other people. She wants help with regard to her withdrawal pattern and feelings of discomfort. By stating that there are girls who would like to be with others who are having fun, the therapist tells Marian that she understands her problem, and thus reassures the girl and helps the transference relation. Rhoda boasts about her accomplishment in overcoming her own difficulty. As her problem is one of behavior disorder, it is not too difficult for her to do this. Marian asks advice from Rhoda, who prescribes a method for overcoming her self-consciousness, a technique that can hardly suit Marian, who is psychoneurotic. She would have to overcome first some of her inner conflicts. However, it is helpful to her in the fact that she discovers it is possible to overcome such difficulties; this gives her a more hopeful feeling about herself.

Clara's participation in the discussion is rather interesting. She jumbles her words so that no one can understand her. Through this, she strikes a compromise between her fear and desire to participate in the discussion. This conflict she resolves by participating, but in a way that did not threaten her: no one understood what she was saying and could therefore not react to it. Just what the therapist sought to accomplish when she told Clara that she understood her, is not quite clear. Clara did not want to be understood, and it might have been better if she were left alone at this point.

(I) Now the girls tell us what is really in their minds. The source of their hostility is that the school prohibits free contact with boys. This blocks what Dr. Spotnitz calls the "reproduction constellation," which irks them. The fact that they speak so freely about it is valuable. Ventilating these feelings eventually leads to a better understanding with the school, the therapist, and with each other. The girls now have a common ground; they identify with one another. Even Marian joins in with the others, but she is still protective of the school and is unable to face her feelings of hostility openly. Rhoda's ambivalence again comes through when she says it may be good for some people but not for others; Clara is more positive on this point. She cannot understand how anybody can like the school. The therapist encouraged the girls on two occasions to come forward with their feelings. This is very helpful, because by asking such leading questions she accepts their hostile feelings and aggression toward the school and, therefore, toward herself.

We also recognize here universalization, identification, and catharsis, which eventually will lead to insight.

If we analyzed further the girls' attitudes toward the school we may find that the hostility is similar in every respect to the hostility that patients have toward their mothers. They complain about restrictions and the unkindliness of the school in exactly the same manner as adolescent girls complain about their mothers at home. Thus, the school becomes the mother figure. Just what the place of the therapist is at this point is not too clear. She is not the mother figure excepting in so far as she represents the school. It is quite possible that the girls complain about her as the one who blocks them from free access to the boys on the campus.

(J) Rhoda gets what she wants. She acts out her Oedipal conflict in relation to the school. She sees her boy friend despite the rules. Marian confirms our suspicion that her impersonal questions concerning girls who are not attractive but are chosen by boys related to herself. Marian admits that she has no boy friend. She again defends the staff because of her fear of aggression. When the worker very advisedly asks the meaning of their belligerency, the girls come through with their nuclear problem, namely, their relation to their fathers, but, in this instance, the father substitute is the director of the school. He is seen by them as the father figure, as the school is the mother figure.

(K) Their interest in the relationships of boys and girls brings them to talk about the incident when a group of boys visited a group of girls in their cottage at the latter's invitation. Marian brings forward this subject to defend the staff. Actually, she is probably quite resentful of the fact that she was not included in the party. The two other girls are provoked and critical. This probably also expresses their envy for not being among the girls who enjoyed the boys' visit. On the other hand, it may be also intended to assure one another that they are not interested in boys, but in one another, which helps the sibling transference and brings forth their homoerotic interests.

Perhaps the most interesting point in this discussion is Rhoda's identification with maleness, which we have suspected. The fact that Rhoda has masculine drives is quite evident from her entire behavior. Here it comes to the surface, when she actually says she would put herself in a boy's place and then proceeds to justify one who would take advantage of a girl who encourages him. This creates considerable conflict in her mind and she suggests that further exploration be made of the relationship of boys and girls, which probably also indicates her confusion of the masculine-feminine aspects of her own personality. But when the therapist acquieces the girls remain silent. They are taken aback, because they expected the therapist, like their own mothers and the school itself, to prohibit this ventilation of their feelings about boys. Rhoda is the first to recover and justifies their interest as natural for girls. In other words, guilt is aroused by the worker's permissiveness, and Rhoda has to justify their impulse. Here, it seems, anxiety had been aroused in a girl with a behavior disorder. The element of surprise or shock has entered in, and, despite her complaint against it, the restraint of the school has made her feel secure.

Myrna comes in late. She is resistant to coming to the group. Both Myrna and Mary (who was absent) are under individual treatment by the group therapist, while the other three members are under treatment with other caseworkers. It is, therefore, understandable that they would be resistive to sharing the therapist with others. Mary does not come at all, and Myrna finds an excuse for not coming. Further, she is defiant about it, also a little frightened. When she says she would not leave the art group for anything, she says it in a semihumorous, yet also a defiant, manner. Thus, she is afraid of losing the good-will of the therapist, but at the same time she is hostile toward her for accepting other children. (Later on the transference was worked through with them and both girls came to the group regularly.)

In seeking for a suitable time for a group meeting in the future, a considerable amount of resistance is displayed. Each girl has some reason for not coming, with the exception of Marian. She is anxious to have a group, which can help her. This is characteristic of a psychoneurotic who is anxious to be helped. There is probably also the possibility that Marian is seeking a way out of individual treatment, which she finds rather difficult. The girls face reality in making a choice and weighing values. The worker helps them clarify this when she tells them that situations arise where one has to make a decision. Again Rhoda expresses ambivalence when she says she had not decided whether she wants to continue with the group.

DISCUSSION

Interview groups in an institution for "delinquent" girls present problems that are not encountered in an out-patient clinic of a city, where the patients are not acquainted and, except for group sessions, seldom have contact with one another. Catharsis is blocked here because the girls are afraid of gossip that may make their problems known to the community. The fact that the girls in this particular group live together in cottages and on the same campus creates difficulties in this respect. The presence of adolescent boys on the same campus with whom they associate, intensifies the girls' fears in this regard, since their "reputations" may defeat their natural need to be accepted and have boy friends.

Such difficulties are not found in a clinic or hospital of a large city, but it may be expected that similar situations may arise in small towns where patients know one another in the community.

It is clear that therapy groups in a non-institutional setting need to be kept quite apart from the ordinary social groupings, unless patients establish friendships (ego-supportive relations), which they carry on outside the group sessions. We have found that these friendships in the community are short-lived, lasting only as long as the group exists, and very frequently terminated before that time. They are understandably only temporary interpersonal associations in the service of the therapeutic process and are dropped as soon as certain needs disappear through psychotherapy. We have always failed in our efforts to transform therapy groups into social clubs after treatment is terminated. The factors of social and psychological homogeneity necessary for social cohesiveness are lacking in therapy groups.

The institutional group, unlike any of the others, displays a remarkable unanimity in hostility toward the school, the staff, and especially the male director. This facilitates conversation, since all have the same hostility target and the same reasons for "griping," which serves to accelerate identification, though it is only in a limited area. Hostility is freely expressed, and its expression is initiated much earlier here than in city groups. Because of their common target and resultant identification, the girls were, according to the caseworkers and group therapist (who had treated two of the girls also individually), much more productive in the group than in individual treatment.

The early interviews consisted almost entirely of complaints and charges against the staff and the institution. Involuntary sequestration from the natural community and one's family necessarily mobilizes hostility and aggression toward the institution, which is, in the minds of the residents, the agency of punishment and restraint. The difficulty is that realistic grounds for dissatisfaction are always present in an institution to give validity to fancied wrongs and imaginary discriminations. Patients vent these dissatisfactions upon the group therapist, and since negative transference tends to be intensified because of the high degree of patient identification and support, the therapist may at times be hard put to it. It requires greater skill and experience to conduct analytic therapy groups in a "restraining" institution than in a voluntary out-patient clinic in a city. There are even in these groups some patients, usually the psychoneurotic, who act as neutralizers. They act as the group superego, as it were, and tend to inject an element of reasonableness and tolerance. Marian is an example of this.

Among the difficulties encountered in the practice of analytic group psychotherapy in an institution is the inevitable contact of patients and therapist at times other than the regularly set sessions and the resultant fact that patients find it hard to disassociate the therapist from the restraining and sometimes punishing role of the other members of the staff. This situation greatly complicates the transference relation. It mobilizes its negative aspects and intensifies and prolongs resistance. Still another difficulty is the meaning attached in the school community to one who belongs to a special group from which others are barred. Being included in these groups is in some instances considered a special privilege, whereas in others it constitutes a stigma. These difficulties, however, are encountered only early in treatment and soon disappear as the patients become accustomed to the group.

In the beginning, suspicion on the part of the school residents makes them resistive to attending group sessions, and considerable seduction has to be used, which is less necessary in out-patient treatment in a city or in private practice. If the therapist were to remain passive and impersonal, few, if any of the residents, would avail themselves of these groups. The therapist has to overcome the initial suspicion by convincing the prospective group members of his interest in them. One cannot exert administrative pressure to force attendance without sacrificing the therapeutic value of the group. The therapist and the referring staff members rather have to entice and seduce the patients into attendance. Once the initial resistances are overcome, and the patients attend several sessions, their interest seems to be sufficiently aroused to insure their return. Because of the initial resistance to group therapy in institutions, regularity in holding sessions is of utmost importance. Skipping sessions, no matter what the pressures are or the explanations given, intensifies the resistances and confirms the patients' convictions of the group's uselessness. What is even more serious is that they are confirmed in their desire to believe that the therapist is not really interested in them.

One of the striking psychodynamics manifested by this group of girls is the displacement of their feelings toward their mothers upon the institution as such. Restraint and prohibition of sexual gratification give rise to hostility and resentment. On the other hand, the attitude toward the male director of the institution is similar to their attitude toward their fathers. They are ambivalent about him and the girls have actually always behaved seductively toward him. The pattern of these attitudes is transparently similar to the Oedipal conflict. Marian, the psychoneurotic girl, became aware of these unconscious attitudes when she said, "Maybe it is because he is director [father] that we don't like him."

In this group of adolescents, more so than in the others reported in this volume, acting out is evident on the surface. Rhoda is openly defiant, Clara refuses to join the group, Marian is throughout submissive and placating, Myrna delays coming, and Mary does not come at all. Each of the girls displayed her anger and displeasure in the group interview, as is seen from their conversation, but they did this also in a number of other ways, such as physical and postural expressions, clenching of fists, shuffling of feet, stiffening of bodies and moving about in their seats. As already indicated, neuromuscular discharge of psychic energy detenses the whole organism and supplies equilibrium through release. This is, however, only a minor step in therapy. Therapy has to be achieved through insight, as well as abreaction. In view of the fact that this was the first session, the therapist was not able to go far in this direction, but the skill and the timeliness with which she probed the patients and suggested lines for the interview are indeed praiseworthy.

There are several possible reasons for the unusually high degree of direct acting out. Since this is the first session, the patients are testing out the situation and the therapist. They are bolder in this than are out-patients, because they have realistic cause for resentment against the therapist as a member of the school staff, and they know her because she lives on the campus. They are, therefore, less shy and less restrained. They are also certain of support from each other, since they are at one in hostility and identify with one another, that is, sibling transferences had been established in this group before the transference toward the therapist. Perhaps the more telling reason is the fact that this group includes a predominant number of delinquent girls accustomed to acting out hostilities, and they continue to do so in the group.

CHAPTER FOURTEEN

SELECTION AND GROUPING OF PATIENTS

THE CRITERIA for selection of suitable patients for analytic group psychotherapy are still inadequately defined and much of the choice is based on the judgment and bias of various practitioners. There is considerable variance in this regard and one would be justified in saying that sometimes errors are made which may have serious consequences.

The criteria employed in the selection or rejection of patients for individual treatment are with some exceptions applicable also for groups. These criteria can be divided into three categories: (1) negative, (2) positive-negative, and (3) positive.

Negative indications are states or attitudes of patients that clearly make them unfit for group treatment. In the positive-negative group fall those patients for whom individual treatment is desirable, but because of their inability or unwillingness to accept it, group treatment is employed either as preparation or concomitant with individual treatment. In the positive category are included patients for whom group treatment exclusively is indicated.

Criteria for fitness for group psychotherapy can also be clinical and non-clinical. In the former are included specific diagnostic categories on the basis of which patients are classified, such as behavior disorders, the various psychoneuroses, character disorders, and border-line cases. Frequently non-clinical considerations, as well, have to be taken into account.

Negative criteria are organic and constitutional defects, and extreme regressive states. Patients with extreme resistances such as found in narcissistic neuroses and psychoses have to be excluded from groups as they frequently are also from individual psychotherapy. Manic patients, patients with a tendency toward depression, potential or overt perverts, suicidal patients, psychopaths, involutionary, compulsive, and obsessional patients, and patients who hallucinate are all unsuitable for groups for obvious reasons. Each will in his own way disrupt, dominate, or exploit the group, or the group, conversely, may activate the pathologic processes and aberrant behavior to the detriment of the patient himself. Obsessional and compulsive patients, for example, are excessively articulate and monopolize the interviews to such an extent that treatment for all others is blocked. Their needs for regression to anal levels as part of treatment may be difficult for the others in the group to countenance or support. The narcissistic and paranoid components in such patients are so strong that the pressure of their fellow members in no way inhibits their fluency and acting out, and they develop intense antipathies and hostilities too difficult to deal with in a group setting. The bizarre behavior of such patients disturbs others who already suffer from anxiety or whose anxieties are readily aroused.

While group treatment is by and large indicated for the transference neuroses, severe psychoneurotics may well be inaccessible by this method. Great caution should be exercised in assigning severe adult psychoneurotics, particularly, to groups. Because of the nature of the character neurosis in which the ego itself is involved, patients suffering from such neuroses would seem unsuitable for therapy groups. While there is great diversity of opinion in the literature on the understanding and treatment of character neuroses, there is unanimity on the fact that they make difficult patients in any type of psychotherapy because of their inflexibility and, especially, because of the difficulty they have in seeing their problem. Because the ego itself is a part of the condition, the neurotic constellation is not isolated or focused; it is rather structured in the personality. In the treatment situation such patients are unreasonable, stubborn, and defensive—not because they are afraid to reveal themselves, but because they cannot recognize themselves as problems. In groups they are overassertive, loquacious, self-centered, argumentative, and power-driven. They have the same effect on a group as do psychopaths, dominating the discussions and blocking the catharsis of the other patients. It is, therefore, inadvisable to include them in groups.

However, patients come for treatment who do not suffer from out and out character neuroses but rather from character deviations and lacks as a result of inadequate growth-producing opportunities in childhood of various kinds. Reva [1] is one appropriate example of this. We have found that, as far as children and adolescents are concerned, in the actual experience with realistic situations such as a group supplies, character malformations can be corrected. Except for congenital and hereditary factors, character is shaped and conditioned by experience; it can therefore be corrected by adaptations to meaningful situations. This is especially true of children.[2]

Psychopathic personalities are unsuitable for group treatment. Both experience and theory support the view that patients of this type cannot adjust to group life and interfere with the therapeutic opportunities of the others. The need for object relationships and a striving to change that patients must have in order to make progress in treatment is lacking. Psychopaths, being narcissistic with defective superego formation and little social hunger, exploit the permissive and tolerant attitudes in the group for their egotistic ends to the detriment of fellow members. They are exhibitionistic, dominate the interviews, block the catharsis of the others, are provocative, and not infrequently directly attack or ridicule the therapist. Unlike the neurotic patients, who behave in much the same manner, they irritate the group members, who become resentful and attack them. Because of the egotistic nature of this state, the patient cannot tolerate such rejection and quits the group. Institutionalization is recommended for psychopaths. They require external pressures which a voluntary therapy group cannot provide. The pressures and rigidities of institutional life, punishment for transgressions, and discipline hold in check the psychopath's self-indulgent trends and his disregard for others. It is quite possible also that as a result, he internalizes some of these restraints and, even when he does not develop a real superego, he may acquire some degree of control over his aberrant impulses and narcissistic indulgence.[3]

[1] See p. 172.

[2] For a more detailed discussion of group treatment for such patients see present writer's "Group Therapy with Character Deviations" in *Practice of Group Therapy*, ed. S. R. Slavson, New York, International Universities Press, 1947.

[3] S. R. Slavson, "Counter-Indications of Group Therapy for Patients with Psychopathic Personalities," *ibid.*

Still another consideration in assigning patients to groups is their general readiness for group participation, that is, for multiple relations. This is a factor difficult to determine in advance, and one has to rely on one's judgment. Patients who have not had minimal satisfactions in childhood with primary relations (with parents, or other important adults, and siblings) and whose rivalry and jealousy are extreme may find it difficult or impossible to participate in a group interview without disturbing the therapeutic atmosphere and gaining little for themselves from the experience. There are also patients who are so inhibited and whose feelings of shame and guilt are so strong that they are unable to reveal themselves in the presence of others. Identification therapy alone is not enough. Then there are the hostile persons who hold themselves in check, are silent and withdrawn as a defense against acting out hostilities. Patients naturally overbearing and verbose (oral aggressive) have an undesirable effect on a group. To gain from a therapy group, patients must have a minimal capacity for group participation and social hunger.

It is evident from the foregoing that in selecting patients more than the clinical diagnoses have to be considered. In some instances, the intensity of the problem is as much a factor as its nature. While by and large psychoneurotic children, and children with neurotic traits, for example, are suitable for group therapy, the disturbances of some may be so intense as to render them unfit. They may require individual treatment either exclusively or concomitant with group psychotherapy. The psychoneurotic child with intense Oedipal involvements and strong incestuous drives obviously needs to be treated individually. A boy who had been exposed to his mother's seductiveness, who slept in the same bed with her, and whose personal needs were taken care of too long develops strong sexual ties toward her. He needs to displace his libidinal ties from the mother on another object, which would require a relation with another woman in individual psychotherapy as well as some insight.

In the *positive-negative* category of patients, and there is a considerable number of them, are those whose resistances and defensiveness against an individual therapist stem from intense distrust, fear, competitiveness, or uncontrollable antagonism toward all persons in power (parental figures). Though many such patients require individual treatment, they cannot accept the relation and should be referred to groups, where the transference is diluted and support from fellow patients is present. Some may be treated in groups exclusively, while for others the group serves as a transitional stage toward individual psychotherapy.

Among the *non-clinical positive* indications for group treatment most frequently encountered are lack of sibling experiences, negative sibling attitudes, absence of opportunities for participation, destructive family relations, danger and fear of homosexual involvement with an individual therapist, resistance to individual treatment, patients with character disorders, and generalized social maladjustment.

One of the important considerations in selecting patients is the intelligence level. Interview group psychotherapy can be beneficial only for persons of at least minimal intelligence. Patients must be able to formulate and verbalize their problems and have some understanding of interpretation. Our experience with a small number of dull patients in groups seems to indicate that the intelligence level need not be very high. This is partly due to the fact that in groups the identification index is high, especially where the emotional difficulties are the same. Dull patients participated in the discussions of the group only occasionally, but seemed to derive considerable benefit from the group discussions.

Adolescent girls with low intelligence ratings have also fitted surprisingly well in groups with much brighter girls. Our earlier hesitancy to include them has proved unjustified. While duller patients fall behind in discussions, by and large, they keep up with the general trend. Frequently, mothers with low intelligence made better strides in handling their children than did the more intellectual and articulate.

That they can act out their feelings in the group is of definite advantage for dull patients. Whereas they may not be able to express themselves verbally, discharge of emotions through anger, rage, disgust, and quarreling serves these adolescents and adults in the same way that activity catharsis serves the child, and reactions from others in the group is as real to them as they are to children.

The selection of children is much simpler than is the case with adults. The general consideration is based on the fact that all children gain from group association. The therapist must determine whether a specific child also has a need for concurrent individual play therapy. The clinical diagnoses as a guide for grouping are also less important in the selection of children. What is important is to prevent exposing a particularly frightened and withdrawn child to excessive aggression or persecution by others in the group. Schizoid personalities and children suffering from childhood schizophrenia should be eliminated, for they would find acting out by their group—mates too distressing and frightening. Children with particularly violent primary behavior disorders, especially of the pre-Oedipal type, are also unsuitable for groups and where the hostility toward the mother is unusually intense, the direct attacks on the therapist are too disturbing for the others and too difficult to cope with by the therapist.

In one of our groups a boy between five and six years of age was inordinately violent in his physical attacks and in less direct hostile acts against the woman therapist. We recognized in his behavior a retaliatory motive. Apparently he resented sharing her with the other children. We suggested that the therapist see the boy for twenty to thirty minutes individually preceding the group sessions. When this was arranged, the boy at once ceased his destructive and violent behavior. This illustrates the point we have already made that where the primary relations are too disturbed or inadequate an individual transference becomes imperative.

The determining factors as to whether a patient should receive group treatment exclusively or a combination of individual and group treatment lie both in the nature and the intensity of his disturbance. When the anxieties are centered in the relations with parents an individual transference upon the therapist through which the earliest emotionally charged and traumatized feelings can be worked through is necessary. In cases where the secondary outcomes such as feelings of inadequacy, sibling rivalry, and social maladjustments are the presenting problems, the earlier difficulties with parents can be allayed by exclusive group treatment. Where both types of treatment are indicated, the individual and group therapist must be one and the same person. Division of transference is undesirable, in fact, would be quite difficult for a patient to achieve.

While the diagnosis of psychopathic personality for very young children is at best a tenuous one, there are some who, either because of constitutional predisposition or inordinately pathological home environment, are, or behave as though they were, psychopathic. The defect in the superego formation in these children and their lack of consideration for people makes them unsuitable for inclusion in groups.[4] The point need not be pressed that placing psychotic with non-psychotic children is counterindicated.

Confused identification often manifests itself in the patients desire to function in an overmature role, in phantasies of being an adult and in self-maximating acts and ideas. This is a borderline condition between a neurosis and a character disorder. Individual treatment may be necessary in some selected cases, but group therapy was found most effective because of the opportunities offered for corrective identifications.

In behavior disorders the focus of treatment is to help the patient develop meaningful relationships with people and thus correct his superego formation. The characteristic difficulty here is that the patient resented the treatment he had received from his parents and adopted retaliatory and attention-getting aggression as a life pattern. The first step in the treatment of these patients is to establish a relation with them. The dilution of the transference, the impersonal nature and the fluid relationships, and the comparative freedom in groups makes it much easier for them to establish relations than in intensive and direct contact with an adult. They see him as a friendly, pleasure-giving person, and not as an enemy to be opposed and fought.

The second step in the treatment of primary behavior disorders is applying restraint to unreasonable and destructive behavior. This has to be carefully timed to accord with a patient's frustration tolerance and must be commensurate with his willingness to surrender pleasures derived from destructive acts for the approval of the therapist and acceptance by the group (reality principle). The surrender is made because of the desire for social acceptance (social hunger), or because of positive identifications, growing self-esteem, and the educational guidance group members give one another

[4] See p. 230.

through discussions. The value of activity groups [5] for primary behavior disorders is to be found also in the other groups described here. Primary behavior disorders, Oedipal type, are more accessible than are the pre-Oedipal.

Our present impression is that groups are particularly suited for adolescent girls even with serious emotional problems, provided they are able to accept and participate in a group, as already described. Many of these youngsters may require individual treatment as well, but there are a large number who do not require individual therapy, and can be treated in groups exclusively. In some instances group treatment may be a preparation for individual therapy.

The record material in this volume clearly demonstrates that adolescent girls with confused sexual identifications [6] have gained much from the association with a group of girls. Such patients have various types of character deviations, changes in which are more easily wrought by experience and corrective identifications, and analytic group psychotherapy is indicated here.[7]

The only available statistical study of improvement in analytic group psychotherapy in relation to clinical entities has been made by Schilder, who pioneered in the application of the psychoanalytic technique to group interviews with adult patients in a hospital and he has reported what seems to be unusually good results as shown by the following table: [8]

[5] See Saul Scheidlinger, "Activity Group Therapy with Primary Behavior Disorders," in *The Practice of Group Therapy* (New York, International Universities Press, 1947).

[6] Girls whose mothers have been rigid, unaffectionate, domineering and rejecting, but whose fathers were mild and friendly become confused as to their own role. Paula is an example of such a case. Sometimes identification and competition with a brother causes such identity confusion. The confusion becomes intensified as adolescence is reached and sex urges are activated. In our experience, treatment of such patients (which involves fundamental libido development and an inverted Oedipal conflict) is prolonged and difficult. Whenever such primary elements of human personality are involved, the more important dynamic of treatment is transference and corrective identifications, which groups can provide. Insight derived from group interviews concomitant with sibling transference and identifications is adequate in these cases.

[7] See S. R. Slavson, "Group Therapy with Character Deviations," in *The Practice of Group Therapy* (New York, International Universities Press, 1947).

[8] Paul Schilder, "Results and Problems of Group Psychotherapy in Severe Neuroses," *Mental Hygiene,* January, 1939; "Introductory Remarks on Groups," *Journal of Social Psychology,* August, 1940, and *Psychotherapy* (New York, W. W. Norton and Co., 1938), pp. 157–159, 197–225.

	Total	*Cured*	*Improved*	*Unimproved*
Social Neuroses	12	3	7	2
Obsessional Neuroses	9	2	7	—
Anxiety Neuroses	3	2	1	—
Hysteria	4 *	2	—	1
Hypochondria	3	—	—	3
Totals	31	9	15	6

* One stopped treatment.

Schilder worked with small groups of five and six patients who were also undergoing individual treatment. A cursory examination of the table yields rather interesting results, because they partially confirm theoretic predictions. The most striking features are (1) the high percentage of cures among the hysterical and (2) no improvement in hypochondria. Hypochondriasis being a narcissistic neurosis can be expected to yield least to group treatment where the relationship factor is so important, while the hysteric (not anxiety hysteria) is a product of over intense repressions, and release (catharsis), facilitated in a group, would cause the patient to respond to such treatment. We also see a high percentage of improvement in "social neuroses" (84 percent), though we would not expect such a high rate of improvement (100 percent) in the obsessional neuroses. Since the patients were also receiving individual treatment, however, it would be necessary to separate the effects of the group from those of the individual treatment before a full evaluation could be made. Note that compulsive neuroses were omitted, as among the conditions unlikely to yield to group psychotherapy. However, this entire field requires considerable experimentation with larger numbers of patients.

Ackerman suggests that "Group dynamics are more specifically adapated to 'externalized' than to 'internalized' patterns of emotional conflict, namely those conflicts in which the struggle is mainly between the person and his environment, rather than between two opposing forces within the psyche." [9] This conclusion confirms Schilder's indication of accessibility by group therapy of patients with "social neuroses," namely, "the struggle . . . between the

[9] Nathan W. Ackerman, "Some General Principles in the Use of Group Psychotherapy," in *Current Therapies in Personality Disorders,* ed. Bernard Glueck (New York, Grune and Stratton, 1946), p. 279.

person and his environment," though I cannot agree to the differentiation between the externalized and internalized patterns. Externalized patterns manifest themselves because of internal conflicts or malformations. The focus of treatment is the subjectum, and one can easily go astray in directing treatment toward the behavioral (externalized) pattern rather than toward the internalized difficulties. Our experience with some 2,700 patients in various groups proves that definite intrapsychic changes occurred, as shown by the Rorschach Test even through activity group therapy.[10] Particularly noteworthy in this respect is the progress reported on Georgia.[11]

The present writer is among those who believe that the basic conflicts of the full-blown psychoneurotic can be resolved only by psychoanalysis. But much of psychotherapy aims to eliminate not the conflict or trauma itself but its derivative personality difficulties and over-intense affect as manifested in behavior and the conscious. Analytic group psychotherapy is well able to do this.

There are also large numbers of patients who seek help but who do not have discernible neurotic symptoms, such as one finds in the conversion, obsessional, compulsive or anxiety neuroses. Even when disturbances originate in a neurotic background and as a result of early traumatizing relations, some patients do not suffer from full-blown neuroses. There are also patients who have become inured in the habit of problem-creating behavior and attitudes through early identifications. Patients also come for treatment whose values in life are faulty and attitudes toward themselves unwholesome. The difficulty in determining the suitability of these patients for groups lies in the symptoms and the ease with which one may confuse behavior superficially observed with more basic emotional problems. In fact much of the confusion that now exists in psychotherapy is that sometimes persons suffering from deeply rooted neuroses receive superficial psychotherapy while many are in psychoanalysis who could gain from a less intensive form of treatment.

It is clear that, where psychological reeducation and improving the self-image are necessary, groups are more effective because of

[10] Miriam G. Siegel, "The Rorschach Test as an Aid in Selecting Clients for Group Therapy and Evaluating Progress," *Mental Hygiene,* July, 1944.

[11] Betty Gabriel, Hyman Spotnitz, Miriam G. Siegel, and S. R. Slavson, "Interview Group Therapy with an Adolescent Neurotic Girl," in *The Practice of Group Therapy.*

the opportunities for identification, the ideological change, and the reality testing offered. The cognative content of the group discussions helps each individual to understand his problems and evaluate his behavior in a new light, thereby leading to general improvement. We have here another criterion for indication for group treatment; the individual's faulty ideological and attitudinal orientation and habits.

Frequently even with patients with full psychoneuroses only limited objectives can be undertaken because of specific personality or constitutional factors, the situations under which they live, their unwillingness to enter on a course of prolonged and intensive treatment or because practical considerations make it impossible. Help can be offered to such persons through groups where they can find relief in some of the peripheral areas of their lives, even though the nuclear conflicts or problems are only partially affected.

On a number of occasions in the preceding pages, as well as in a number of papers elsewhere, I have emphasized the great importance of grouping. In view of the fact that the total group climate is set by the network of feelings among the members and individual relations which form the background for the therapeutic process, matching of the personnel of the group is of utmost importance. Experience shows that the presence of even one unsuitable patient not only changes the atmosphere of a group and the content of the interviews, but its effectiveness as well. The effect upon a social group or gathering of a disturbing person is well known to everyone and, because patients in a therapy group are less stable, selection is even more important here. However, one is hard put to it when asked to describe specifically the criteria and considerations in matching patients. Much has still to be left to the intuition and judgment of the therapist, a judgment that grows keener and more unerring with practice.

One of the chief aims of grouping is to achieve a permissible quantum of pathology and hostility density. For if these are too high for tolerance by patients who are disturbed as it is, the resultant tensions may be too great not only for the patients, but for the therapist as well. Groups should include persons who can act as neutralizers, that is, who dilute tensions and introduce an element of quiet and control when situations become too difficult or disturbing. Emotions like rage, anger, distress, self-pity, hopelessness are common and infectious, and unless there is enough rationality and self-control in some of the group members, these emotions may become reinforced and overintensified. Thus the group should include a variety of persons, though they should have *the same psychologic syndromes.*

No therapist can deal with one patient at any given time and the group acts *as one patient* when all the members in it are preoccupied with some central problem or whose traumatic syndromes are alike even if the symptoms are different. This is essential for several reasons. In the first place identification therapy and identification transferences are possible only when such homogeneity exists. Divergence in the problems and the nature of psychological constitution also diminish the possibilities for interpersonal therapy since the unconscious content and the conscious preoccupations differ. Perhaps a good illustration of this is the reaction of a schizoid patient who was placed in a group of psychoneurotics. He remained quite inactive for several sessions. After one of the sessions he approached the therapist and asked, "Doctor, why do these people talk so much about their parents and how bad they were to them? My parents never did anything like that!"

Some patients suddenly break off the group interviews because of a topic which they cannot tolerate, or which seems puzzling to them. Reva, for example, during the earlier interviews, was quite puzzled and seemed lost when sexual matters came under discussion. What is of utmost importance is that patients activate each other's unconscious and this they can do only when the psychological constellations, or syndromes, are the same. This is well illustrated in the discussion between Mrs. Allen and Mrs. Farmer[12] because both were preoccupied with their relations toward their fathers.

Perhaps a good illustration of what is meant here is furnished by the following incident. We once planned to organize a group for fathers of children under treatment, where they seemed to be the major source of the youngsters' problems. Only a woman therapist was available, and the suggestion was made that fathers of a certain type be selected—those who needed a "better relation with a

[12] See p. 192.

woman," that is, men who treated their wives impersonally, unfeelingly as though they were unimportant incidents. Some of these men were good providers and discharged all responsibilities well, but were too indifferent and cold. Upon further analysis it was found that this symptom or behavioral pattern was misleading. There were many reasons for the seeming indifference by the men toward their wives, such as guilt in relation to an unresolved Oedipal conflict with their mothers, latent homosexuality, sadomasochism, schizoid character structure, and others. What was necessary was to combine patients according to similarity in the causal psychologic syndrome, even if they presented symptoms other than the one under consideration, for only under this condition can group interviews be meaningful to all in terms of their unconscious.

Another illustration from experience is the use of a symptom as a criterion for grouping. Several psychiatrists decided to pool their patients to form a therapy group. After the very first session they became aware that something was wrong with the group, though they were unable to find the reason. They consulted the present writer before the second session. It was found that the criterion for selection and grouping of the patients was "anxiety." Patients who suffered from anxiety had been placed in the group without prior consideration of the meaning and the etiology of the symptom in each patient. When the group was reorganized on the basis of common syndrome rather than similarity of symptom, the interviews became more fruitful and later reports showed gratifying improvement in the patients.

Another young psychiatrist experienced similar difficulty when, in the attempt to treat a number of patients with a special social maladjustment, he placed psychoneurotic patients together with others having character disorders. When this was called to his attention and he separated the two, he reported "a startling change" in the nature of the interviews and the results obtained.

It will be noted that, with respect to syndromes, the choice of patients for interview groups differs from that for activity groups. In the former the syndromes must be the same, namely, the nuclear problem of the patient and the foci of the traumatic constellations must be sufficiently similar to assure a measure of identification and render interpretation meaningful to all. In activity groups for children in latency, on the other hand, dissimilar syndromes are essential. In such groups balance is necessary. Thus, withdrawn children are grouped with the outgoing and aggressive, the fearful with the more courageous. Mild psychoneurotics, primary behavior and character disorders, and under specific conditions moderately schizoid and even the latent schizophrenic can be included in the same group.

Because the activity, rather than verbalization, is the pattern in these groups, the interaction of the various types of individuals is helpful to all. Through imitation and demonstrated action by others, each of the children gains confidence, overcomes fears, or regulates his overt actions to levels acceptable to the group. Intrapsychic changes also occur through the direct face-to-face relations of children diverse in their personality organization. Specific intrapersonal as well as interpersonal difficulties are worked through because of this diversity, whereas if all patients in these groups were alike, intensification of a given problem or syndrome would occur. Neutralization and dilution, not intensification, are sought in these groups.

In interview groups, on the other hand, similarity of syndromes is important because insight through communication is the aim, and identification and universalization are the relevant mechanisms. The sharpness of this contrast in grouping patients is considerably lessened in analytic groups for pre-pubertal children. In these groups, as well, diversity of clinical diagnoses and psychological syndromes is permissible, but in view of the presence of intensely psychoneurotic children, the range of diversity must of necessity be less than in pure activity groups.

Because of improper grouping some therapists find it necessary to turn their attention to individual members. In fact they interview the patients in rotation or order. Syndrome homogeneity diminishes the strain on the therapist from carrying on individual treatment during a group session, for this is not only strenuous, but confuses the patients and supplies them with avenues of escape.[13] It would seem that this technique leans heavily on spectator or identification therapy. But identification therapy occurs only when

[13] See p. 95.

patients have similar basic problems with which they can identify, and when this is the case there is no need for the "call method" or rotation system. Free association and interpatient therapy occur quite spontaneously where the problems and constellations in the unconscious are similar.

Any rotation system eliminates the very essence of psychotherapy, namely, spontaneity and free association; it is necessary only when the matching of patients is faulty. Small wonder one group psychotherapist who had employed the rotation system gave up group treatment because of a feeling of exhaustion after each session. The same complaint was voiced by other practitioners of this method. If one stops to consider the amount of frustrating and control of the patients the therapist has to exercise in these circumstances the reason for the fatigue is not too difficult to understand.

Still another aim to be sought in grouping of patients is their capacity for mutual catalization. We have stressed the value of neutralization and control that patients should exercise upon one another. Equally important is the catalytic or releasing effect they have upon each other. To achieve this, one must look for (a) similarity of problems (identification); (b) varying degrees of inner conflict; (c) mutual support, with a consequent decrease of anxiety (neutralization), and (d) diminishing of the homoerotic drives.

Grouping of young children presents fewer difficulties than in the case of adolescents and adults. A greater variety of problems and syndromes can be included in children's groups. It is generally recognized, however, that the age factor in pre-pubertal children is of utmost importance. This is equally true of early, middle, and later adolescence. But one finds in adult groups, surprising age-span among the patients—sometimes as much as twenty to thirty years; one therapist in an out-patient clinic includes parents and their grown children in the same groups.

It has been our practice to place pre-school children in groups whose age difference was but a few months; certainly not more than a year. This rule was adhered to also as far as possible with children in the latency period. Pubertal children were placed together, and we avoided grouping youngsters in middle adolescence with those in later adolescence. Thus children between the ages of thirteen and fifteen, fifteen to seventeen, seventeen and eighteen, were placed together. The records of the group interviews included in this volume seem to support these criteria. Organic, intellectual, emotional, and social maturity, sophistication and the intensity of aggression may make it necessary to assign an individual to a somewhat older or younger group.

Similarly, the age differential in adults should also be kept within limits, though here it can be much greater. However, assignment to groups of patients of twenty-five years of age with sixty-year-olds, as is sometimes done, is counterindicated. Perhaps a good criterion is that patients whose age-relation is that of child and parent should not be grouped together.

The question of open or closed groups is one that needs to be considered and some experimentation in this area is necessary. This is important because some patients may feel uncomfortable when new members are added in the course of the group treatment. To gain most from treatment, patients should be as nearly as possible on the same levels of personality development. Individuals with too wide a range in maturity and ego integration ought not to be grouped together. Even when the similarity of syndromes favors grouping, the degree of immaturity and the levels of infantile fixation of the patients must also be considered. It is, therefore, understandable why a patient who is far along in treatment or is on the point of recovery would find himself disturbed when others of lesser developmental levels were added to the group. The new patients, as well, may be overwhelmed by the integration and maturity of the others. This is particularly true where the therapy is conducted entirely on an interview basis.

Levels of activity in young children are not as distinct as are the thoughts and ideas of adults or adolescents. It would, therefore, be wiser to keep the groups of adults and adolescents closed. This does not preclude adding patients at the early stages of group treatment when the patients had not as yet worked through some of their deeper problems. We have found that in play groups for very small children, as well, the discrepancy in growth levels of the young patients creates difficulties; by and large we would recommend that these analytic therapy groups as well be closed groups.

Whether men and women should be grouped together is one of the matters that still require investigation. There are at present differences of opinion with regard to this, which probably stem from differences of practice. Some therapists include patients of both sexes largely because they lack enough patients of one sex to form groups. Others believe that in mixed groups patients activate each other's catharsis and communication. On theoretical grounds, however, it would seem to be more advisable to separate the sexes. Sexually homogeneous groups find it easier to break through resistances, particularly in matters of sex, sexual practices, deviant sexual behavior, and others subjects of a similar nature. The shyness present among persons of different sexes is exaggerated in most of the patients that come for treatment. There is also greater possibility of identification and universalization among patients of the same sex.

The natural hostilities among men and women and their distrust militates against free communication, though these attitudes in themselves can be used as part of the therapeutic process with benefit. In a mixed group of psychoneurotic patients the therapist sensed a degree of reserve and an effort on the part of the men and women to impress one another as sexually adequate and desirable. This served to block free catharsis. Once when all the men happened to be absent from a session, the women patients were much freer in their verbalization and revealed some characteristics that were not evidenced before. For the first time, one of the most productive and seemingly more secure of the patients broke down and wept, something she had never done in any of the preceding sessions. Though in itself inadequate proof, this incident confirms our assumption that the sexes should be separated in adult and adolescent groups.

At some stages of treatment patients may ask that members of the opposite sex be introduced into the group. This very interesting phenomenon needs to be analyzed and understood. In one such instance where psychoneurotic men had made such a request, we found that two factors operated to activate it. One was the presence of a female stenographer at the sessions, which in my opinion is undesirable; the men sought protection against their feelings toward this rather attractive young woman. The more important cause, however, was the mounting anxiety stemming from their latent homosexuality.

At no time did women patients ask that men be added to their groups. This is more or less in keeping with the general pattern, namely, that women are more comfortable and more satisfied with each other's company than are men—feelings that stem from the relations with their mothers. Men, on the other hand, crave the company of women largely due to the fact that their earliest satisfactions were experienced through the mother.

Another problem which often troubles group psychotherapists is whether husbands and wives should be placed in the same groups. Some preliminary experiments have been made in this direction. Sometimes husbands and wives are placed in groups with single patients. In one instance four couples were grouped together exclusively. These experiments, however, have not been either extensive or conclusive, and more investigation is necessary to establish the validity of the procedure. On general principles one is justified in saying that it is undesirable. The very intense mutual hostility among neurotic and otherwise disturbed married couples is so great that there would undoubtedly arise very great interference with or distortion of the catharsis. In many instances where the suppressed or controlled resentments are brought to the surface, active disharmony and even breakup of the marriage may result before the group treatment can affect intrapsychic changes to prevent it. The interviews at sessions may degenerate into quarreling and the injury to self-esteem in the marriage partners is likely to destroy the relation beyond repair. The deep-rooted, hostile, destructive, mutually debasing, and contemptuous feelings that often exist between husbands and wives, if unmasked and brought to the surface, may make it impossible to repair the conjugal relation. For these and other considerations, we can assume that grouping of husbands and wives, as a principle, is undesirable, but this should not preclude experimentation with great caution and wisdom.

Therapy groups, to be effective, must be structured groups. They cannot be accidental or convenient conglomerates of individuals. As far as it is humanly possible, the therapist should envisage in advance what role each of the patients accepted for treatment will play in the complex of interpersonal dynamics in the group. But above all, he must aim at syndrome homogeneity.

CHAPTER FIFTEEN

THE USE OF GROUPS IN THE TREATMENT OF PSYCHOTICS

GROUP treatment for psychotics is less widespread and less understood than for non-psychotic personality disturbances. This is largely due to the fact that the foundations for the treatment of transference neuroses were clearly laid down by Freud and are only now beginning to be understood as treatment of psychoses. Recent work with pharmacotherapy, the convulsive therapies (better known as shock therapies), and psychosurgery have opened new fields. Hypnotherapy and various narcotherapies, also of recent development, are thought to be less therapies in themselves than means for reducing resistances. The actual therapeutic process is verbalization (catharsis) and insight. These ancillary techniques can, therefore, be considered rather as means for establishing the conditions necessary for psychotherapy—transference and catharsis—and thus as accelerants of the therapeutic process. Psychotics, being in a state of narcissistic regression, cannot ordinarily establish the transference relations without which therapy is impossible. Hypnosis and narcoses are therefore used to break through these narcissistic barriers; in themselves they cannot be considered as adequate therapeutic agents. It is also believed by some that shock therapy, as well, has temporary effect unless followed by psychotherapy.

Before these recently developed methods had been introduced, mental hospitals relied almost entirely upon the spontaneous recovery that very frequently occurs in patients, probably as a result of being removed from the oppressive actuality from which the psychotic retreats. When patients were fortunate enough to have a kindly and sympathetic physician, nurse, or orderly, or the friendship of other patients less disturbed, recovery—temporary and permanent—was facilitated. When the treatment was cruel and unsympathetic, the condition usually remained unchanged, though even under these adverse circumstances a small percentage of patients were discharged as partially or completely "cured."

Another past practice that militated against developing sound treatment methods with psychotics was reliance on blanket and categorical diagnoses rather than an understanding of the dynamics and etiology of each. The trend now is in the latter direction.

As far as group psychotherapy is concerned, one needs to differentiate between organic, toxic, and functional psychoses. Toxic psychoses require appropriate medical care to reestablish normal metabolism. Organic psychoses are incurable unless the precipitating condition is repaired; but since the physical deteriorations, such as in encephalitis, paresis, and senility, that produce psychotic states are usually irreversible, little hope is commonly held out for permanent or appreciable recovery or improvement of such patients. Nonetheless, even these patients need a conditioned environment where pressures and demands are commensurate with their capacities. They need a life of attenuated and simple realities, as do children, and the protection and guidance of trained, sympathetic, and resourceful people.

The psychotics that gain most from group living, in fact for whom it is an essential if not a major tool of treatment, are those suffering from functional psychoses. As far as is known at present, the functional psychoses are abnormal mental states that are not caused by structural abnormalities or pathological metabolism. They are rather regressive forms of adaptations, perhaps defenses, against stress under which the individual is unable to bear up. Fundamentally, psychoses are forms of withdrawal to a narcissistic, infantile stage in which actuality is denied. The psychotic has been subjected to pressures of actuality, but finding them too painful to bear, escapes by withdrawing to an autistic stage characteristic of infancy, when there was no need to deal with these pressures and difficulties.

We are justified in suspecting that the choice of escape into psychosis, instead of some other form of defense, has some organic or constitutional foundation. But such constitutional "faults," to borrow a term from geology, may remain latent throughout the lives of many people, provided the demands and frustrations are not too great for them to bear. When these become too difficult, such as on a battlefield, for example, the psyche breaks where the fault exists, as is the case also in geological earthquakes. Pressures, however, need not come from such dramatic or sudden occurrences.

> There is almost sure to be evidence that from very early life, perhaps birth, the [psychotic] child was poorly equipped to successfully deal with the emotional stresses of even the relatively protected life of little children. If, in addition, the child's unusual reactions result (as might be expected) in rejection or retaliation by frustrated and antagonized parents, siblings, and neighbors, the problems may all be aggravated. It seems as though this retaliation (which originally was the result of the patient's own innate difficulties) is what precipitates a psychotic adjustment.[1]

The function of hallucinations and delusions is to recapture a world in which the patient can satisfy his infantile, narcissistic phantasies. Through them he denies the demands that he cannot, or will not, bear. The violence and aggressive behavior characteristic of some psychotics is another effort to mold the environment in accordance with an infantile, omnipotent will. Both the hallucinations and the violence of the psychotic have the same function, and are analogous (though not similar) to the aggressions of children with primary behavior disorders. In fact the analogy can be carried further into the area of treatment. Children with primary behavior disorders are permitted to act out freely their aggressions. The therapist is entirely permissive and tolerant. The similarity to this is strikingly illustrated in the hospital treatment of a particularly violent woman suffering from a psychosis with delusional manifestations. The patient thought herself a queen with royal prerogatives who was being illegally detained. She had on many occasions viciously attacked the nurses and other members of the staff. These assaults received the treatment that was necessary to allay her excitability but was not in any way punitive or vindictive. The nurses maintained quiet and equanimity throughout the many violent outbreaks, until one day following a particularly vicious attack, after a year and a half of hospitalization, the patient turned to the

[1] Charles Bradley, "Psychoses in Children," in *Modern Trends in Child Psychiatry,* ed. Nolan D. C. Lewis and Bernard L. Pacella (New York, International Universities Press, 1945), p. 148.

nurse and said: "You have taken this from me for so long, and still you don't dislike me. I think I'll try your way. Maybe I'm wrong." "From this time on," the report reads, "she accepted suggestions and eventually made a complete recovery." [2]

Another report deals with a schizophrenic patient who, even in a catatonic stupor, was aware of relationships. The physician first asked the nurse to take the patient's temperature, but changed her mind and took the temperature herself. The patient, after recovering from the stupor said to her: "You didn't know if you loved me or not, but you do." Dr. Bradley has also found in his work with children that "A tolerant attitude by adults toward the asocial, bizarre, irritable, and at times resistive activities of [psychotic] patients encourages them to relate themselves to reality. Surroundings in which the atmosphere is intellectually stimulating but not subjected to social pressure have definite therapeutic value." [3]

The value to group psychotherapy of reality awareness, despite the tendency toward reality denial, will receive consideration presently. Before we can enter into a discussion of this and other topics relative to it, it will be helpful to establish a few more etiological factors in psychoses.

Functional psychosis is a means through which the psyche resolves overintense difficulties and conflicts with which the ego is unable to deal. Tolerance to frustration, fear, and anxiety varies in different people, and everyone who reaches the limit of that tolerance reacts with flight or avoidance. Psychosis, therefore, can be considered a result of an especially intense avoidance drive, or flight reaction, of the ego when it feels too strongly threatened. The threat may originate outside the personality, such as catastrophic loss of the supportive elements in one's life—one's business or mate for example; or its origin may be an intense intrapsychic conflict and anxiety too strong for the ego to resolve. The most common of these are incestuous impulses and homosexual drives.

The history of psychotics in the functional category show strong deprivations in ego-development, intense frustration in basic psychobiological strivings, defective identifications, and destructive

[2] Donald M. Hamilton, "The Psychiatric Hospital as a Cultural Pattern," in *Current Therapies of Personality Disorders*, ed. Bernard Glueck (New York, Grune and Stratton, 1946), pp. 23–24.

[3] Charles Bradley, "Psychoses in Children," p. 150.

home relations. These lead to poor ego development and frequently to overintense superego, which causes overwhelming conflict within the psyche, a conflict that it cannot bear or resolve. The only solution is denial of its existence. When such a denial also involves the psychological instruments of perception, a state of insanity sets in. Fear, threat, and frustration cause regression to an early state at which these pressures were not present—that is, to infancy and its narcissistic defenses. The psychotic process may be cumulative and slow. The narcissistic regressive processes may continue for long periods and culminate at some crisis, or the break may be brought on suddenly through shock in the presence of predisposing factors that may not have been apparent in the past.

The treatment of psychoses such as schizophrenia, depressions, manic reactions, paranoia aims mainly at strengthening the ego so that it need not retreat from reality, but rather grow able and *willing* to cope with it. The important element in psychoses is that the ego is involved, which is not the case with psychoneurotics. In the latter the ego is intact, though weak, and it functions within boundaries. In the psychotic, the ego boundaries are undefined and the ego is itself cathexized. Reality, as well, needs to be viewed in its dual manifestation—the inner and the outer. Hospitalization helps the psychotic in his trend to escape the outer realities (actualities). With these pressures removed, recovery can sometimes be affected in very much the same manner as in physical illness when noxious bodies are eliminated. Here we rely upon the natural trend in the organism toward health and wholeness. This type of passive therapy was for generations the only one known to psychiatry. Freud, however, led the way, unintentionally perhaps, to a more active psychiatry. His basic contributions to psychodynamics and psychopathology, generally, and to the treatment of the transference neuroses, also opened up possibilities for the treatment of "narcissistic neuroses" (Freud), that is, psychoses.

In the treatment of psychoses, as in the treatment of neuroses, relationship is the pivot. This is in a way a recent and startling discovery, since it is attempting to replace the age-old attitude that lurks even in the modern mind, including the physician's, that psychotics need to be treated sternly, if not cruelly. This may or may not stem from the uncertainty in all of us as to our own sanity, or it may be an application of the prevalent educational attitudes that children must be disciplined, regimented, and punished, which points to an intuitive recognition that psychotics and children have much in common. Certainly the facial expressions, grimaces, and behavior of adult psychotics and little children have a striking similarity. The stern attitude toward insanity persisted for centuries, despite Socrates' admonition that the mentally ill need the ministration of "sweet words."

Certainly psychotics, despite their occasional outbursts of violence, are as helpless and dependent as little children. They crave the same attention and some return even to an intra-uterine state, as in the catatonic stupor. The difficulty in applying relationships to the treatment of psychoses is that in terms of transference one encounters a blank wall, as it were. The patients are not always responsive to the therapist's overtures. There seems to be a need for some preliminary experiences in emotional orientation before a therapeutic relation is possible. These can be designated as activating experiences, and the periods during which such experiences occur as *periods of activation.* The psychotic can be considered as living in a dream or fog. He does not see the actualities of the world about him as does the average person. Because of his defensive withdrawal, his perceptions are as blurred as his conceptions are distorted. Any technique that helps activate outward interest is useful here. Occupational therapy has been employed for this purpose. Spontaneous relationships on a ward were observed to be very valuable for some patients and many such relationships spring up without any encouragement or planning on the part of physicians or other staff members. This spontaneous trend should be utilized for the activation of patients preparatory to establishing relations.

Group activities are important in this connection. Participation in every way possible in the hospital community should be encouraged. If hospital treatment is to be considered an educational opportunity for the psychotic, patients should take an active part in groups.[4] The more these activities bring the patients in contact with reality and each other, the better, and progressive education should

[4] Since the above was written I have come upon an admirable statement of this approach to hospital treatment in a paper by Dr. Hamilton to which the reader's attention is called. (See p. 249, footnote.) See also J. M. Klapman, *Group Psychotherapy: Theory and Practice* (New York, Grune and Stratton, 1946). Despite its general title,

16

have many suggestions for this work. Dr. Lauretta Bender pioneered in this direction with children in a hospital ward with good results. The educational group experiences have been helpful not only as a means of discipline and group management, but they have activated young patients and built up group morale.[5] Dr. Hamilton particularly has given a very comprehensive statement in the paper already referred to of the effectiveness of the "cultural pattern" in a hospital as a therapeutic agent.

According to Ernest Harms [6] the value of groups for psychotics was recognized in the latter half of the last century and according to him a book entitled, *Social Psychotherapy*, dealing with this subject was published by Arthur Kronfeld and Sidney Wronskey in 1929. Harms has this to say:

> Purely environmental group therapy exemplified by the procedure of placing severely sick mental patients in a well instructed healthy farmer-family, was first successfully carried out in Norway by Ragnar Vogt. The interfamilial form of group therapy, as Robert Sommer has formulated it—i.e., working out a case of mental disease in a family by an interfamiliar therapeutic arrangement—had, aside from this great German pioneer, other advocates in Forel and Dubois. However, it is difficult to draw the line between the old clerical family worship forms and those advocated as primarily educational patterns, as we find them in Pestalozzi and Jean Paul or even Goethe, on the one side, and the beginning of medical social help. They all advocate help through family ties in neurotic and psychotic conditions. Another form, that of influencing patients therapeutically outside of institutions through other patients, and of influencing acutely ill patients through cured ones, was practiced as far back as 1918 by physicians like Knud Alborn and Harold Schulz Henke, among others. And what has now been imported to America and trade-marked as "psychodramatics" was actually brought from Denmark to central Europe under the name of *Stegreif-Buhne*. The real originator was a Danish psychiatrist, Joergensen, who as early as 1915 applied what he called "dramatic diagnosis and therapy" with great success.[7]

---

the latter volume deals entirely with ward treatment of psychotics. It is confined to the tutorial or "class" method of education, which limits its usefulness.

[5] See Lauretta Bender, "Group Methods of the Children's Wards as a Method of Psychotherapy," *American Journal of Orthopsychiatry*, March, 1947, and her "Techniques of Child Psychiatry," in *Current Therapies of Personality Disorders*, ed. Bernard Glueck (New York, Grune and Stratton, 1946).

[6] Ernest Harms, "Group Therapy: Farce, Fashion, or Sociologically Sound?" *The Nervous Child*, April, 1945, p. 186.

[7] *Ibid.*, p. 188.

J. H. Pratt successfully employed the "class method" for the treatment of psychosomatic disorders in Boston at the turn of the century. Pratt later published a number of reports on his work. His method has been employed in the treatment of psychotics as well as psychogenic organic illnesses. Among the many who used the "class method" with psychotics are E. W. Lazell, A. A. Low, H. I. Harris, Austen Riggs, Mary G. Schroeder, Louis Wender, J. M. Klapman, W. Rhoades, Ira M. Altschuler, Donald M. Hamilton. In England, J. Beirer employs "Therapeutic Social Clubs" with ward and extramural psychotic patients.[8] With the exception of Wender, Altschuler, and Hamilton, group techniques used were the "class method," namely teaching, lecturing, and discussions. Some English psychiatrists use social clubs and other group activities, but the predominating plan is the discussion and demonstration.

In addition to the effects of the group upon patients listed by Harris [9] Schroeder found that:

> (1) Group discussion of mental hygiene problems helps to direct the [psychotic] patient's thought away from personal problems. (2) Group therapy is an effective and economical addition to treatment in large institutions. (3) Many mental hygiene subjects can be more successfully handled with groups than individually. (4) Identifying the patient's conflict with the universal problem of adjustment of the individual to environment, gives the patient courage to try to work out a solution.[10]

Riggs, quoted by Schroeder, characterizes the tutorial method succinctly when he says that the lectures to the patients and staff together on matters of mental health and mental illness are carried on "in an atmosphere . . . of the college classroom, but somewhat less formal." Altschuler uses voluntary participation by patients in a musical program in addition to group discussions, while Hamilton provides the patients with a cultural setting in which full participation in the total life of the hospital is encouraged.

The experience with social and special interest clubs for in- and

[8] For a fuller discussion of these and other current practices of group psychotherapy, as well as a bibliographical listing, see S. R. Slavson, "Group Therapy," in *Progress in Neurology and Psychiatry,* ed. Ernst Spiegel (New York, Grune and Stratton, 1946), Vol. I; S. R. Slavson and Saul Scheidlinger, "Group Psychotherapy," *ibid.,* Vol. II (1947), and "Group Psychotherapy," *ibid.,* Vol. III (1948); S. R. Slavson and Emanuel Hallowitz, "Group Psychotherapy," *ibid.,* Vol. IV (1949).

[9] See p. 4.

[10] Mary G. Schroeder, "Group Psychotherapy in a State Hospital," *Elgin Papers,* Elgin, Illinois, State Hospital, 1936.

out-patients at St. Bartholomew's Hospital, Guy's Hospital, Southend General Hospital, and East Ham Memorial, all in London, was summarized as follows:

1. Some patients are placed in mental hospitals because they are a danger to themselves or to society. The responsibility resting on those in charge of such hospitals is great, hence a conservative attitude over risking a quick discharge of patients. The longer they stay in hospital the less normal their life becomes. In some cases the less normal their life the worse they grow. The social club is a successful way of breaking, or even preventing this vicious circle.

2. The stigma that at times tells so heavily against the patient, both while he is in and after he is discharged from a mental hospital. The social club is a successful antidote, and helps to remove the dividing-line between the man who is or has been a patient and the man who has not had that misfortune.

3. Many people who break down lack much freedom of action, initiative, and responsibility. The social club gives an opportunity to train them to use initiative and to shoulder responsibility.

4. The number of persons attending out-patient departments of hospitals and coming into mental hospitals who have great difficulty in adapting themselves socially is overwhelming. The social club proves to be one of the easiest ways to overcome this difficulty.

5. The problem of every psychotherapist to-day is how to make the discoveries of modern psychotherapy applicable to the masses. The social club, as part of a bigger scheme of group psychotherapy, appears to be one of the most promising solutions.

The symptoms that yielded to this treatment were (a) shyness and loneliness; (b) general and social inferiority feelings; (c) sexual maladjustment; (d) lack of incentive and aim in life; (e) inability to co-operate with others; (f) anxiety and phobias; (g) parental domination; (h) acute disappointment; (i) psychological effects of physical defects.[11]

As we analyze the work done in groups of psychotics by various practitioners we find that the aims and results, whether consciously sought or unintentionally achieved, are activation and social education, in its broader meaning. Groups serve to activate the psychotic out of his semi-stupor, give him a motive for improving, and generate interests in some aspects of reality. Perhaps motivating the life of the functional (as well as the organic) psychotic is the most important need in his treatment, and requires utmost skill and resourcefulness. "The modern hospital for the treatment of psychia-

[11] E. B. Strauss, A. Strom-Olsen, and J. Bierer, "A Memorandum on Therapeutic Social Clubs in Psychiatry," *British Medical Journal* (London), December 30, 1944.

tric disorders," says Dr. Hamilton, "creates an environment, a kind of culture of the race best fitted together in a pattern neatly arranged for the special needs of patients. It is an asylum in the sense that it is a haven from the storms outside the bulwark of its breakwaters." [12] And, "the psychiatrist is at the controlling center of an elastic culture which can be manipulated to a great degree so as to fit the patient's needs, providing a milieu for those at the most primitive levels of adjustment up through more complicated levels until the highest modern civilized state is reached." [13]

As we study the statements based upon the experiences of the various practitioners, we find that groups universalize the problems for the patients as they do also in the treatment of neurotics. Schroeder, for example, says:

> By directing the patient's attention away from her own problems, it is hoped to encourage habits of thought which may break the sequence of the depressing emotions so disturbing to bodily functions and clear thinking. By realizing that failure may be used as a means of growth, the patient may come to approach this same problem with courage. Each one is about to feel that her own experience has been the most tragic and difficult that could happen to anyone. By emphasizing the fact that no one, however fortunate, can hope for life free from trouble—we try to influence the group to take a less personal and more constructive attitude.[14]

Through these means, and especially the active use of the total environment as a living culture, reality is made attractive to patients and they are rendered disposed toward accepting it and participating in it. In this connection the relationships with people are of paramount importance, and since the psychotic finds it difficult to submit to authority and relate to individuals, the impersonal milieu of a group and the indirect relationships in common activities are essential transitions. Thus, groups and activities in groups serve to "socialize" the patient. It has been my conviction for many years that activity groups, including the refreshment period, the free choice of occupations, and the absence of a planned group pattern, which have so far been used only with non-psychotic children, would be appropriate for treatment of adult psychotics in and out

[12] "The Psychiatric Hospital as a Cultural Pattern," in *Current Therapies of Personality Disorders*, p. 22.

[13] *Ibid.*, p. 25.

[14] "Group Psychotherapy in a State Hospital." *loc. cit.*

of institutions. Such groups, together with therapeutic social clubs, occupational therapy rooms, didactic instruction, and special interest and discussion groups (used with specially selected patients, according to their needs and readiness) could be made the core of the hospital treatment of mental patients. Even the withdrawn and delusional patients who, by and large, prefer individual and isolative occupations, can gain much from pursuing activities in the presence of others. Being with others opens possibilities for social interaction at the moment when they become ready for it.

We found, for example, that activity groups have a salutary effect upon schizoid children and some with latent schizophrenia and schizophrenic personality structure. At the beginning, these children are withdrawn, isolated, wary, and distrustful, but because the environment is permissive, of low pressure, and non-threatening, in varying degrees they ultimately take part in the group activities. However, unless this growth is supported in the home, little progress can be made with these patients. Intensive educational work with parents, and sometimes with siblings, is therefore indicated. The psychotic gains from the informal, free, and friendly relations that arise spontaneously in groups. Especially is the refreshment period important.

Elsewhere I have described a group in an out-patient clinic.

In one such group for adult psychotic women, the members brought along their knitting, crocheting, and sewing, and worked together. The agency provided the coffee and the ingredients for cakes and pastries. Members who were expert at any of the activities demonstrated to the others. Upon the request of some of the members, trips were arranged to various points of the city. This became a major and valuable self-motivated interest for the group.

At later meetings members helped each other with their knitting and other manual work, and learned to share things with one another. There were a number of quarrels and in one case a fist fight, which was resolved by the group itself. One of the members, a patient in a local clinic, was afraid to travel and whenever she left the house, walked holding on to walls. After a few months she traveled to and from the meetings by herself and even talked to some of the members of the group. Some of the patients brought their children to the meetings (but never their husbands). As the group progressed there was definite and observable improvement in the individuals composing it.

The program of this group consisted almost entirely of manual activities. It would be possible, however, to include discussions . . . and thus extend the possibilities of group therapy to adults as well as to children. Such an extension requires criteria for intake and grouping that are not so sharply defined at present as those for children.[15]

The sphere of occupational therapy could be greatly extended if utilized at appropriate stages, for inter-personal relations, and group association in addition to the manual and art occupations it provides. That there is value in the craft occupations and skill activities there is little doubt. They are as useful here as in the education of children through which ego and feelings of self-esteem are built up, powers are mobilized, and libido drives externalized. Such activities are strong motivators for extraversion and aid psychomotor balance. They also serve as catharsis and sublimation, especially where patients cannot verbalize.[16] Creative achievement assures one of group status, since patients who stand out in any one craft are called upon by the others for help. Such interaction and relationships should be both the aim and means of occupational therapy. Since the aim of treatment is to counteract the psychotic's autism and withdrawal, patients would gain greatly from a setting in which isolated and individualistic occupations were turned into group projects, when possible, and spontaneous cooperation encouraged.

To employ such procedures, criteria for grouping even psychotic patients would need to be better understood than they are now. With a given patient, the diagnostic categories, and especially patterns of behavior, must be considered as well as the value of and capacity for group association. As with other types of patients, groups may not only be unbeneficial, but harmful. The function of the hospital is to protect patients from strain, threat, and attack, not to increase them, which can be easily the case when choice and grouping are faulty. These criteria still have to be established empirically, but despite risks and dangers, the natural trend to association among psychotic patients must be utilized in the therapeutic scheme. It is a matter of common observation that wardmates make

[15] S. R. Slavson, *An Introduction to Group Therapy* (New York, Commonwealth Fund, 1943), p. 330.

[16] Margaret Naumburg, *Studies of the "Free" Art Expression of Behavior Problem Children and Adolescents as a Means of Diagnosis and Therapy* (New York, Nervous and Mental Disease Monographs, No. 71, 1947).

friends, relate to and confide in one another even when they are inaccessible to the hospital staff. With such patients especially, interpatient therapy should be encouraged.

Altschuler and Klapman have reported ward patients who were inaccessible to individual psychotherapy and who also refused to take part in group activities for a long time. Some of the patients jeered and made fun of those who did so, but later joined in with the others. Even catatonic patients were found to respond to group activities. Human relations are important to everyone. Social hunger is a motivating force among psychotics as it is among non-psychotic patients and normal people, even though it must first be unearthed. The paranoiac, for example, adopts his way of life not because people mean nothing to him; rather because they mean too much.

At present all of the group treatment of psychotics in hospitals is carried on a mass basis, and I suggest that the term *mass therapy* be employed to designate it.[17] Treatment in large groups is considered an economy measure by some, but, as has been pointed out already, economy is not an adequate reason for adopting this procedure. In mass therapy large numbers of patients are taught basic physiology, mental hygiene, elementary psychiatry and general cultural subjects. The physician explains to the patients the organic processes that take place during emotional disturbances. Some psychiatrists use solid models of the human body, others use figures projected from lantern slides, moving pictures, and marionettes. In some forms of mass therapy, discipline and authority are employed as well.

We have already emphasized that group psychotherapy, on the other hand, addresses itself to a small group of five to eight patients where direct and intense interaction takes place and where transference to the therapist and among the members is possible. One of the major difficulties in organizing such intimate interview groups with psychotics is to determine the fitness of patients for groups and the criteria for grouping them with therapeutic validity. Answers to these questions await further practice and experimentation. One

[17] See S. R. Slavson, suggestion in "Group Psychotherapy," in *Progress in Neurology and Psychiatry, 1946* (New York, Grune and Stratton, 1947), and S. R. Slavson, "General Principles and Dynamics" in *The Practice of Group Therapy,* ed. S. R. Slavson (New York, International Universities Press, 1947).

of the surest criteria is the spontaneous response to groups on the ward.

In treating the psychotic, the first task is to activate his psychic energies outward, to de-cathexize the ego. Then follows the step toward socialization, or reintegration, and when the ego grows stronger, individuation can occur. The last is both the most difficult and the most important stage. The psychotic's ego is poorly developed and in extreme instances almost non-existent, as in the vegetative psychoses like catatonia. The ego is strengthed when the patient functions dynamically in relation to his environment, accepts responsibility, and becomes a self-directive entity. It is these very things, however, that he sought to escape through a psychotic pattern, and to motivate his reentering a world of reality is the real task of treatment.

Active living in a specially set, or conditioned, environment, where one receives praise and recognition and the inducement to take part because of empathy with other participants, is the most reliable means of achieving this. In this scheme interview groups have their place, but their significance should not be overemphasized as against the natural and spontaneous reaching out toward relationships on the part of patients. There are, of course, many patients who remain withdrawn and inert, despite any environmental opportunities offered to them. They are unable to mobilize and externalize their energies, and need stimulation (activation) by some outside agent. Attachment to a hospital staff member is one of the best means for achieving this. Another is to place well-suited patients near each other at the dining table, in recreation, and at work assignments. Still another is the use of group discussions and classes.

The passivity and neutrality of the therapist advocated for nonpsychotic patients has to be greatly modified for the psychotics, and very frequently abandoned. Like children, they crave love and attention. The hospital staff, including the group therapist, must be more active and more assertive than is recommended for other types of groups. Frequently the group therapist may find it essential to take the initiative for a period of time and actively stimulate group interviews and activities. If he fails to do this, silence and boredom ensue.

In the treatment of psychotics in groups (as well as individually) it is most imperative that their defenses should not be tampered with or assailed. This holds also in the treatment of psychoneurotics, but vastly greater caution has to be exercised with the former. If psychosis is a defensive pattern, the very life of the psychotic is founded on it. The psychoneurotic defends himself against anxiety, the psychotic against life itself. The aim of group interviews is to strengthen the ego so that the patient wants to live; he must be aroused out of the haze—the dream world—in which he has immersed himself as protection. This requires a sort of active indirection, much tact, and much patience. In summary, the use of groups in the treatment of psychotics the following types emerge:

Work and Living Groups. These groups, either planned or rising spontaneously out of the living needs in the hospital, include groups in gardens, on the farm, in maintenance and repair, in the kitchen, laundry, sewing rooms, and office, and similar community functions.

Recreational Groups. Planned groups for recreational purposes include sports and games according to the needs of each patient, as well as art, science, crafts, literary, dramatics, music, dancing, current event discussions, and the many other types of recreational activities to be found in a neighborhood recreational center.

Socialized Occupational Therapy. Occupational therapy rooms provide opportunities for patients who cannot, or do not wish to participate in larger group contacts. Here they can work individually and develop relations with the therapist and other patients. Association and patient interaction should be encouraged.

Classroom Groups are indicated for patients who wish to undertake a program of an academic nature. These groups should be small. Free discussion and the question-and-answer method should prevail. Patients can be expected to be punctual and attend to their work.

Mass Discussions have already been described in preceding pages. Dr. Klapman [18] gives a detailed outline of psychiatric subjects and discussion plans that he employs but which seem to the present writer extremely advanced. The reader is advised to review the topics used by the other writers referred to in this chapter as well.

[18] *Group Psychotherapy: Theory and Practice* (New York, Grune and Stratton, 1946).

Interview Groups have already been discussed and the difficulties outlined. See particularly in this connection the writings of Schilder and Wender.[19]

Relational Groups. Since the problems have been activated and brought to culmination through the critical and rejecting attitudes of members of the patients' families, their education in the care of the patients is essential preparatory to the latters' return home. Groups can be very effective here for reasons already indicated in our discussion of the treatment of mothers.[20]

[19] See Bibliography in *Group Therapy,* published by the American Group Therapy Association, 1950.

[20] Harris B. Peck, Ralph Rabitovitch, and Joseph Cramer, "A Treatment Program for the Parents of Schizophrenic Children," *American Journal of Orthopsychiatry,* October, 1949; W. D. Ross, "Group Psychotherapy with Patients' Relatives," *American Journal of Psychiatry,* April, 1948, and "Group Psychotherapy with Psychotic Patients and Their Relatives," *ibid.,* November, 1948.

*GLOSSARY**

Action interpretation. The reaction, or lack of it, on the part of the group psychotherapist aimed to convey meaning of the conscious intent or unconscious motivation of a patient's statement or act.

Active restraint. Direct restraint of activity or behavior from a person or persons. See also *Passive restraint.*

Activity catharsis. Catharsis that arises from physical activity or "acting out" as differentiated from verbal catharsis.

Activity-interview group psychotherapy. Same as group-play psychotherapy, but designed for seriously disturbed children of school (latency) age.

Aim attachment (in transference). The therapist's objective or aim for his patient or group.

Anti-nodal behavior. The lowest point or quietus in a group's behavior or activity. See also *Nodal behavior.*

Associative thinking. Ideas and thoughts of events or feelings related to each other not in a regressive relation, but as contemporaneous occurrences. The term is used as a distinction from free association.

Basic transference. The fundamental and permanent transference feelings a patient has toward the therapist as differentiated from transitory transference. See also *Transitory transference.*

Blanket groups. Groups which are not planned with a special aim in view.

Call system. The practice of calling in turn on individuals in a therapy group to react to a specific problem.

Catalysis. The effect through which one person is activated by another resulting in accelerated catharsis.

Catalytic agent. Individuals in groups who activate the emotional activity of the other members of a group or their catharsis.

Cathexis displacement. The displacement of emotional or sexual drive from one center or focus on to another.

Class method. A form of education of groups oriented toward enlightening patients as to their illness and symptoms and provide motivation for recovery.

* See also "Group Therapy Terms and Phrases," in S. R. Slavson, *An Introduction to Group Therapy* (New York, Commonwealth Fund, 1943), p. 342.

Closed groups. Therapy groups to which no new patients are added in the course of treatment. See also *Open groups.*

Collective experience. Common emotional experiences of a group of people.

Compresence. The presence of two or more persons in physical proximity.

Deflection. The process of redirecting attention from oneself to another member of the group. See also *Escape.*

Derivative insight. Insight arrived at by the patient himself without interpretation by the therapist (as in activity group therapy).

Didactic group psychotherapy. A strictly tutorial practice in which definite outlines, texts and visual aids are used for teaching patients in special subjects.

Directional function. The function of the group psychotherapist by which he gives purpose to the interviews and canalizes them.

Escape. The various means employed by patients to prevent anxiety. Chief among these are deflection, projection, selective silence, and absentism.

Extensional function. The function of the group psychotherapist through which he helps the group to overcome a block or stereotypy.

Group balance. The result of grouping patients in accordance with clinical and personal criteria to prevent intensification of a specific problem or set of problems.

Group fixity. The pattern of group association in which each individual assumes or is assigned a specific role, function, or position in relation to the other members of the group.

Group mobility. A group pattern in which activity and relationships are free, fluid and spontaneous, that is, where no fixed or planned patterns exist.

Group-play psychotherapy. Small groups of children of pre-school age where activity catharsis is made possible and is interpreted by the psychotherapist or other members of the group.

Hostility density. The quantitative and qualitative degree of hostility and its intensity on the part of members of a therapy group reflected in their interpersonal relations.

Identification therapy. The corrective effect of a situation on one patient as a result of his identifying with another actively participating in treatment; also referred to as *Spectator therapy.*

Identification transference. The attitudes and relations derived from identifying with other members of a therapy group or the desire to emulate or be like them.

Interpretive function. The function of the group psychotherapist in helping patients acquire insight.

Interview group psychotherapy. Groups for adolescents or adults in which the catharsis and free association are on the verbal level.

Libidinal transference. The transference which is derived from and charged with libidinal drives such as that of a patient toward the therapist.

Libido-binding activities. Tools, materials and games that serve to arrest the interests and energies of children during their activities. Refers chiefly to activity group therapy.

Libido-evoking materials. Materials, toys and games used in the psychotherapy of children which serve to evoke their libidinal (sexual) impulses and phantasies. See also *Libido-revealing materials.*

Libido-revealing materials. Materials, games and toys through which children reveal libidinal (sexual) phantasies and interests.

Mass therapy. Various group therapy techniques, particularly the didactic, recreational and class methods, used for large audiences.

Multipolarity. The phenomenon in a group through which more than one focus of transference is present such as in inter-patient transference in addition to transference on the therapist.

Nodal behavior. The peak of hyperactivity in a group. See also *Antinodal* behavior.

Nuclear problem. The central problem of a patient arising at a point of maximal trauma; especially the mechanism, psychic dynamism or striving that interfere with wholesome response or adaptations.

Open groups. Therapy groups to which new patients are added in the course of treatment. Also referred to as *Continuous groups.* See also *Closed groups.*

Passive restraint. Restraint to activity or behavior derived from a situation or planned arrangement of a setting rather than from a person or persons. See also *Active restraint.*

Primary group code. The basic and more or less prevalent understanding of function and relationships existing among members of a group.

Projection. The process of attributing to another person one's own feelings of hostility, destruction and aggression. See also *Escape.*

Rotation system. The practice of treating one patient in a group while the others are spectators.

Selective silence. The phase of withdrawal of a patient in a group from the discussion of a specially anxiety or guilt evoking topic. See also *Escape.*

Self-image. The perceptions the individual has of himself as to his weakness, strength, worthiness or unworthiness.

Social hunger. The desire or craving on the part of an individual for companionship, for being with, or part of, a group.

Sibling transference. The attitudes and feelings patients have toward other members of a therapy group similar to those they have had toward their siblings.

Stimulative function. The function of the group psychotherapist through which the group is activated to catharsis.

Structured groups. Groups in which patients are assigned with a view of their therapeutic effect on each other or to prevent excessive hostility or pathology. It also applies to group balance. See also *Blanket groups.*

Support. The security derived by a patient from the other members in a group either in his negative transference, deficiency of ego strength, or through sanctioning of his behavior.

Target multiplicity. The multiple possibilities existing in a group for projecting or displacing hostility.

Transference dilution. The diminution of the intensity of transference toward the therapist due to the presence of sibling and identification transferences in a group.

Transitory transference. The periodic and short-lived transference feelings toward the therapist which are different from or in opposition to the prevalent basic transference. See also *Basic transference.*

Universalization. Commonness of a problem, attitude, feeling or urge among the members of a group.

Visual suggestion. The suggestion for activities or occupations derived from exposing to view materials and tools and the planned arrangement of a therapy room.

INDEX